Password English 1re

Coordination pédagogique

Juliette Ban-Larrosa
IA-IPR, Académie de Paris

Claudine Lennevi
Professeur, Académie de Caen

Auteurs

Yannick Abgrall
Professeur, Académie de Caen

Sylvain Basty
Professeur, Académie de Créteil

Benjamin Baudin
Professeur, Académie de Créteil

Boucif Benyacine
Professeur, Lycée Pierre Mendès France de Tunis

Pascale Fontaine
Professeur, Académie de Versailles

Claudine Lennevi

Pour la langue orale

Jeremy Reyburn
IA-IPR, Académie de Caen

Pour la grammaire

Bérengère Rivoallan
Professeur, Académie de Montpellier

didier

Les auteurs et l'éditeur remercient particulièrement Janet Sadler, lecteur critique, pour la remarquable précision de son travail. Un grand merci également à Philippe Garillot, qui a aimablement accepté de relire, de tester les chapitres de ce manuel et de partager expériences et réflexions.
Les auteurs remercient vivement les élèves des académies de Caen, Créteil, Paris, Versailles et du lycée français de Tunis.

Photographie de couverture : Angleterre, Londres, 2006. Greenwich park.
Philippe Brault/Agence VU

Illustrations : Lucie Albon (pp. 176, 179, 181) ; Clémentine Berthier (pp. 16, 17, 28, 56, 58, 158, 171) ; Camille Beurton (p. 39) ; Thérèse Bonté (pp. II, 34, 49, 64, 117, 147, 167, 207, 208, 212, 213, 215) ; Viravong Chanthapanya (pp. 22, 36, 50, 66, 77, 84, 101, 132, 148, 168) ; Christopher (pp. 86, 87), Michel Galvin (pp. 70, 144) ; Nathalie Tousnakhoff (pp. 70, 105) ; Agathe Raciazeck (pp. 92, 172, 175) ; Aude Samama (pp. 112, 113) ;
Cartes et schémas : Anne Horrenberger
Conception maquette intérieure et couverture : Elhadi Yazi
Mise en page : Catherine de Trégomain
Photogravure : IGS-CP

PAPIER À BASE DE FIBRES CERTIFIÉES

éditions didier s'engagent pour l'environnement en réduisant l'empreinte carbone de leurs livres. Celle de cet exemplaire est de :
950 g éq. CO_2
Rendez-vous sur www.editionsdidier-durable.fr

 – ISBN : 978-2-278-06934-7

Achevé d'imprimer en août 2013 par La Tipografica Varese (Italie) / Dépôt légal : 6934/05

Avant-propos

AVEC **Password 1re** ENTREZ DANS LA LANGUE ET DANS LA CULTURE DES PAYS ANGLOPHONES

Au fil des dix chapitres, saisissez toutes les occasions qui vous sont offertes de pratiquer l'anglais et de communiquer.

- Communiquer, c'est échanger – être capable de lire des textes de nature différente, de comprendre des messages oraux variés et pouvoir en retour s'exprimer personnellement. **Password** vous aide à développer vos compétences dans tous ces domaines, et ce faisant à découvrir et à comprendre la culture de l'autre.
- Prendre la parole ou la plume pour s'exprimer personnellement, c'est se mettre en action. Chaque chapitre du manuel est jalonné par des tâches d'entraînement et se conclut par deux « tâches finales » à réaliser dans une situation et un contexte définis.
- Chacun des dix chapitres vous conduira à explorer une question et un thème particuliers, et vous permettra d'enrichir vos connaissances et votre réflexion sur le monde anglophone.
- Nous espérons que **Password** vous donnera de multiples occasions de faire vivre la langue anglaise dans toutes ses dimensions !

Les auteurs

Visite guidée...

Chacun des 10 chapitres de **Password 1re** explore un thème particulier et met l'accent sur l'une des cinq activités langagières.

Une double progression, culturelle et actionnelle

- ***Un thème abordé sous forme de problématique,*** pour s'impliquer et réagir personnellement.
- ***Deux tâches finales*** en fin de parcours, l'une en compréhension, l'autre en production, dans l'activité langagière dominante du chapitre et celle qui lui est associée.

Entraînements

Dans chacune de ces double-pages, à partir de documents à écouter, visionner, regarder ou lire, les élèves explorent un aspect spécifique du thème et consolident leurs compétences de communication.

- ***Une tâche d'entraînement*** clôt la double-page et permet de réinvestir compétences et acquisitions linguistiques, tout en se préparant aux tâches finales.

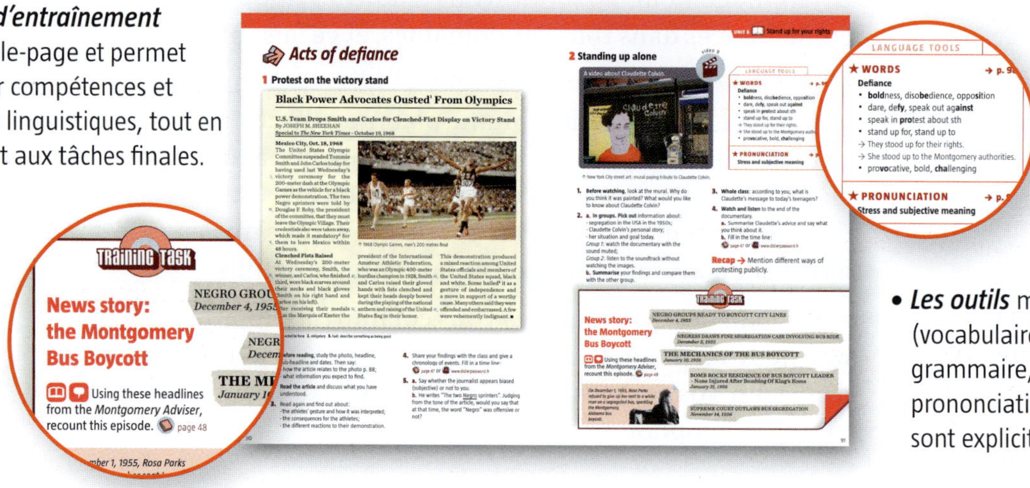

- ***Les outils*** mobilisés (vocabulaire, grammaire, prononciation) sont explicités.

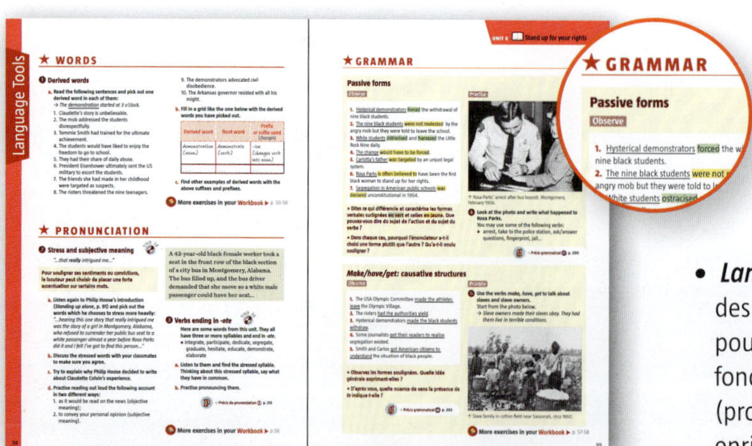

- ***Language Tools :*** des exercices en contexte pour mieux comprendre le fonctionnement de la langue (prononciation, grammaire) et enrichir son vocabulaire.

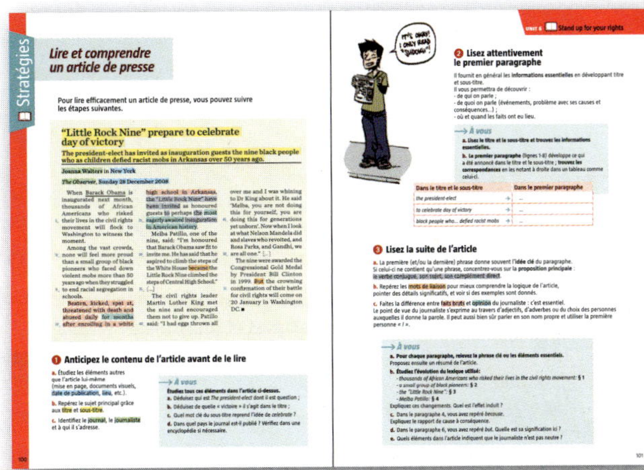

- ***Les pages Stratégies***, dans l'activité langagière dominante du chapitre, développent conseils et aides méthodologiques qui seront utiles au moment de réaliser les tâches finales, mais aussi tout au long de l'apprentissage.

Auto-évaluation et évaluations

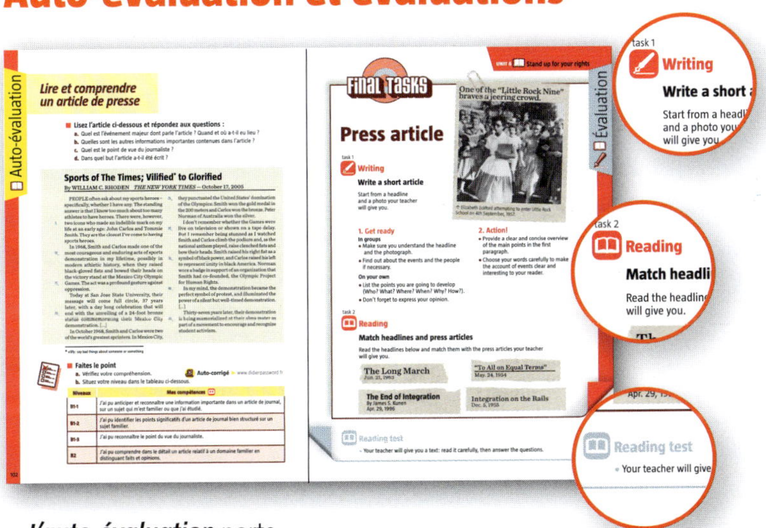

- ***Les Final tasks*** sont l'occasion :
  - de donner libre cours à son inventivité, de s'exprimer personnellement et de communiquer de manière authentique en anglais, en mettant en œuvre ce qu'on a appris au cours de la séquence ;
  - d'évaluer ses compétences à travers la réalisation de deux tâches communicatives, en compréhension et en production, à l'oral ou à l'écrit.

- ***L'auto-évaluation*** porte sur l'activité langagière privilégiée dans le chapitre. Elle permet de s'entraîner et de faire le point sur les acquisitions en cours, juste avant l'évaluation.

L'auto-corrigé est disponible sur www.didierpassword.fr

- ***Un test de compréhension,*** à l'oral ou à l'écrit, est aussi systématiquement proposé à l'issue de chaque chapitre.

→ Appareil d'évaluation, critères et barème dans le guide pédagogique.

Bien repérer

- Compréhension orale
- Compréhension écrite
- Production orale
- Production orale en interaction
- Production écrite

track 7 — Écouter la piste correspondante du **CD audio** de l'élève

page 7 — Aller à la page correspondante dans le **Workbook**

vidéo 7 — Visionner la séquence correspondante du **DVD** classe

Aller sur le **site Internet** www.didierpassword.fr sur lequel sont proposés les supports utiles à la réalisation de certaines activités et les grilles d'auto-évaluation.

Sommaire

Chapitres | Culture Documents | Activités langagières

Activité langagière dominante du chapitre : couleur foncée *(exemple pour unit 1)*

Activité langagière associée : couleur claire *(exemple pour unit 1)*

Langue	Tâches d'entraînement	Stratégies	Évaluations finales
Lexique • *Tourism* • *Responsibility* • *Business* • *Buying and selling* • *Environment* **Prononciation** • Intonation dans les énumérations **Grammaire** • Permission, obligation, interdiction • La voix passive	Écouter des touristes pour juger de leur comportement : responsable ou non ? Justifier ses choix → p. 15 Choisir et rédiger les entrées d'un guide touristique → p. 17 Identifier le tableau décrit dans un enregistrement et justifier sa réponse → p. 19	Comprendre un message oral (1) → p. 22-23	**Tâche** Faire la voix-off d'un documentaire vidéo **Tâche** Suggérer la meilleure destination de voyage pour trois profils de touristes différents ***Listening test*** → p. 25
Lexique • *The Internet* • *Self portraying* • *Revealing* • *Group activism* **Prononciation** • Accentuation et comparaisons • Noms composés avec *self-* **Grammaire** • Durée : *for/since* • Questions *(how long? how often?)*	Convaincre ses camarades de devenir membres d'un réseau social → p. 29 • Discuter de l'impact des réseaux sociaux sur l'individu → p. 31 • Discuter du rôle des réseaux sociaux dans l'espace mondial	Exprimer son opinion et convaincre → p. 36-37	**Tâche** Prendre part à un débat télévisé **Tâche** Associer réseaux sociaux et utilisateurs potentiels ***Reading test*** → p. 39
Lexique • *Power* • *Criminal activities* • *Attitudes* • *Trust, suspicion, admiration* **Prononciation** • Accentuation des mots avec préfixe • Accentuation pour marquer la différence entre le passé et le présent **Grammaire** • Questionnement • Questions courtes • *Tag questions*	Rechercher et échanger des informations sur des gangsters célèbres pour découvrir leurs points communs → p. 43 • Écrire une lettre pour relater des événements de son propre point de vue → p. 45 • Rédiger un dialogue entre un père et son fils à partir d'une situation donnée (roman graphique) → p. 47	Rédiger un dialogue narratif → p. 50-51	**Tâche** Rédiger une scène dialoguée pour une histoire inspirée par la Mafia **Tâche** Associer critiques et affiches de film ***Listening test*** → p. 53

Activité langagière dominante du chapitre : couleur foncée *(exemple pour unit 1)*

Activité langagière associée : couleur claire *(exemple pour unit 1)*

Langue	Tâches d'entraînement	Stratégies	Évaluations finales
Lexique • *Travel and holiday* • *Memories and feelings* • *Dreams* • *Landscapes* **Prononciation** • Noms de lieux • Intonation et sentiments **Grammaire** • Les comparaisons • *Past/present perfect/present*	Après discussion en groupes, concevoir la pochette d'un CD puis la présenter en expliquant ses choix → p. 57 Enregistrer un message publicitaire pour la radio → p. 59 Identifier cinq lieux remarquables et les associer aux photos correspondantes → p. 61 Rédiger une lettre pour relater des faits en exprimant sentiments et réactions → p. 63	Comprendre un message oral (2) → p. 66-67	**Tâche** Choisir et présenter un lieu célèbre sur la Route 66 en justifiant son choix **Tâche** Associer des diapos à leur commentaire enregistré ***Listening test*** → p. 69
Lexique • *Impressions and reactions* • *Doubt and uncertainty* • *Fear and apprehension* • *Incident* • *Habits* • *Integration* **Prononciation** • Accentuation des formes négatives **Grammaire** • Discours rapporté • *be + V-ing*	Poster un commentaire en ligne pour relater une expérience personnelle et faire part de ses réactions → p. 75 • Imaginer et écrire les pensées d'un personnage dans un texte étudié → p. 77 • Imaginer et rédiger un dialogue entre deux personnages (dont le narrateur) → p. 79 Préparer une conférence de presse et y prendre part → p. 81	Écrire un récit en adoptant un point de vue → p. 84-85	**Tâche** Réécrire une histoire en changeant le point de vue **Tâche** Dans différents témoignages écrits, identifier la phase du choc culturel correspondant à chacun ***Reading test*** → p. 87
Lexique • *Defiance* • *Violence and heroism* • *Fear and resistance* • *Tribute and legacy* **Prononciation** • Accentuation et sentiments/convictions • Mots se terminant par *-ate* **Grammaire** • Formes passives • *make/have/get* : structures causatives Joan Baez, *We shall overcome* (song) *Obama overcomes*	Raconter un événement en s'appuyant sur des titres de journaux → p. 91 Rédiger un court article et son titre pour relater et expliquer des faits et des opinions → p. 95 • Prédire et discuter les points marquants d'un discours commémoratif → p. 93 • Discuter de la portée collective d'actes individuels en étayant son propos avec des exemples historiques → p. 97	Lire et comprendre un article de presse → p. 100-101	**Tâche** Rédiger un court article de presse à partir d'un titre et d'une photo **Tâche** Associer gros titres et articles de journaux correspondants ***Reading test*** → p. 103
Lexique • *Dreams and aspirations* • *Modernity and tradition* • *Values* • *Surprise and astonishment* • *Gloom and pleasure* **Prononciation** • Intonation et opinions **Grammaire** • Expression du but • Présent simple	Faire le commentaire d'une vidéo touristique → p. 109 Après quelques recherches, créer une brochure pour des visiteurs → p. 111 Imaginer et rédiger un dialogue faisant suite à un récit ; jouer la scène → p. 113 Rédiger un court article sur un aspect d'une société utopique → p. 115	Écrire un texte descriptif et explicatif → p. 118-119	**Tâche** Imaginer et présenter par écrit un aspect de sa « société idéale » **Tâche** Dessiner, d'après sa description écrite, le plan d'une ville utopique ***Reading test*** → p. 121

Activité langagière dominante du chapitre : couleur foncée *(exemple pour unit 1)*

Activité langagière associée : couleur claire *(exemple pour unit 1)*

Langue	Tâches d'entraînement	Stratégies	Évaluations finales
Lexique • *Description* • *Conflict, betrayal and loyalty* • *Desire, dilemma and reproach* • *Pain, hope and despair* • *Peace* **Prononciation** • Lire un texte à voix haute • Rythme et sens **Grammaire** • Suppositions et probabilités • *What I know is that...*	Faire un bref exposé sur un personnage ou sur un événement historique → p. 125 • Décrire et commenter une photo à tour de rôle pour élaborer une histoire → p. 127 • Proposer en groupe une illustration pour un texte poétique. La présenter et répondre aux questions de la classe → p. 129	Faire un exposé sur un document iconographique → p. 132-133	**Tâche** Présenter une fresque murale et l'événement historique dont elle témoigne **Tâche** Esquisser une fresque murale d'après sa description sonore ***Listening test*** → p. 135
Lexique • *Body and health* • *Scientific progress* • *Genetic engineering* • *Respect and disrespect* • *Similarities and differences* **Prononciation** • Intonation subjective • Vraies questions et questions rhétoriques **Grammaire** • Différents sens de *can* • *If... will/would*	Anticiper la teneur d'un article à partir de son titre et en rendre compte par oral → p. 139 En tant qu'auditeur, réagir à des opinions exprimées à la radio → p. 141 Saisir puis discuter le message de dessins humoristiques → p. 143 Écrire au courrier des lecteurs pour exprimer son opinion → p. 145	Identifier les opinions exprimées dans un texte argumentatif → p. 148-149	**Tâche** Participer à un débat télévisé sur les conséquences du génie génétique **Tâche** Identifier les opinions de différents participants à un débat, en vue d'organiser le « plan de table » ***Reading test*** → p. 151
Lexique • *Courtroom vocabulary* • *Introducing arguments* • *Reparation* • *Deliberating* • *Responsibility* **Prononciation** • Intonation dans les dialogues **Grammaire** • *Not only, hardly... when, never...* • *Do* dans les phrases affirmatives	• Faire une courte plaidoirie à partir de notes → p. 159 • Légender le plan d'un tribunal, expliquer le rôle des protagonistes → p. 161 Écrire et « jouer » une plaidoirie → p. 163 Prendre part aux délibérations d'un jury. Donner et défendre son point de vue → p. 165	Argumenter pour convaincre → p. 168-169	**Tâche** « Jouer » un procès en classe **Tâche** Identifier les auteurs de dépositions (témoin, juge, avocat, etc.) ***Reading test*** → p. 171

UNIT 1 Tourism in a sacred place

In the Australian Outback, an Aboriginal ranger helps tourists understand the world's oldest living culture.

How can tourism benefit indigenous people?

Read the title of the chapter and **look** at the picture. **Comment** on them; what questions do they bring to mind?

FINAL TASKS

P. 25

Promoting tourism

Speaking
Make a video commentary

Listening
Suggest the best tourist destination for three visitors

CULTURE

- Discovering why Australia is an attractive tourist destination.
- Exploring tourism impact on indigenous people.
- Discovering indigenous culture.
- Literary work: B. Chatwin, *The Songlines*

COMMUNICATION

- Understanding specific information and explanations given in video reports and interviews.
- Giving a brief presentation of a place I have studied and explaining its significance.
- Understanding information and opinions in an article and in a narrative text.

TOOLS

★ Words
- Tourism and responsibility
- Business
- Heritage
- Buying and selling
- Environment

★ Pronunciation
- Intonation of lists

★ Grammar
- Permission, obligation, prohibition
- Passive forms

Stratégies
→ *Comprendre un message oral (1)*

A debated issue

1 Oz tourism

video 7

A report on the Australian tourism industry.

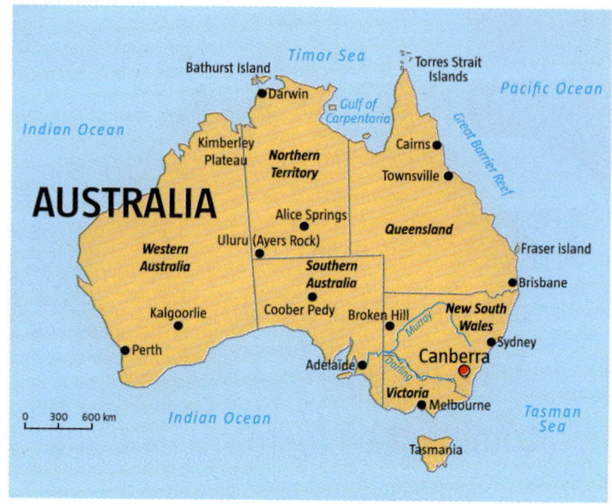

1. **Look** at the photo and the map. What comes to your mind?
2. **Watch the report** and discuss what you have understood.
3. **a. In groups**. Watch again and focus on:
   - the pictures; explain what makes Australia an attractive tourist destination *(group 1)*.
   - the commentary; explain why tourism is important to Australia *(group 2)*.

   b. Report your findings back to the other group.
4. Would you like to visit Australia? Give your reasons, concentrating on what most or least appeals to you.

2 Tourism ad "tramples all over our culture"

Aboriginal elders[1] from northern Australia are upset at a tourism campaign based around the movie *Australia* that they say suggests it is "OK to trample[2] all over our culture".

Ambrose Mungala Chalarimeri, a Kwini tribe elder from Oomarri country in the east Kimberley, made the comments after seeing a Tourism Australia advertisement showing people swimming above King George Falls.

"The waterfalls hold special tribal and spiritual significance, with a burial site located near the top of the falls which is protected by our ancestral spirits," Mr Chalarimeri said.

He said that although tourist boats were permitted at the base of the waterfalls, people were forbidden from climbing to the top.

Tourism Australia has invested in a $40 million campaign, including two ads directed by Baz Luhrmann [...].

WA[3] Aboriginal Lands Trust chairman Doc Reynolds said he was concerned the ads showed images of people in culturally sensitive areas without seeking permission from traditional owners.

"It seems to be hypocritical to promote indigenous tourism but not uphold[4] the values and traditions and sensitivities of these areas," he said.

But a Tourism Australia spokesman denied the campaign was promoting illegal entry onto Aboriginal land.

"The advertisements do not make any reference to a specific location," he said. "Rather, they are about the emotional impact of visiting Australia and the type of experiences people can have here."

Jewel Topsfield, November 19, 2008,
www.theage.com.au

1. community leaders **2.** damage **3.** WA: Western Australia **4.** support, defend

The King George Falls, →
in the Kimberley region
(Western Australia),
have a special and spiritual
significance for Aborigines.

LANGUAGE TOOLS

★ **WORDS** → p. 20

Tourism

- a **ho**liday-maker, an ad**ven**turer, a **back**packer
- tour a **coun**try, go **sight**seeing
- go off the **bea**ten track ≠ **vi**sit a **po**pular site

Responsibility

- ap**pro**priate, res**pect**ful, res**pon**sible be**ha**viour ≠ inap**pro**priate/of**fen**sive be**ha**viour
- show res**pect** for (the traditions)
- pol**lute**, **da**mage = spoil, **ru**in

★ **PRONUNCIATION** → p. 20

Intonation of lists

★ **GRAMMAR** → p. 21

Permission - obligation - prohibition

→ Tourists must take local culture into account.

1. **Look** at the photo above, then read the headline and the first paragraph of the article on p. 14 (lines 1 to 4). What is it about?
2. **Read the whole article** and discuss what you have understood.
3. **a. In groups**. Read the text again and highlight information about:
   - the Aboriginal elders' concerns *(group 1)*;
   - Tourism Australia's comments *(group 2)*.

   page 5

   b. Report your findings back to the other group.
4. **Explain** why Doc Reynolds uses the word "hypocritical" to refer to the campaign (line 25).

Recap → Why is tourism a debated issue in some parts of Australia?

TRAINING TASK

Responsible tourists?

track 3

1. Listen to four tourists talking about their holidays. Make notes. page 6

2. In groups, discuss and decide which of them are responsible tourists, i.e. respectful of the environment and the local culture.

3. Explain your choice to the other groups.

1 Grace

2 Ryan

3 Emily

4 Harry

Aboriginal tourism

1 Uluru-Kata Tjuta National Park

WELCOME TO ABORIGINAL LAND

Uluru-Kata Tjuta National Park

Rock-art at Uluru

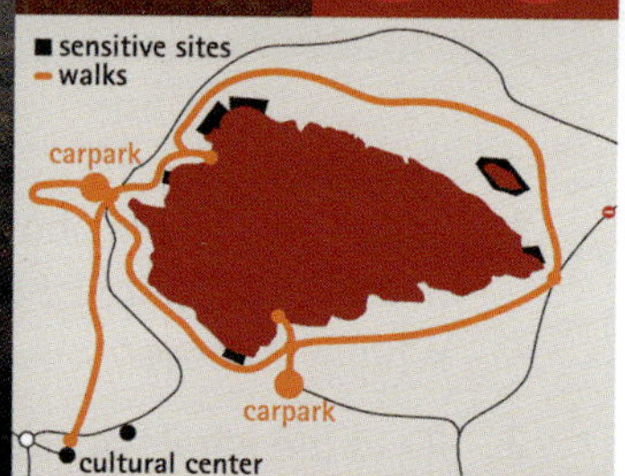

Towering 348 metres above the red desert in the heart of the Australian Outback, Uluru is both Australia's most visited icon and one of its most sacred places.

A few key dates about Uluru-Kata Tjuta

Early 1900's The area around Uluru and Kata Tjuta was declared an Aboriginal Reserve.

1950 Uluru (Aboriginal name)/Ayer's rock (name given by an English explorer) was declared a National Park. The land was taken away from the traditional owners by the Australian government.

1985 The handback: the Australian government gave the land back to the Aborigines, who signed an agreement leasing the park back to the Australian Parks and Wildlife Service for 99 years.

- **Skim-read the document above.**
  Say what you have learnt about Uluru-Kata Tjuta National Park.

2 Park management

video 2

A documentary
about Uluru-Kata Tjuta National Park.

1. **Watch the video**. Discuss what you have understood.
2. **a.** Watch the video again. Find out more about:
   - the management of the park, now and before 1985;
   - the benefits for indigenous people.

   b. Organise your findings and report them back to the class.

3 Indigenous tourism opportunities

track 4

A Newslines Radio programme about the indigenous tourism industry, 2009.

LANGUAGE TOOLS

★ WORDS → p. 20

Business

- a **bu**siness = an ac**ti**vity, an **en**terprise
- **ma**nagement, staff, **ran**gers, tour **op**erators
- run a **bu**siness, **ma**nage a park
- make a **li**ving = earn a **li**ving
- pro**vi**de oppor**tu**nities
- **be**nefit

→ They benefit from tourism, tourism benefits them.

★ GRAMMAR → p. 21

Passive forms

→ This business is run by indigenous people.

1. **Before listening**: what do you expect this radio programme to be about?
2. **Listen to the programme**, picking and memorising as much as you can. Tell your classmates what you have understood.
3. a. **In groups**, listen again and pick out information about:
   - the indigenous tourism industry *(group 1)*;
   - the benefits of tourism for indigenous people *(group 2)*.

   b. Organise your findings and share them with the other group.
4. **Explain** why the indigenous tourism industry can be an asset (i.e. something useful and valuable), for indigenous people and for Australia as a whole.

Recap → List the benefits of tourism for indigenous people.

TRAINING TASK

Visitor's guide

Keep in mind what you have learnt about Uluru-Kata Tjuta National Park and suggest a few possible entries for the contents page of a *Visitor's guide*.

1. In groups: choose one of these entries and develop it into a few lines. Don't hesitate to browse the Internet to get more information.

2. Whole class: read all the entries. Choose the best ones and discuss how you will organise them.
Write the contents page – you can add pictures if you wish.

Keeping culture alive

The Songlines[1]

Bruce, the narrator of this story, is touring Australia to try to learn more about Aboriginal culture. He is now in the Alice Springs area, in Mrs Lacey's Desert Bookstore, where a couple of American tourists are buying souvenirs. Stan is a Pintupi[2] elder and artist who has come to sell one of his paintings.

Mrs Lacey switched to her second pair of glasses and said: "What you got here, Stan?"

"Honey-ant[3]," he whispered in a hoarse voice.

"The honey-ant", she turned to the Americans, "is one of the totems[4] at Popanji. This painting's a honey-ant Dreaming[5]."

"I think it's beautiful", said the American woman thoughtfully. We could buy it."

"Now, dearest," said the husband in an effort to calm her. "First we have to ascertain if this honey-ant painting is for sale. And if so, how much?"

Mrs Lacey fluttered her eyelashes and said, harshly, "I couldn't say. You'll have to ask the artist."

Stan rolled the whites of his eyes to the ceiling and rustled his lips. Obviously, he was thinking of a price–the price he'd get from Mrs Lacey–and doubling it. [...] He then lowered his head and said, "Four hundred fifty."

"Australian dollars," Mrs Lacey chipped in.

"Fair enough," said the man, looking rather relieved. [...] "But now I want to know what's going on. In the painting I mean."

I crept up behind the Americans and watched Old Stan point his bony finger at the large blue circle on the canvas.

It was the Eternal Home, he explained, of the Honey-ant Ancestor at Tatata. And suddenly it was as though we could see the row on row of honey-ants, their bodies striped and gleaming, bursting with nectar in their cells beneath the roots of a mulga tree. We saw the ring of flame-red earth around the entrance to their nest, and the routes of their migration as they spread to other places.

"The circles," Mrs Lacey added helpfully, "are honey-ant ceremonial centres. The 'tubes', as you call them, are Dreaming-tracks."

The American man was captivated. "And can we go and look for these Dreaming tracks? Out there, I mean? Like the Ayer's Rock? Some place like that?

"They can," she said. "You can't.

"You mean they're invisible?"

"To you. Not to them."

" Then, where are they?"

" Everywhere," she said, "For all I know there's a Dreaming track running right through the middle of my shop."

"Spooky," the wife giggled.

"And only they can see it?"

"Or sing it," Mrs Lacey said. "You can't have a track without a song."

"And these tracks run every place?" the man asked. "All over Australia?"

"Yes," said Mrs Lacey, sighing with satisfaction at having found a catchy phrase. "The song and the land are one."

Bruce Chatwin, *The Songlines* (1986)

1. tracks/lines the mythical Ancestors followed as they sang the world into creation

2. an Australian Aboriginal group

3. Honey ants look like small crawling honey pots.

4. an animal or a plant which is the emblem of a clan and sometimes revered as its ancestor

5. The "Dreaming" or "Dreamtime" is the Aborigines' mythical time when the Ancestors walked across the land to create life.

1. **Read the introduction**. Identify the place, characters and situation. Guess what the excerpt might be about.
2. **Read the text**. Discuss what you have understood.
3. a. **In groups**: read the text again. Highlight details about:
   - the different characters' behaviours or reactions *(group 1)*;
   - the description and meaning of the painting *(group 2)*.

   pages 7-8

   b. Report your findings to the other group.
4. a. **Explain** what the painting may have helped the American man understand.
   b. **Comment** on Mrs Lacey's words: "The song and the land are one." (line 42).

Recap → How can tourism help indigenous people keep their culture alive?

LANGUAGE TOOLS

★ **WORDS** → p. 20

Buying and selling
- a **cus**tomer
- a **sou**venir, an **ar**tefact, a me**men**to, **art**works
- trade, **bar**gain
- au**then**tic = **ge**nuine
- for sale, on sale

→ Stan's painting is for sale at a fair price.
→ Stan's paintings are now on sale: they are sold at a reduced price.

Environment
- land, earth, a rock, a track, a tree, a shrub, a sand dune, **wild**life conser**va**tion
- take care of, pro**tect**, pre**serve**

TRAINING TASK

Identifying an Aboriginal painting

track 5

1. Listen to the description of one of the two paintings on this page. Identify the painting described.
2. Discuss why it matches the description.

★ WORDS

❶ Link words

a. Read the following list of link words:
• if - even - unless - as - provided - although
Check their meanings in a dictionary if necessary.

b. Complete the following sentences using one of these link words.
1. The site is not dangerous ... you follow the safety instructions.
2. Tourists won't be welcomed by the local population ... they behave appropriately.
3. A lot of tourists think package tours are not expensive ... they include transport, accommodation and entrance fees.
4. Some tourists don't respect the local traditions ... they know about them.

c. Sort the link words under one of these headings:
condition — paradox — cause

d. Using some of the link words above, comment on tourism in sacred places.
→ *Some sacred places are open to visitors provided they respect the rules.*

↑ Rock art.

❷ Heritage

a. Read this list of words referring to the Australian Aboriginal cultural heritage:
• rock art, engravings, sacred, dot painting, rituals, drawing, spirit, dreaming stories, track, soil, mountain, cave, ceremonial sites, waterfalls, music, totem, songlines

b. Sort them under one of these headings:
land and places of significance — art — beliefs

c. Use the picture above to present Aboriginal heritage to a group of tourists.

More exercises in your **Workbook** ▶ p.9-10

★ PRONUNCIATION

❸ Intonation of lists

track 6

"...tourists spend money on transport, accommodation, food, entry fees to places, souvenirs..."

L'intonation permet à celui qui parle de faire comprendre qu'une liste est ou n'est pas terminée.

a. Listen to this extract from the video *Tourism in Australia* (track 6. a) and say when the intonation is rising (↗) or falling (↘).
"Tourists spend money on transport (?), food (?), accommodation (?), entry fees to places? (?), souvenirs (?)..."

b. What do you notice?

c. Listen to another example (track 6. b) to confirm your conclusion.

d. Now practise pronouncing this sentence with the right intonation:
→ There are so many tourist attractions — for example the views, the weather, the architecture, the friendliness, the sports and of course the beaches.

More exercises in your **Workbook** ▶ p.10-11

★ GRAMMAR

Permission - obligation - prohibition

Observe

If you visit a sacred place you must be aware of the local traditions and values. You can visit different sites but you can't behave as if you were in your own country. For example when visiting some places, tourists must pay particular attention to the way they dress: women mustn't go bare-armed and have to wear long skirts and men are not allowed to wear shorts, explained the guide.

Classez les différentes formes verbales surlignées selon leur sens : permission, obligation ou interdiction.

g → Précis grammatical ⑫ p. 194-196

Practise

4 Rephrase the following sentences using a modal or an equivalent (several answers are possible):

a. Tourists are forbidden to take photos.
b. Visitors are allowed to climb Uluru provided they respect the place.
c. Indigenous people were denied the right to stay on their lands.
d. No smoking in this area.

5 List your obligations as a "responsible" tourist, starting from the list below:

- litter - clothes - photographs - shopping - wildlife - culture

Passive forms

Observe

National parks are usually large areas of land that are protected because they have unspoilt landscapes and a diverse number of native plants and animals. This means that commercial activities such as farming are prohibited and human activity is strictly monitored.

Repérez dans cette définition les verbes à la voix active et ceux à la voix passive. Comment reconnaît-on ces derniers ?

g → Précis grammatical ⑱ p. 200

Practise

6 Put the verb in brackets in the appropriate form:

a. The cultural centre *(build)* right in the middle of the park and it *(make)* of mud.
b. The area *(restrict)* because it is a sacred site but it *(not forbid)* to climb it.
c. Many people eagerly *(watch)* the colour changes on the rocks with the sun behind them.
d. Tourists always *(not tell)* how to behave in special places.

7 Put the verb in brackets in the appropriate form.

Fancy a Free Ranger-Guided Mala Walk?
A Mala Walk *(conduct)* daily by Park rangers. Meet at the Mala Walk sign. You will *(take)* along the base of the rock, and *(tell)* the story of the Mala Tjukurpa. Joint management of the Park, rock art, and traditional Anangu culture will also *(discuss)*.

← Mala Walk, Uluru, Autralia.

8 Write your own definition of sacred places.

More exercises in your **Workbook** ▶ p. 11-12

Stratégies

Comprendre un message oral (1)

À l'oral, comprendre un message en anglais peut sembler difficile mais ne doit pas vous décourager. Voici quelques conseils et stratégies qui vous aideront.

1 Entraînez-vous régulièrement

a. Écoutez de l'anglais le plus souvent possible : dans la classe mais aussi en dehors (émissions de radio sur Internet, DVD, etc.).

b. Enrichissez votre vocabulaire oral
Lorsque vous apprenez des mots et expressions, mémorisez leur sens, leur orthographe et leur prononciation.
Répétez-les en veillant aux sons et à la syllabe accentuée, puis vérifiez la prononciation dans le dictionnaire si besoin.

→ À vous
Mémorisez la prononciation des mots appris dans le chapitre.

2 Préparez-vous à l'écoute

Étapes	Indices	Exemple
1. Identifiez le contexte et la situation	Un titre, une image, ce qui a précédé dans la conversation ou les activités de classe, la source...	• programme de *BBC Radio 4* titre de l'émission : *Elvis by Bono*
2. Anticipez, faites des hypothèses.	• nature du document (reportage, publicité, interview, conférence, flash d'information, conversation, débat...) • le sujet dont il va être question • qui parle : une personne ou plusieurs ? • dans quel but ? (expliquer, raconter, décrire, convaincre) • les mots que l'on est susceptible d'entendre	On peut supposer : • qu'il s'agit d'une émission de musique, • que Bono va raconter aux auditeurs la vie d'Elvis Presley, • qu'il va expliquer pourquoi il aime ce chanteur, • qu'il répondra à des questions, • qu'on entendra des mots tels que : *great, rocker, fan, idol, born, Memphis, guitar, voice, fifties, song...*
3. Rassemblez les indices dont vous disposez.	Les éléments listés ci-dessus, votre propre expérience et vos connaissances générales.	Vous avez pu faire des hypothèses sur Bono et Elvis Presley à partir de ce que vous connaissez d'eux.

→ À vous
Faites des hypothèses, les plus larges possibles, à partir de ces titres d'émission :

Great explorers

Age of the genome

Have your say: *does tourism bring positive changes to your country?*

3 Soyez actif lors de l'écoute : mémorisez

Écouter, ce n'est pas « ne rien faire ». Lorsque le son passe il faut savoir le retenir, donc exercer sa mémoire pour pouvoir s'affranchir des notes, sauf quand le document est long.

→ À vous

track 8

Écoutez l'enregistrement et mémorisez le plus d'éléments possible.

4 Repérez pour faire du sens

Lors d'écoutes successives, vous pourrez recueillir de nouveaux indices pour vérifier vos hypothèses. N'essayez pas de tout comprendre mais de trouver des réponses aux questions que vous vous êtes posées :

Éléments à repérer	Objectifs
l'environnement sonore (bruits de fond, musique, applaudissements...)	Identifier la **nature** du document
les voix (leur nombre, homme/femme, adulte/enfant...)	Identifier les **personnes qui parlent**
Le ton, l'intonation	Faire des premières hypothèses sur les **sentiments ou opinions** des locuteurs
Les mots que vous connaissez ou que vous avez déjà anticipés	Avoir une idée du **sujet**
Les dates, les heures, les chiffres (à mettre en lien avec : le temps des verbes et les adverbes de temps ; les éléments quantifiés)	Avoir une première idée : • du **temps** • de la **quantité**
Les questions posées s'il s'agit d'une interview	Anticiper les réponses avant une nouvelle écoute
Les mots-clés sont toujours accentués et souvent répétés	Importants pour le sens

→ À vous

track 9 part 1

Global Trends radio phone-in programme

Repérez et listez les éléments que vous avez saisis.

5 Mettez les indices en relation pour construire le sens

Étapes	Faire du sens
1. Vérifiez vos premières hypothèses et émettez-en de nouvelles.	Qui parle ? à qui ? où ? quand ? de quoi ? qui dit quoi ?
2. Cherchez des points communs entre des éléments repérés à différents endroits du document.	Mots répétés, champ lexical, une opinion avec son argument, un exemple, un fait et son explication, etc.
3. Notez vos nouvelles hypothèses de sens, elles serviront de guide lors de la prochaine écoute du même document.	Qui parle ? dans quel but ?

→ À vous

track 9 part 1

Global Trends radio phone-in programme

Réécoutez le document et résumez ce que vous avez compris.

Comprendre un message oral (1)

↑ Mass tourism in Angkor, Cambodia: escalating a temple

Talk show: *Do you think tourism should be restricted?*

track 10

a. Préparez-vous à l'écoute d'une émission à l'aide des *Stratégies* pp. 22-23.

b. Écoutez l'extrait (3 fois) : qu'avez-vous repéré et compris ?

Faites le point

a. Vérifiez votre compréhension. **Auto-corrigé** ▶ www.didierpassword.fr

b. Situez votre niveau dans le tableau ci-dessous.

Niveaux	Mes compétences
B1-1	J'ai pu me préparer et faire des repérages pour comprendre globalement la position adoptée par quelqu'un dans une discussion sur un thème que je connais bien.
B1-2	J'ai pu comprendre globalement quels arguments utilise une personne dans une discussion sur un sujet que je connais bien.
B1-3	J'ai pu repérer et comprendre tous les avis formulés.
B2	J'ai pu comprendre correctement le ton, l'humeur des locuteurs.

FINAL TASKS

Promoting tourism

task 1

Speaking

Make a video commentary

video 3

Provide a commentary for a video promoting responsible tourism in Australia.

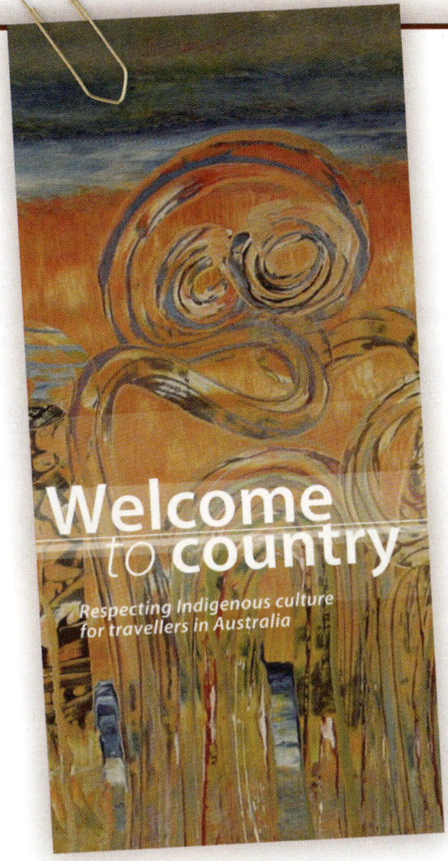

1. Get ready

In pairs

- Watch the video three times, making notes.
- Organise your notes and ideas.
- Watch the video once again and complete your notes.
- Rehearse what you are going to say, paying particular attention to pronunciation.

2. Action!

Individual work

- Record your commentary.
- Remember to speak clearly and to stress the important words.

task 2

Listening

Suggest the best tourist destination for three visitors

- Listen to holiday ads and look at these three tourists' profiles.
- Which destination is best for each of them? Justify.

Listening test

- Listen to a recording, then answer the questions your teacher will give you.

UNIT 2 Social networks

↑ Making friends

How has social networking changed our lives?

Look at this picture and the title of the chapter.
Do you use social networking sites?
Tell the class about your experiences and views.

FINAL TASKS

P. 39

Talk Show

Speaking
Take part in a TV talk show

Reading
Match social networking sites with their potential users

CULTURE

- Exploring 21st century online communication:
  - the rise of social networking,
  - its impact on personal lives.
- New relationships with the world.
- Social studies:
  - Christine Rosen : *"Virtual Friendship and The New Narcissism"*
  - David Kirkpatrick, *The Facebook Effect: The Inside Story of the Company That Is Connecting the World*

COMMUNICATION

- Discussing social networking sites.
- Discussing the changes social networking has brought to our lives.
- Understanding the evolution of social networking sites from various sources.
- Understanding key information and arguments in a press article and in a narrative.
- Giving a short presentation, backing up what you say with relevant explanations.

TOOLS

★ Words
- The Internet
- Self portraying
- Revealing
- Group activism

★ Pronunciation
- Stress and comparisons
- Compound nouns with *self-*

★ Grammar
- Questions (How long?/How often?)
- *For* et *since*

Stratégies
→ *Exprimer son opinion et convaincre*

Social networking times

1 Keys dates and figures

▶ **2003** The social networking site boom begins (MySpace, LinkedIn, Hi5...).

▶ **2004** Mark Zuckerberg, a 19 -year-old student at Harvard, starts a Web service from his room: Thefacebook.com, an "online directory that connects people through social networks at college". Flickr appears in the virtual world.

▶ **2005** Bebo and YouTube are launched.

▶ **2006** Twitter and Windows Live Spaces are born.

▶ **2007** In March, MySpace hits 100 million monthly unique users worldwide.

▶ **2010** In February, Facebook announces it has 400 million active members. That's larger than the population of the US and UK combined. In a single day, about a billion new pieces of content are posted on Facebook.

2 0 1 0

The rise of Facebook

Mark Elliot Zuckerberg has been elected *TIME*'s 2010 Person of the Year "for connecting more than half a billion people, for creating a new system of exchanging information, and for changing how we live our lives". ■

PERSON OF THE YEAR
Mark Elliot Zuckerberg is connecting more than half a billion people.

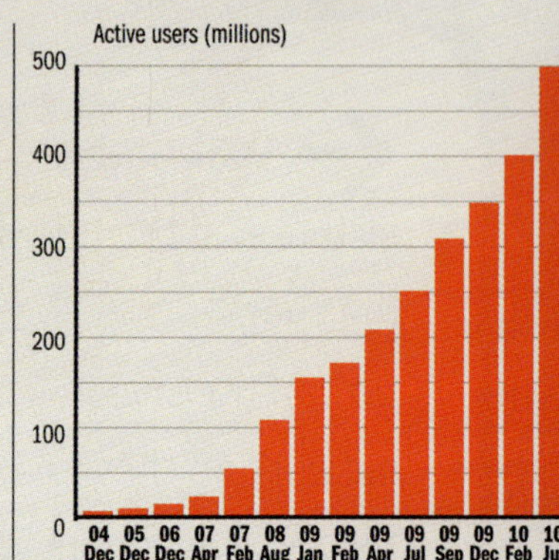

Source: Facebook

1. **In groups**:
   - study the chronology *(group 1)*;
   - study the article *(group 2)*.

   Report your findings to the other group.
2. **Whole class**: explain the possible reasons for the success of social networking sites.

2 Social network users

track 11

An NPR* radio programme, 2007

* National Public Radio: a US media organisation with about 750 member stations. NPR's programmes are renowned for their quality.

1. **Before listening**, list all the words you expect to hear.
2. **Listen to the programme**. Discuss what you have understood.
3. Listen again:
   a. First, concentrate on the people who use social networking sites.
   b. Listen once more, concentrating on how social networking sites work.
   c. Share your findings with the class.
4. **React**: comment on the photo on the left to summarise what you have learnt.

3 What Americans use the Internet for

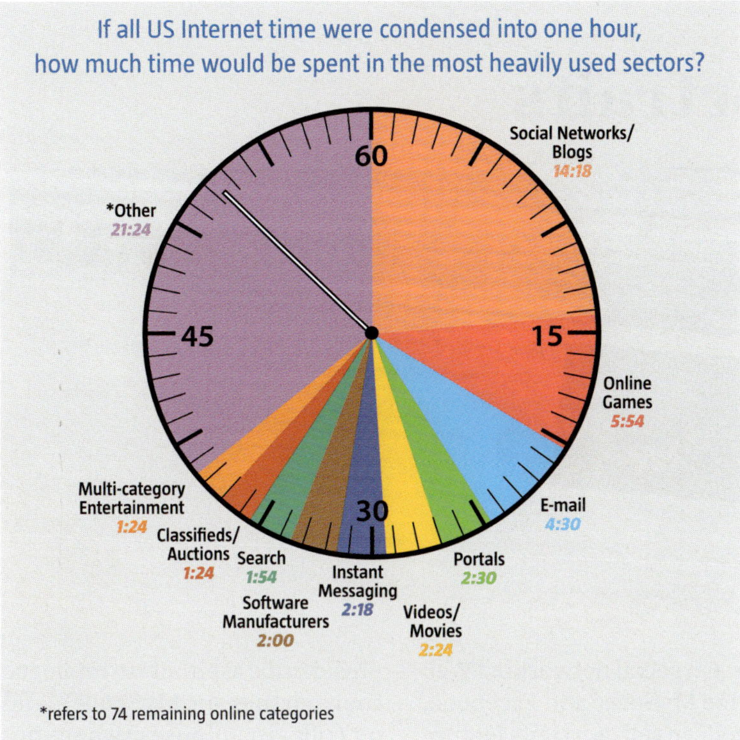

1. **Study the chart:**
   a. In your own words, say what you understand or list your questions.
   b. Summarise what the chart shows.
2. **React**: compare your own use of the Internet with that of the Americans surveyed.

Recap → Define what social networking sites are and give the reasons why so many people use them.

LANGUAGE TOOLS

★ WORDS → p. 34

The Internet

- a **pro**file, a **so**cial **net**working Web site, **friend**ship, a com**mu**nity, an ac**count**, an **up**load
- be on**line**, surf, **face**book, post, **so**cialise, share text

→ "Facebook me!"

★ PRONUNCIATION → p. 34

Stress and comparisons

★ GRAMMAR → p. 35

Questions

→ how long? / how often? / how much time?

For/since

→ I have been chatting since 2 o'clock.

→ It's 6! You've been chatting non-stop for four hours!

TRAINING TASK

My favourite site

1. In groups, do some brief research about one of these social networking sites.

2. Give your classmates three reasons to become a member.

LibraryThing What's on your bookshelf?

bebo

twitter

flickr

LinkedIn

My online self

Modern self-portraits

For centuries, the rich and the powerful documented their existence and their status through painted portraits. A marker of wealth and a bid for immortality, portraits offer intriguing hints about the daily life of their subjects—professions, ambitions, attitudes, and, most importantly, social standing [...].

Self-portraits can be especially instructive. By showing the artist both as he sees his true self and as he wishes to be seen, self-portraits can at once expose and obscure, clarify and distort. They offer opportunities for both self-expression and self-seeking. They can display egotism and modesty, self-aggrandizement and self-mockery.

Today, our self-portraits are democratic and digital; they are crafted from pixels rather than paints. On social networking Web sites like MySpace and Facebook, our modern self-portraits feature background music, carefully manipulated photographs, stream-of-consciousness musings, and lists of our hobbies and friends. They are interactive, inviting viewers not merely to look at, but also to respond to, the life portrayed online. We create them to find friendship, love, and that ambiguous modern thing called connection. Like painters constantly retouching their work, we alter, update, and tweak our online self-portraits; but as digital objects they are far more ephemeral than oil on canvas. Vital statistics, glimpses of bare flesh, lists of favorite bands and favorite poems all clamor for our attention—and it is the timeless human desire for attention that emerges as the dominant theme of these vast virtual galleries.

Joshua Grigby (English landowner), by Thomas Gainsborough, circa 1760.

Although social networking sites are in their infancy, we are seeing their impact culturally: in language (where *to friend* is now a verb), in politics (where it is de rigueur for presidential aspirants to catalogue their virtues on MySpace), and on college campuses (where not using Facebook can be a social handicap). [...]

But we are only beginning to come to grips with the consequences of our use of these sites: for friendship, and for our notions of privacy, authenticity, community, and identity. As with any technological advance, we must consider what type of behavior online social networking encourages. Does this technology, with its constant demands to collect (friends and status), and perform (by marketing ourselves), in some ways undermine our ability to attain what it promises—a surer sense of who we are and where we belong? The Delphic oracle's guidance was *know thyself*. Today, in the world of online social networks, the oracle's advice might be *show thyself*.

Christine Rosen, "Virtual Friendship and the New Narcissism", *The New Atlantis* (2007)

1. **Before reading the article**, look at the facebook page and the portrait on page 30. How can they be linked to the title of the article?
2. **Read the article** and discuss what you have understood.
3. a. **Focus on lines 1 to 50**. Compare painted and digital portraits; highlight:
   - the common points;
   - the differences.

   pages 13-14

   b. Discuss your findings with your classmates.
4. **Read from line 51 to the end.**
   a. Highlight the elements showing the impact of social networking sites.

   pages 13-14

   b. Discuss your findings with the class.
5. Comment on lines 81 to 82 "the oracle's advice might be *show thyself*".

Recap → Explain and discuss how online social networking influences people's behaviour.

LANGUAGE TOOLS

★ WORDS → p. 34

Self-portraying
- **e**gotism = **nar**cissism
- **mo**desty = re**serve**
- **self**ishness, **self**-admi**ra**tion = **self**-**in**terest
- show off, boast = brag

→ She is showing off with her new iPhone.
→ Facebook boasts 500 million members.
→ He always brags about how many friends he has on MySpace.

Revealing
- re**veal** = dis**play**; ex**hi**bit
- dis**tort** = misrepre**sent**
- leak = *s'ébruiter*

→ She was very upset that personal information leaked out to the public.

★ PRONUNCIATION → p. 34

Stress in compound nouns with *self-*
→ self-portrait, self-interest

TRAINING TASK

Have your say!

Discuss the possible consequences of social networking, starting from these cartoons.

New relationships with the world

"Digitally fueled activism"

In 2008, Oscar Morales, a civil engineer from Colombia, wanted to publicly voice his outrage at FARC* and their policy of taking hostages. He decided to create a Facebook group called "Un millión de voces contra las FARC" – "One Million Voices Against FARC". This is what ensued:

↑ A march of protest against FARC, Medellin, Colombia, 2008.

After midnight on January 4, Morales created the group. He made it public so that any Facebook member could join. His personal network included about one hundred friends, and he invited them all. He was tired. At 3 A.M. he went to bed.

At 9 A.M. the next morning he checked his group. Fifteen hundred people had joined already! "Woooooooo!!!" Morales howled in delight. This was an even better response than he had expected! That day at the beach he told his extended family about the group and asked them to invite their own Facebook friends to join. Most of them were avid Facebook users as well, and they hated FARC, too. By the time Morales returned home in the late afternoon, his group had four thousand members.

"That's when I said to myself, 'Okay, no more beach, no more going out." He was ready to get serious. "I felt, 'Oh my God! This is what I want! A committed community around the message." [...]

As more and more Colombians joined the group, members started talking not only about how mad they were about FARC, but what they ought to do about it. On January 6, just the second full day, a consensus on the page was emerging that the burgeoning group should go public. By the time it hit eight thousand members, people were posting on the discussion board, over and over, "Let's DO something."

Late on the afternoon of the 6th, his newfound Facebook friends, especially two he was speaking to by phone, convinced Morales that he should propose a demonstration. When he did, the idea was received on the wall and discussion board by acclamation. By the end of the day the group, still operating only out of Morales's upstairs bedroom, had decided to stage a national march against FARC. It would be February 4, one month after the formation of the group. Morales, who was used to being left out of things since he lived in a provincial city, insisted the march take place not only in Bogota, the capital, but also many other places throughout the country, including of course his hometown of Barranquilla.

So Morales created an event called the National March against FARC. He and his co-organizers, several of them already as consumed by the project as he was, immediately got pushback from unexpected quarters. Members in Miami, Buenos Aires, Madrid, Los Angeles, Paris, and elsewhere argued that it should be a global demonstration. Morales didn't even realize people

*FARC: Revolutionary Armed Forces of Colombia, a revolutionary guerrilla force engaged in armed struggle against the government of Colombia.

living outside Colombia had joined the group. These Colombian émigrés were on Facebook partly to stay in touch with things back home. They wanted to be involved in this movement, too. So it became a global march.

What ensued was one of the most extraordinary examples of digitally fueled activism the world has ever seen. On February 4, about 10 million people marched against FARC in hundreds of cities in Colombia according to Colombian press estimates. As many as 2 million more marched in cities around the world. The movement that began with an impassioned midnight Facebook post in one frustrated young man's bedroom led to one of the largest demonstrations ever, anywhere in the world.

David Kirkpatrick, *The Facebook Effect: The Inside Story of the Company That Is Connecting the World* (2010)

1. **Read the introduction**. Explain what you have understood and imagine what happens next.

2. **a.** **Read the text** and highlight:
- the dates;
- the numbers of people who joined Oscar Morales;
- the cities mentioned.

pages 14-15

b. Explain what Oscar Morales achieved.

3. Read the text again and explain its title.

Recap → Discuss how virtual relationships can influence the real world on a global scale.

LANGUAGE TOOLS

★ WORDS → p. 34

Group activism
- a march = a demon**stra**tion, a **pro**test
- com**mit**ment = in**vol**vement
- as**sem**ble = **ga**ther, con**vene**
- **sum**mon
- Join/get in**vol**ved in/take part in

→ The demonstrators were summoned via email.

TRAINING TASK

Group activism

1. Give examples of large-scale protests or events organised through social networking.

2. Discuss the positive and negative aspects of such events.

International Pillow Fight Day
New York, March 22, 2008.

Unfriend Coal: a 2011 Internet campaign by Greenpeace to convince Facebook to use only 100% renewable energy.

★ WORDS

❶ Speaking about activities involving new technology

a. Observe the following sentences:
1. I spend my time **surfing** on the Internet.
2. I can't help **checking** my email every hour.
3. **Texting** has become a popular way of **communicating**.

b. Write down five sentences to talk about activities that can be done with mobile phones or computers.

❷ Turning verbs into nouns

You may have read or used these verbs in the chapter. Add the right ending to turn them into nouns. Use a dictionary if necessary.

demonstrate	*a demonstration*
commit	
mobilize	
develop	
employ	
involve	*involvement*
judge	
alter	
admire	

More exercises in your **Workbook** ▶ p. 16-17

★ PRONUNCIATION

❸ Stress and comparisons

track 12

"...it used to be the territory of people at high school... but now that's not the case anymore..."

Dans une comparaison, un locuteur met en relief les éléments comparés en les accentuant plus fortement.

a. Listen to a person talking about how communication has changed.
1. I spend more time on the phone now than I ever used to.
2. It's now becoming difficult to find phone boxes in towns, and not long ago they were everywhere.
3. You not only talk to people in other countries but now you can see them as well.
4. Christmas cards used to cost a fortune; now you send them all by email.
5. Some people I know still write letters and put them in envelopes.

b. Take notes of the stressed words which reinforce these comparisons.

c. Practise saying some of the sentences you have heard on track 12.

d. Now practise doing the same: talk about some changes in your life.

❹ Compound nouns with *self-*

track 13

You have seen a number of compound nouns starting with *self-* in this chapter:
• self-portraits, self-mockery, self-confidence, self-seeking, self-expression...

a. Listen to these words and underline the syllables which are stressed. Check with your classmates that you all agree.

b. Try and decide together on the stress patterns: (O o), (O O) or (o O)?

c. Say what conclusions you can draw.

d. Practise pronouncing them.

More exercises in your **Workbook** ▶ p. 17-18

★ GRAMMAR

For et *since*

Observe

A. No wonder he was late for school this morning. He was on Facebook ***for*** 4 hours last night.

B. She's doing some research for her homework and has been on the Internet ***since*** 2 o'clock. We haven't heard her ***for*** two hours.

C. I haven't had any news from them ***since*** they stopped using Facebook.

- **Que précisent *for* et *since* dans ces phrases ?**
- **Quand emploie-t-on *for* ? Quand emploie t-on *since* ?**
- **Comparez et expliquez les formes verbales soulignées dans les phrases A et B.**

g → Précis grammatical ⑬ p. 196

Practise

5 Complete the following sentences with *for* or *since*.

a. Our campaign for a shorter school day has gathered strong support ... we launched it on the school website in September.
b. Facebook has been very popular ... four years and its success is growing everyday.
c. ... months now, people have been warned about the dangers of social networking.
d. I used to play video games ... hours. I haven't played ... the doctor told me it could hurt my eyes.
e. ... when have parents been able to check what sites their children visit on the Internet?

6 Write down five sentences, using *for* and *since* to talk about your Internet activities.

Questions

Observe

A. *How long* was he stuck to his computer?
He was stuck to his computer for 10 hours.

B. *How many times* has he changed his e-mail address?
He is so cautious he has changed his e-mail address at least four times so far.

C. *How much time* does he spend on Facebook every week?
He usually spends 10 hours a week on Facebook.

D. *How often* is he allowed to connect?
He is allowed to connect twice a week.

- **Que veut-on savoir exactement lorsque l'on utilise *how long..., how many times..., how much time...* ou *how often...?***
- **Comment sont formés les mots interrogatifs soulignés ?**
- **Connaissez-vous au moins un autre mot interrogatif formé de la même manière ? Lequel ?**

g → Précis grammatical ⑮ p. 198

Practise

7 You want to conduct a survey about the amount of time young people spend on the Internet. Jot down five questions you would ask.

8 Look at the cartoon below and imagine the questions Twitter could ask her parents.

"MOMMY AND DADDY MET ON A SOCIAL NETWORKING SITE. THAT'S WHY WE NAMED YOU TWITTER."

More exercises in your Workbook ▶ p. 19

Exprimer son opinion et convaincre

Lors d'une discussion vous serez souvent amené à exprimer votre opinion. Les techniques oratoires suivantes vous permettront de prendre une part active au débat et d'être convaincant.

Entraînez-vous à partir du sujet suivant :
It is possible to live without mobile phones.

Arguments possibles

For	Against
→ *Our parents didn't have mobile phones.* → *Real contacts are better.* → *You are not disturbed all the time.*	→ *You should keep up with the times.* → *Useful in case of emergency.* → *You are not part of a group.*

1 Impliquez votre interlocuteur

Technique	Exemples
1. Mettez-le dans une situation où il sera incité à adopter votre point de vue.	→ *"Imagine you are driving in the middle of a desert and your car suddenly stops..."*
2. Reprenez ses arguments à votre compte en utilisant la concession ou la comparaison.	*however - yet - still - nevertheless - although...* → *"You say that... but/however/yet... "* → *" I agree with you but..."* → *"You are right, however I think that..."* → *"Although you are right, I think..."*

→ À vous

Choisissez dans le tableau des arguments possibles un point avec lequel vous n'êtes pas d'accord.

a. Formulez vos propres arguments de manière à impliquer votre interlocuteur.

b. Donnez votre opinion en utilisant la concession ou la comparaison.

2 Posez des questions

Technique	Exemples
1. Demandez des éclaircissements et des exemples précis qui pourront amener votre interlocuteur à se contredire.	→ *"Can you give me an example?"*
2. Amenez votre interlocuteur à être d'accord avec vous en utilisant des questions rhétoriques.	→ *"Don't you think that having a mobile is really useful in case of an emergency?"* → *"Can you deny the fact that...?"* → *"Do you really think that...?"*

→ À vous

Choisissez deux arguments dans le tableau p. 36 puis posez des questions à votre interlocuteur afin de le contredire.

3 Mettez en valeur vos arguments

Technique	Exemples
1. Utilisez les verbes appropriés : • pour exprimer votre opinion • pour marquer votre désaccord	→ *I think, I agree, in my opinion, as far as I'm concerned, I don't doubt, I know...* → *I don't agree, I disagree, I can't believe, I don't share your point of view...*
2. Illustrez vos arguments avec : • des exemples précis, • des anecdotes, • des chiffres, etc.	→ *"Less than 20% of teenagers don't have a mobile phone..."*
3. Accentuez certains mots afin d'être plus convaincant.	→ *"Today, everybody has a mobile phone."* → *"Do you know one person who doesn't have one?"*
4. Utilisez l'intonation descendante pour affirmer votre point de vue.	→ *"Do you really believe that?"* ↘ → *"What a strange idea!"* ↘ → *"I really think that..."* ↘

→ À vous

Imaginez une anecdote en utilisant le tableau des arguments p. 36 puis exprimez votre opinion. N'oubliez pas d'utiliser l'intonation et l'accentuation !

4 Nuancez vos affirmations

Évitez les exagérations : nuancez vos affirmations.

"Teenagers have become totally illiterate because of text messaging."

→ *Many teenagers now have spelling difficulties because of text messaging.*

→ À vous

Nuancez les affirmations ci-dessous :

a. *Everybody has a mobile phone.*

b. *Teenagers don't read books anymore.*

c. *People who spend their time in front of their computers are completely out of touch with reality.*

Exprimer son opinion et convaincre

Discutez de la citation suivante :

"We have more media than ever and more technology in our lives. It's supposed to help us communicate, but it has the opposite effect of isolating us."

Tracy Chapman, chanteuse américaine

Vous pouvez vous inspirer de la bande dessinée ci-dessous.

a. Listez vos réactions sous forme de notes.

b. Confrontez votre point de vue à celui de vos camarades.

Faites le point

a. Vérifiez votre production. **Auto-corrigé** ▶ www.didierpassword.fr

b. Situez votre niveau dans le tableau ci-dessous.

Niveaux	Mes compétences
B1-1	J'ai pu demander à quelqu'un ce qu'il pensait.
	J'ai pu exprimer poliment mon opinion et dire si j'étais d'accord ou non avec mon interlocuteur.
	J'ai pu interrompre poliment mon interlocuteur quand je n'étais pas d'accord ou quand je ne comprenais pas.
	J'ai pu lui demander de répéter ce qu'il venait de dire.
B1-2	J'ai pu m'exprimer autrement quand mon interlocuteur ne me comprenait pas. J'ai pu exprimer mon désaccord avec une opinion. J'ai pu échanger pour confronter mon point de vue à celui de mon interlocuteur.
B2	J'ai pu exprimer mes idées et mes opinions avec précision et les défendre en fournissant des explications, des arguments et des commentaires.

Final Tasks

Talk Show

task 1

Speaking

Take part in a TV talk show:
How has social networking changed our lives?

Your teacher will hand out role-play cards to form the discussion panel.

1. Get ready!

- Discover your role-play card and jot down notes about your opinion.
- Prepare arguments and examples which will help you answer questions.
- Imagine what the other members of the panel may say and prepare counter-arguments.

2. Action!

- Wait for the TV presenter to allow you to speak.
- Consider the views of the members of the panel before speaking. Take their remarks into account.
- Interrupt politely and ask for explanations if necessary.

task 2

Reading

Match social networking sites with their potential users

- Your teacher will give you descriptions of websites and of potential users' needs and tastes.
- Choose the best website for each user.

Reading test

- Your teacher will give you a text: read it carefully, then answer the questions.

UNIT 3 Mafia gangsters

↑ Poster for ***Once upon a Time in America***, directed by Sergio Leone (1968)

How are mafia gangsters represented in fiction?

← **Read** the title of the chapter and **take a look** at this film poster. **Comment** on them and **tell** the class what you already know about American gangsters.

FINAL TASKS

P. 53

Mafia stories

Writing

Write a dialogue for a scene in a mafia story

Listening

Match film posters and film reviews

CULTURE	COMMUNICATION	TOOLS
• Discovering the real lives of famous mobsters. • Exploring the representation of mobsters' lives in fiction. • Literary works: - Mario Puzo, *The Last Don* - Christopher Gambino, *The Only Son* - *Road to Perdition* (trailer), directed by Sam Mendes	• Writing a letter expressing feelings and moods. • Writing a dialogue. • Understanding a video documentary and interviews about a famous mobster. • Understanding the key events in a film plot from a trailer. Understanding the main events and the characters' feelings in a narrative.	★ **Words** • Power • Criminal activities • Attitudes • Trust/suspicion, admiration ★ **Pronunciation** • Stress on words with a prefix • Stress to contrast past and present ★ **Grammar** • Questions • Tag questions • Short questions **Stratégies** → *Rédiger un dialogue narratif*

Real-life Mafia gangsters

1 Public Enemy #1

Organised-crime networks known as the Mafia or the Mob rose to power through their success in the illicit liquor trade during the Prohibition era (from 1919 to 1933, when it was illegal to make, sell or transport alcoholic drinks in the US).

They operated in cities across the United States, particularly New York and Chicago. One of the most notorious top mobsters was Al Capone.

❶

WANTED:

PUBLIC ENEMY #1

ALPHONSE GABRIEL CAPONE

PUBLIC ENEMY NUMBER ONE

PUBLIC ENEMY NUMBER ONE

DESCRIPTION

Born: January 17, 1899 **Birthplace:** Brooklyn, New York **Height:** 5' 9" **Weight:** 225 **Hair:** Black **Eyes:** Brow
Complexion: Dark, Ruddy **Scars, Marks, Tatoo's:** Visible facial scarring along left cheek

REMARKS

Al Capone, alias "Scarface" so named due to three visible wounds inflicted in a bar fight by a straight razor is currently being sought by the United States Government's **DEPARTMENT of the TREASURY, BUREAU OF INTERNAL REVENUE SERVICE,** for Violation of Federal Income Tax Evasion Laws for the years 1925-1929. A team of United States Prohibition agents nicknamed the **"Untouchables"** headed by Chief agent **Eliot Ness** are investigating the **Capone Crime Organization.**

CAUTION

Al Capone is believed to have masterminded the 1929 **St. Valentine's Day Massacre** in the **Lincoln Park** distric on Chicago's North Side where his henchman, **Jack "Machine Gun" McGurn** & three others wiped out the rival **"North Side" Gang** led by mobster **George 'Bugs' Moran.**

F.B.I. Bulletin #: AC-311787-CD-44551-K Issued by: J. Edgar Hoover, Director Dated: June 15, 1931

❷

January 25, 1947

CAPONE DEAD AT 48

Heart Disease Fatal at Miami Beach Home After Stroke of Apoplexy Last Week

LINKED TO WIDE KILLINGS

Ruler of Chicago Underworld Was Finally Put in Alcatraz for Income-Tax Fraud

❸

The Chicago Daily News FINAL EDITION

October 17, 1931

JURY CONVICTS AL CAPONE

1. What do you know about Prohibition and Al Capone? **Read** the introduction and **explain** why the Mafia expanded its US operations in the 1920s.

2. Look at document ❶. Share what you have understood with your classmates. Where would such posters be seen? Why?

3. a. Read the headlines (documents ❷ and ❸). What can you guess about Al Capone's life:
- his origins?
- his family?
- his crimes...?

b. Start filling in Al Capone's ID card:
page 20 or ▶ www.didierpassword.fr

2 Capone's life in close-up

video 4

A TV documentary about Al Capone's life and times

↑ Al Capone with family and friends at a picnic, Chicago Heights, 1929.

1. **Before watching**: say what you expect to find out.
2. **Watch the documentary**. Use the pictures to help you understand what is said. Briefly discuss your findings.
3. Watch again and find out more about:
   - Al Capone's origins and youth;
   - Al Capone's success;
   - Al Capone's personal and business relationships.
4. **Discuss** your findings and complete Al Capone's ID Card.
   page 20 or ▶ www.didierpassword.fr
5. **React** to what you have learnt in this documentary.

LANGUAGE TOOLS

★ WORDS → p. 48

Power
- a chief = a **lead**er, a boss
- **pow**erful, **in**flu**en**tial ≠ **pow**erless

Criminal activities
- drug **traf**ficking, racke**teer**ing, theft, il**le**gal **gam**bling
- com**mit** a crime = break the law
- a **crim**inal: someone who breaks the law
- a **mur**derer = a **kill**er
- **blood**thirsty, uncon**trol**lable, en**raged**

★ PRONUNCIATION → p. 48

Stress to contrast past and present

★ GRAMMAR → p. 49

Asking questions

→ Where was he arrested?

Recap → Using your Mobster ID Card, present Al Capone, insisting on significant aspects of his life.

TRAINING TASK

Famous criminals

1. a. Group work. Here are three famous mobsters. Select one and research his life and crimes. Use your mobster ID cards.
pages 20-21 or ▶ www.didierpassword.fr

b. Prepare questions to interview the other groups about the gang leader they have chosen.

2. a. Interview the other groups.

b. Whole class. What do these mobsters have in common?

Paul Castellano

John Gotti

Lucky Luciano

Success story

The last Don

The Last Don ***is the fictitious story of a powerful mobster family. In this extract, Dominico Clericuzio, the "Don" (the powerful head of a Mafia family), has gathered his sons and his nephew for a reunion.***

The Don and his sons sat around the white wrought-iron table in the trellised garden at the back of the mansion. The oldest, Giorgio, was tall, with a small, fierce mustache and lanky frame of an English gentleman, which he adorned with tailored clothes. He was twenty-seven, saturnine, with savage wit and a closed face. The Don informed Giorgio that he, Giorgio, would be applying to the Wharton School of Business. There he would learn all the intricacies of stealing money while staying within the law.

Giorgio did not question his father; this was a royal edict; not an invitation to discussion. He nodded obedience.

The Don addressed his nephew, Joseph "Pippi" De Lena, next. The Don loved Pippi as much as he did his sons, for in addition to blood – Pippi being his dead sister's son – Pippi was the great general who had conquered the savage Santadio*.

"You will go and live permanently in Vegas," he said. "You will look after our interest in the Xanadu Hotel. Now that our Family is retiring from operations, there will not be much work for you here to do. However you will remain the Family Hammer."

He saw Pippi was not happy, that he must give reasons. "Your wife, Nalene, cannot live in the atmosphere of the Family, she cannot be accepted by them. You must build your life away from us." Which was all true, but the Don had another reason. Pippi was the great hero general of the Clericuzio Family, and if he continued to be "Mayor" of the Bronx Enclave, he would be too powerful for the sons of the Don when the Don no longer lived.

"You will be my Bruglione in the West," he told Pippi. "You will become rich. But there is important work to do." [...]

The Don then turned to his youngest son, Vincent [and] smiled at him. "I am about to decide your destiny," he said, "and set you on your true path. You will open the finest restaurant in New York. Spare no expense. I want you to show the French what real food is all about." Pippi and the other sons laughed, even Vincent smiled. The Don smiled at him. "You will go to the best cooking school in Europe for a year."

Vincent, though pleased, growled, "What can they teach me?"

The Don gave him a stern look. "Your pastries could be better," he said. "But the main purpose is to learn the finances of running such an enterprise. Who knows, someday you may own a chain of restaurants. Giorgio will give you the money." [...]

"Giorgio," the Don said, "You will be my successor. You and Vinnie will no longer take part in that necessary part of the Family which invites danger,

* Leader of a rival crime family.

except when it is absolutely necessary. We must look ahead. Your children, my children, and little Dante and Croccifixio must never grow up in this world. We are rich, we no longer have to risk our lives to earn our daily bread. Our Family will now serve only as financial advisors to all the other Families. We will serve as their political support, mediate their quarrels. But to do this we must have the cards to play. We must have an army. And we must protect everyone's money, for which they will let us wet our beaks."

He paused. "Twenty, thirty years from now, we will all disappear into the lawful world and enjoy our wealth without fear. Those two infants we are baptizing today [Dante and Croccifixio] will never have to commit our sins and take our risks."

Mario Puzo, *The Last Don* (1996)

1. **Before reading**, focus on the title of the text, the introduction and the picture. Discuss what this title may imply.

2. **Read the text** and identify who the Don is talking to. Tell the class what you have understood.

3. **a.** **In groups**, highlight information about:
- the Don: material success, decisions, thoughts *(group 1)*;
- the young men: relationships, physical portraits, roles/occupation *(group 2)*.

pages 22-23

b. Share your findings.

4. Now focus on the young men's moods, feelings and attitudes. Discuss their states of mind throughout the meeting and explain their reactions.

pages 22-23

5. Read the last two paragraphs again (lines 39 to 51). Pick out the repeated verbal forms used by the Don. What do they reveal about his personality and aspirations?

Recap → Explain and discuss Mario Puzo's opinion about the success of Mafia stories:

"I think it's a story with warm personal family feeling, and I think also it's everybody's wish, I mean, that they would have somebody they could go to [...] somebody fixing up your world for you."

LANGUAGE TOOLS

★ WORDS → p. 48

Attitudes
- **loy**alty ≠ dis**loy**alty, **treach**ery
- o**bey** ≠ diso**bey**

→ You have to obey the Don.
- o**bed**ient, sub**mis**sive ≠ re**bel**lious
- im**pos**ing, im**press**ive ≠ insig**nif**icant

★ GRAMMAR → p. 49

Tag Questions

→ Al Capone was an impressive character, wasn't he?

TRAINING TASK

Letter to a friend

After this meeting, Pippi writes a letter to his best friend, telling him how he feels about the Don's decision.

Dear Marco,

You have met Giorgio and Vincent, haven't you? Well, we've just had a meeting with their father, and I must tell you what happened and how I feel about it.

. . .

The Fall

1 The Godfather's only son

As the Italian Mafia Grows, so Do the Bosses

Felicia, the Godfather's wife, is talking to Vinny, their only son.

Vinny got home that night around five-thirty and found Felicia in the kitchen, crying. As soon as she saw her son, she rushed over and hugged him tightly. Her heart was pounding and she was clearly fearful and upset.

"Mom, what's the matter with you?"

"Vinny, I have to talk to you about something and you must promise me that you won't say anything to your father or he'll hurt me."

"Mom..." Vinny thought she was being a little dramatic.

"This is hard for me to explain to you, Vincenzo, and I wanted to wait until you were older but I have no choice." Felicia's voice was desperate.

"What is it?" Vinny asked.

"After the argument your father and I just had, I know I have to tell you."

"Tell me what?"

"Your father is involved with some nasty people. You've met a few of them – which Mr. Capers you were so fascinated with is one of them." Then speaking almost to herself, Felicia said under her breath, "God help me if Sonny finds out that I told you this..." she whispered.

"Mom, tell me, Dad won't find out, I promise." Vinny reached out for her, but she took a step back and looked at him.

"Vinny, your father has other plans for you than for you to finish college." She said.

"Why? What plans are you talking about?"

Felicia pulled out a newspaper clipping that dated three days earlier. She would cut it from the paper so Vinny would not see it, but thought it best that he did. Handing it to Vinny, it read:

"As the Italian Mafia Grows, So Do the Bosses"

"Sonny Denucci, Godfather who took over the New York Mafia crime family five years ago, is becoming the most powerful boss ever. [...] Our inside sources say that when young Vincenzo is ready, Sonny will retire from routine local dealings, passing the torch to his son, and handle only major family business."

"Does this mean what I think, Mom?"

She started to cry.

"Is this true, Mom?"

Christopher Gambino, *My Only Son*, (2004)

1. Before reading the text, concentrate on the newspaper headline and the introduction: discuss what Vinny and Felicia are probably going to talk about.

2. Read the whole extract. Tell the class what you have understood about their conversation.

3. a. Highlight information about:
- Felicia's attitude;
- Vinny's reactions;
- the consequences of Sonny's plan on his family.

pages 23-24

b. Share your findings with the class.

4. Discuss the options Vinny and Felicia may have, taking into account the family context.

2 Road to Perdition

video 5

A trailer for the film *Road to Perdition*, directed by Sam Mendes, 2002

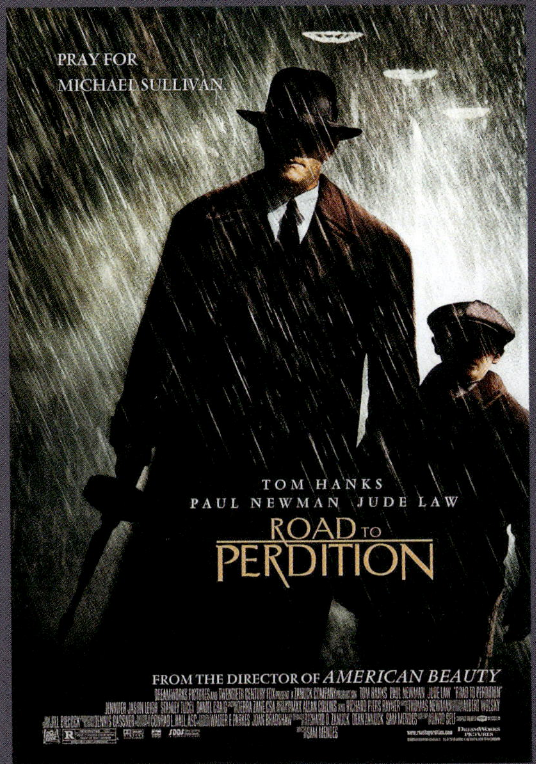

1. **Before watching**, look at the poster and the title. What do you think this film is about?
2. **Watch the trailer** and discuss what you have understood (concentrate on the images and the soundtrack).
3. **Watch the first part again**.
   a. Gather information about:
   - the family;
   - the father;
   - Mr Rooney.

   b. Share your findings and explain the relationships between the different characters.
4. **Watch the second part again**.
   a. Focus on the events and their consequences for the father and the son.
   b. Discuss your findings and react to the last picture "every father is a hero to his son".

Recap → List some consequences of mobsters' activities on their families.

LANGUAGE TOOLS

★ WORDS → p. 48

Trust / Suspicion

- dis**belief** = doubt, **scep**ticism /ˈskeptɪsɪzəm/
- trust ≠ mis**trust**, dis**trust**

→ Never trust to luck!

- **trust**ing, **trust**ful ≠ **scep**tical

Admiration

- fasci**na**tion, ideali**sa**tion
- res**pect**, fear, re**gard**

→ I have respect for his judgement.

- ad**mire** /ədˈmaɪ_ə/

→ I admire him for his audacity.

★ PRONUNCIATION → p. 48

Stress on words with a prefix

★ GRAMMAR → p. 49

Short Questions

→ I don't have the documents. Do you?

TRAINING TASK

Creative writing

This is an extract from the graphic novel *Road to Perdition*. Imagine the end of the conversation between the father and his son (150 words).

"You saw everything?"
"Yes, Sir."
"..."

★ WORDS

❶ Describing characters

a. Here are adjectives referring to:

power | rebellion | obedience

• authoritative, subservient, weak, domineering, rebellious, submissive, oppressive, powerless, forceful, disobedient, unruly, imposing, commanding, yielding, compliant, defiant, headstrong, docile

Sort them out under each heading.

b. Imagine a character in a mafia story and write a few lines (80 words) to describe him/her.

❷ Describing attitudes

a. Here are adjectives referring to violence or moderation:

• easy-going, enraged, uncontrollable, wild, placid, vehement, brutal, collected, composed, ruthless, harmless, nasty, antipathetic, detached, peaceful

Make sure you understand them.

b. Two suspected mafia mobsters have been arrested by the FBI. One becomes very violent, the other remains calm. Use the adjectives above to complete the FBI agent's notes:

Suspect A: violent...

Suspect B: calm...

❸ Describing feelings

a. Here is a list of adjectives describing feelings. Write down a short definition of these words.

• sensitive, disappointed, predictable, sympathetic, endearing, receptive, unpleased, bitter, disdainful, placid

b. Pick adjectives from the list above to talk about two characters, Giorgio and Pippi, from the text *The last Don* (p. 44). Explain why you have chosen these adjectives to describe these characters' feelings.

More exercises in your **Workbook** ▶ p. 25

★ PRONUNCIATION

❹ Stress on words with a prefix

track 17

Here are two-syllable words which you have seen and perhaps used in this chapter.

• commit, support, invite, protect, advise, decide, retire, accept, remain, discuss

a. Listen to them and underline the stressed syllable.

b. Check with your classmates.

c. By using your book ⑧ p. 210, say what conclusions you can draw.

d. Practise pronouncing them.

❺ Stress to contrast past and present

track 18

"...only a small time gangster... now he was ready for something new..."

Lorsqu'un locuteur veut marquer la différence entre un « avant » et un « après », il accentue fortement les éléments qui ont évolué afin de souligner les changements.

a. Listen to an extract from the documentary on Al Capone (p. 43). Try and identify the heavily stressed words.

b. Listen to other parts of the documentary to find some similar examples.

More exercises in your **Workbook** ▶ p. 26

★ GRAMMAR

Short questions

Observe

Jim: I don't have the documents. Do you?
Suzie: Yes, I do. What do you need them for?
Jim: It's none of your business.
Suzie: But I want to know. Can I?
Jim: No, you can't. I'll do business directly with the boss.
Suzie: All right then, but be careful, it might be very dangerous for all of us.
Jim: Don't worry. The boss does not suspect anything.
Suzie: Doesn't he? How can you be sure?
Jim: Come on, you know I won't take any risks. You should trust me.
Suzie: Should I?
Jim. Of course you should. I'll never let you down.
Suzie: Won't you?

Observez les segments de phrases surlignés : quand les utilise-t-on et pourquoi ?

g → Précis grammatical ⑮ **p. 198**

Practise

6 **Read through the following dialogue between an FBI agent and a mobster.**

Agent: You're under arrest for the bloody shooting in Brooklyn last week.
Mobster: Am I? You have no evidence. Or do you?
Agent: As a matter of fact, we do. I want to ask you more questions. Can I?

7 **Continue the dialogue, using short questions.**

Tag questions

Observe

Peter: You're Mary Vincent, aren't you?
Mary: Well, yes. I am. Who are you?
Peter: You've just been released from jail after serving 5 years for racketeering, haven't you?
Mary: So what if I have. What do you want? We haven't met, have we?
Peter: Yes we have. I used to live in your neighbourhood. Don't you remember me?
Mary: No. Why are you here?
Peter: I'm a journalist and I would like to talk to you. You pleaded guilty but you weren't, were you?
Mary: My sister didn't ask you to help me, did she?
Peter: In fact, yes, she did.
Mary: She won't give up, will she?

Observez les questions surlignées : comment sont-elles construites et pourquoi sont-elles employées ?

g → Précis grammatical ⑮ **p. 198**

Practise

8 **Supply the missing tags in the questions below.**

Peter: No, she won't. You know her better than I do, ...?
Mary: Well, I don't know, ...? You've probably talked a lot to her lately. I haven't seen or spoken to her for years. Tell her I'm fine.
Peter: You should get in touch with her, ...?
Mary: You don't understand, ...?
Peter: I know you don't want anything to happen to her. But it's time you told someone the truth, ...?

9 **Continue the dialogue, using as many tag questions as you can.**

More exercises in your **Workbook** ▶ p. 27

Stratégies

Rédiger un dialogue narratif

Les dialogues rendent un récit plus authentique et plus vivant.

When I was five, my father dragged me into my bedroom after I lit a folded pile of his shirts on fire. I sat on the edge of the bed, not looking up, my hands folded mannerly in my lap.

"What's wrong with you?"he asked.

"Nothing," I said.

"You lit my shirts on fire, boy? Where'd you learn that?", he shouted.

"Daycare."

"What? Daycare? You learned how to light shirts on fire at daycare?"

I froze and looked up the ceiling, trying to backtrack. I actually learned how to light matches by watching him light his pipe, but I couldn't tell him that.

"A kid brought matches one day. I told him matches were bad."

"I'm calling your daycare."

"No," I screamed, and he scowled at me.

"Tell me the truth, lad."

I took a deep breath: "I hate your shirts, Dad."

verbes introducteurs
adverbes
personnages
mouvements/attitudes

1 Indiquez clairement qui parle et à qui

a. Ouvrez des guillemets chaque fois qu'un personnage parle.

b. Veillez à la ponctuation (point, point d'interrogation, point d'exclamation, virgule) avant de refermer les guillemets.

c. Allez à la ligne quand vous changez de personnage.

→ ***À vous***

Transformez la conversation ci-dessous en indiquant clairement qui parle et à qui.

Boss, I guess you're right
I'm going to work harder
You'd better
Success depends on hard work
I understand what you mean Boss
You have no choice or...

2 Exprimez les intentions, les sentiments et les réactions des personnages

a. Utilisez des verbes introducteurs, ou *speech tags* : ils indiquent qui parle et de quelle manière.

Manières de parler	Intentions	Sentiments
say, tell someone... — ask, inquire... answer, reply... — add, exclaim, suggest...	*agree, disagree, warn, admit, insist*	*confess, sigh, moan, retort, snap back, implore, beg*
speak loudly = shout, scream, yell speak in a low voice = mutter, whisper, murmur		

b. Employez des **adverbes** : ils précisent la modalité de l'action.
→ *faintly, quietly, hopelessly, stiffly, inquiringly, loudly, disdainfully...*

c. Choisissez des verbes indiquant les **mouvements/attitudes des personnages**.
→ *He nodded, gritted his teeth, rubbed his chin, narrowed his eyes, twisted his lips, folded his arms...*

→ À vous

Reprenez le dialogue que vous avez transformé dans l'étape 1 et complétez-le en insistant sur les intentions, les sentiments et les humeurs des personnages.

3 Rendez votre dialogue plus authentique

Faites en sorte que votre dialogue possède les caractéristiques de la langue orale.

Éléments à utiliser	Exemples
les formes contractées	→ *"I've told you not to do it again, what's wrong with you?"* → *"We can't spend all that time on this!"*
les *tag questions*	→ *"No, it's a waste of time, isn't it?"* → *"I'm the best detective, aren't I?"*
les *gap fillers*	→ *Er... You see... Well, I mean... Let me see...*
les réponses brèves	→ *I hope so... I hope not... I think so... I'm afraid not... Really?*

4 Veillez à la cohérence de votre dialogue

En particulier dans les domaines suivants :

a. l'emploi des pronoms personnels et relatifs
John → *he* → *his* → *him* Jane → *she* → *her*
→ I saw the man *who...* and *whose...*

b. la continuité thématique :
- références au même champ lexical,
- utilisation de synonymes,
- répétition de mots qui aident le lecteur à faire des liens entre les différentes phases du récit et à comprendre le thème.

c. la logique :
emploi de mots de liaison appropriés.
→ *"he was angry ~~so~~* ***but*** *he smiled at me"*

→ À vous

Choisissez une suite cohérente aux phrases A et B parmi trois propositions :

A. What I told him made him really angry.	1. He put his coat on and said "Let's go to the cinema". 2. "Who do you think you are?", he yelled. 3. "I'll go to your birthday party", he said.
B. After Janet had found fingerprints on the crime scene,	1. she went back home and had a shower. 2. she called the forensic unit. 3. he booked a ticket to Hawaii.

Rédiger un dialogue narratif

Lisez les éléments de l'intrigue ci-dessous.

CHARACTERS

Dino Bersconi: Mafia boss
Tony Bersconi: Dino's son
Alicia Bardini: Tony's grandmother

SYNOPSIS

Tony's mother died when Tony was still a young kid. He was told she had a car accident.

He is now 20 and his grandmother has decided to tell him the truth about his mother's death: Dino had his wife murdered.

a. En groupes de 3 ou 4 :
imaginez le contenu de leur conversation.

b. Individuellement :

- écrivez le dialogue entre Tony et sa grand-mère (150 mots) ;
- relisez votre dialogue à l'aide des différents points abordés dans les Stratégies pp. 50-51.

Faites le point

a. Vérifiez votre production. **Auto-corrigé** ▸ www.didierpassword.fr

b. Situez votre niveau dans le tableau ci-dessous.

Niveaux	Mes compétences
B1-1	J'ai pu écrire un texte simple et cohérent sur un sujet travaillé en classe dans une langue relativement correcte.
B1-2	J'ai pu rendre compte des sentiments et réactions des personnages dans ce contexte, avec un bon contrôle grammatical malgré quelques erreurs.
B1-3	J'ai pu raconter une histoire, en mettant en relief la succession et la cohérence des événements et des comportements, sans fautes conduisant à des malentendus.
B2	J'ai pu décrire des événements et des expériences imaginaires en donnant des détails, avec un bon contrôle grammatical.

FINAL TASKS

Mafia stories

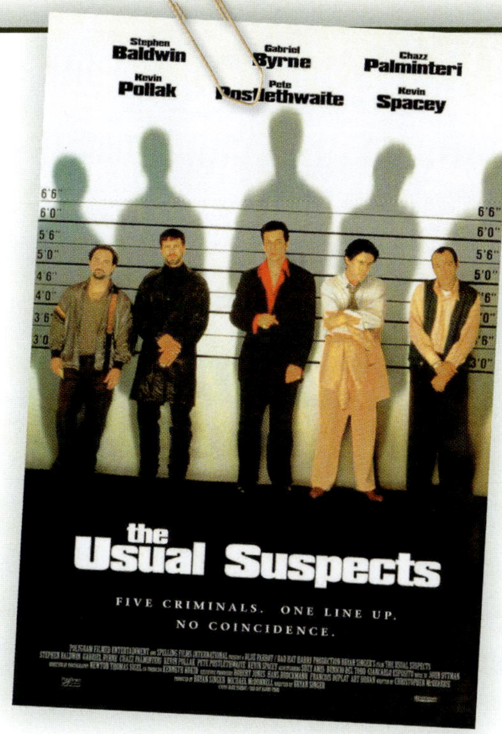

1

task 1

Writing

Write a dialogue for a scene in a mafia story

Your teacher will give you a situation to start from.

1. Get ready

- Think about the situation and the characters' feelings and reactions.
- List your ideas for a dialogue.

2. Action!

- Write your dialogue.
- Don't forget to include indications of:
  - places;
  - movements;
  - reactions and feelings.

task 2

Listening

Match film posters and film reviews

- Listen to four radio film reviews and match three of them with the corresponding posters on this page.

2

3

Listening test

- Listen to a recording, then answer the questions your teacher will give you.

UNIT 4 On the road

Cruising Route 66, near Grants, New Mexico, USA.

Why has Route 66 become a legend?

Read the title of the chapter and look at the picture. **Discuss** what they evoke. In pairs, **list** your questions about Route 66.

FINAL TASKS

P. 69

Slide show

Speaking
Present a slide

Listening
Match slides with commentaries

CULTURE

- Discovering key facts about Route 66 and elements of American history, geography and way of life.
- Exploring some sights and tourist attractions along Route 66.
- Discovering a legendary song.
- Literary work: J. Steinbeck, *Grapes of Wrath*

COMMUNICATION

- Understanding the main points of a song and radio programme.
- Understanding key information as well as specific details in travel videos and documentaries.

Promoting Route 66.

- Understanding a personal account in detail.
- Understanding explicit and implicit meaning in a narrative passage.

TOOLS

Words
- Travel and holiday
- Memories and feelings
- Dreams
- Landscapes

Grammar
- Comparing
- Past - present - present perfect

Pronunciation
- Place names
- Intonation and point of view

Stratégies
→ *Comprendre un message oral (2)*

The iconic American road

1 "Get your kicks on Route 66"

video 6

Travelblog

HOME | THE AUTHOR | THE BIKERS | THE BIKES

Last summer we rode Route 66 from Chicago to L.A. (2,278 miles) on our Harleys and we sure did get our kicks: it was such fun! Look at these photos of our most memorable vacation!

A bit of history

The story of US Route 66 began in 1926 with an act of Congress: many existing roads from Chicago to Los Angeles were joined to create the new highway. Millions of people streamed west along Route 66.
In 1985, the historic road was officially replaced by Interstate 40. But almost thirty years later, Route 66 lives on in books, songs and the American imagination.

Follow Route 66 through:

- Illinois
- Missouri
- Kansas
- Oklahoma
- Texas
- New Mexico
- Arizona
- California

Collected our bikes and headed out of Chicago nervous and excited.

We spent the night in a Motel in Gallup, New Mexico. Most impressive neon lights!

Cadillac Ranch, near Amarillo, Texas. The craziest road attraction!

Speeding freely near San Bernardino, California. Baking hot!

1. **Read this travel blog**. Comment on it and locate the different places mentioned.
   pages 28-29 or www.didierpassword.fr
2. a. **Watch the video** focusing on the pictures only. Which ones do you remember? Share your impressions with the class.
   b. Watch the video again, focusing on the lyrics of the song. Pay attention to place names. Report your findings back to the class.
3. **React.** Would you enjoy yourself, would you "get your kicks" travelling on Route 66? Discuss your opinion with the class.

2 The gateway to the West

track 21

A radio programme about the importance of Route 66 – the highway and the song.

LANGUAGE TOOLS

★ **WORDS** → p. 64

Travel

- a trip (a road-trip), a **jour**ney /ˈdʒɜːni/, an ad**ven**ture
- **tra**vel, take a trip, hit the road, **mo**tor (US), drive (cross **coun**try/west)

★ **PRONUNCIATION** → p. 64

Place names

→ Chicago, Los Angeles...

★ **GRAMMAR** → p. 65

Comparing

→ Cruising Route 66 is more exciting than driving on the Interstate.

1. **Before listening:** why do you think Route 66 – the highway and the song – have become so famous?
2. **Listen** to the radio programme and discuss what you have understood. Focusing on stressed and repeated words will help.
3. **a. In groups:** listen again and find out more about:
   - the highway *(group 1)*;
   - the song *(group 2)*. page 30

   b. Share your findings with the other groups.
4. **Explain** why the American Congress decided to preserve Route 66.

Recap → List some of the reasons why Route 66 is the most famous highway in the US.

TRAINING TASK

Design a CD cover

Countless interpretations of the song *Route 66* have been recorded by artists and groups as diverse as Nat King Cole, The Rolling Stones, Ray Charles, Bruce Springsteen, Bob Dylan or Depeche Mode, to name but a few.

In groups:

a. Google different interpretations of the song *Route 66*. Listen to some and select the one that most appeals to you.

b. Discuss what you would like to include in your cover (text, drawings, colours, photos, maps etc.). Create your CD cover.

c. Present it to the other groups, explaining the reasons for your choices.

A destination in itself

1 So much to see!

video 7

A travel video about Route 66.

← Left, North America's oldest house in Santa Fe, New Mexico.

← Right, Devil's Rope museum, Mc Lean, Texas.

1. **Before watching**: what information do you expect to get from this programme?
   page 30
2. **Watch the video**, focusing on the pictures. List everything you can remember.
3. Watch again, focusing on figures and the names of states and towns. Discuss what you have understood.
4. a. **Note down** on the map what can be seen in the different states. Compare your findings.
   pages 28-29 or www.didierpassword.fr
   b. Watch the video again: correct and complete your map if necessary.
5. **React:** tell the class which place you would or wouldn't like to visit. Why?

2 Travel Arizona's historic Route 66

1. **Skim-read the leaflet** and explain why Arizona's section of Route 66 is a tourist destination.
2. **Discuss** the different types of tourists who might choose this destination.

3 A date with Route 66

video 8

A video report about a Harley Davidson riders' group.

1. a. **Before watching the video**. Work in groups:
   - discuss what the title of the report evokes *(group 1)*;
   - comment on the photograph *(group 2)*.

   b. Share your findings and discuss what the report may be about.
2. **Watch the video**. Discuss what you have understood.
   page 31
3. a. Watch again and find out about:
   - the riders and their views on Route 66;
   - what Route 66 used to be like and what it is like now.
   page 31

   b. Share your findings.
4. **Comment** on the journalist's statement:
   "For Boyd's friends the ride is very much the destination."

Recap → Discuss what makes Route 66 attractive to today's travellers.

LANGUAGE TOOLS

★ **WORDS** → p. 64

Holiday
- va**ca**tion (US), accommo**da**tion, a mo**tel**, a **di**ner /ˈdainə/, a lodge
- **lei**sure /ˈleʒə/, enter**tain**ment, sights, at**trac**tions
- have fun, have a rest

★ **PRONUNCIATION** → p. 64

Intonation and point of view

TRAINING TASK

Radio ad

Promote Route 66 on a radio programme.

In groups of four:

a. Decide who you want to persuade to make a trip on Route 66:

young people | sporty people | families | history lovers | etc.

b. Make notes, listing and organising your arguments; illustrate them with examples. Google *Route 66 landmarks/attractions* for help.

c. Record your commercial or make a live presentation, using intonation to be more convincing.

An unforgettable experience

My first road trip "out West"

SAUGATUCK, Mich. - One of the most indelible memories of my childhood was a trip "out West", as my parents liked to refer to it, via the famous Route 66.

I remember it vividly even to this day, perhaps because my parents took me out of school to accompany them on what my teachers agreed would be an important "educational journey". My first road trip.

I was very young, but I can recall almost every detail of that adventure.

I remember my parents encouraging me to feel the silky texture of a piece of wood from the Petrified Forest in Arizona. I remember the intense heat of the Mojave Desert and my mother dipping cotton towels in melted ice and wrapping them around our heads to keep us cool during that endless drive through that relentless desert. I remember the ghost towns and gold mines that captured my imagination, the Cherokee trading post, my first and only auto court chamber pot and of course, Stuckey's pecans.

There were some sobering moments as well.

↑ At the Petrified Forest, Arizona

I remember clinging to my parents' hands in fear and amazement as I took my first glimpse over the edge of the Grand Canyon. I was awestruck by its magnificence, but terrified by the possibility that my parents might consider descending those canyon walls on the backs of "poor little mules".

↑ Stuckey's pecans

It was there that I discovered my fear of heights and what would become my lifelong love and empathy for animals. I also saw my first serious car accident along a windy mountain road and watched my father – the only doctor to come upon the scene – grab his black leather medical bag and scramble down the mountain side to try to save the family of five that had been thrown from their overturned automobile.

That was the first time I was aware of my father's profession as a physician and surgeon, and it was my first encounter with death. I clearly remember my mother trying to shield me from the scene and my resistance to her efforts. I was mesmerized by my father's command of the situation and the respect shown by the onlookers. I was so proud of him. I think it was the first time I had observed leadership.

That trip was a journey that held many "firsts" for me. I

↑ Crossing the Mojave* Desert

*/maʊˈhɑːvi/

↑ Looking over the edge of the Grand Canyon

believe it played a major role in molding my future, building my character and binding my love of travel with the intellectual aspects of art, history, culture and education.

[...] I will always remember being given the awesome responsibility of "lookout" from the back seat of our yellow Buick Roadmaster convertible to scan the horizon steadfastly with my brand new pink plastic binoculars to alert my parents of any run-away stage coaches, bands of Indians or stampeding herds of bison that might impede our progress west on Steinbeck's "Mother Road", historic Route 66.

Felicia Fairchild

← The Cherokee Trading Post, Oklahoma

1. Before reading: take a look at the photos and read the title of the article. Say what you expect to read.

2. Read the article and discuss what you have understood.

3. a. In groups, highlight information about:
- places and events *(group 1)*;
- the narrator's memories and feelings *(group 2)*.

pages 32-33

b. Report your findings back to the class.

c. Fill in the map.

pages 28-29 or www.didierpassword.fr

4. Explain the narrator's sentence:
"That trip was a journey that held many 'firsts' for me."

Recap → Discuss what can make a journey unforgettable.

LANGUAGE TOOLS

★ WORDS → p. 64

Memories
- a **mem**ory, a re**min**der
- re**mem**ber, re**mind**, re**call**

→ I remember visiting Chicago when I was ten.
→ This postcard reminds me of my visit to Chicago.
→ I clearly recall visiting that part of Chicago.

- **mem**orable, **viv**id, unfor**get**table

Feelings
- **ter**rified, scared = **fright**ened, a**fraid**
- im**pressed** = **awe**struck
- ex**ci**ted, enthusi**as**tic

TRAINING TASK

Spotting places

track 23

You are going to listen to a presentation about five remarkable places, four of which are illustrated on these pages. Listen and match each commentary with its corresponding picture.

A symbol of the American dream

Road to a new life

The Great Depression of the 1930s and the terrible weather conditions (drought and dust storms) forced hundreds of thousands of farmers from Oklahoma to abandon their land and go west in search of better living conditions. In his novel* The Grapes of Wrath*, John Steinbeck describes their situation.

Highway 66 is the main migrant road. 66- the long concrete path across the country, waving gently up and down on the map, from Mississippi to Bakersfield – over the red lands and the grey lands, twisting up into the mountains, crossing the Divide[1] and down into the bright and terrible desert, and across the desert of the mountains again, and into the rich California valleys.

66 is the path of a people in flight, refugees from dust and shrinking[2] land, from the thunder of tractors and shrinking ownership, from the desert's slow northward invasion, from the twisting winds that howl up out of Texas, from the floods that bring no richness to the land and steal what little richness is there. From all of these the people are in flight, and they come into 66 from the tributary side roads, from the wagon tracks and the rutted country roads. 66 is the mother road, the road of flight. [...]

66 out of Oklahoma City; El Reno and Clinton, going west on 66. Hydro, Elk City, and Texola; and there's an end to Oklahoma. 66 across the Panhandle[3] of Texas, Shamrock and Mc Lean, Conway and Amarillo, the yellow. Wildorado and Vega and Boise, and there's an end to Texas. Tucumcari and Santa Rosa and into the New Mexican mountains to Albuquerque, where the road comes down from Santa Fe. Then down the gorged Rio Grande to Los Lunas and west again on 66 to Gallup, and there's the border of New Mexico.

And now the high mountains. Holbrook and Winslow and Flagstaff in the high mountains of Arizona. Then the great plateau rolling like a ground swell. Ashfork and Kingman and stone mountains again, where water must be hauled and sold. Then out of the broken sun-rotted mountains of Arizona to the Colorado, with green reeds on its banks, and that's the end of Arizona. There's California just over the river, and a pretty town to start it. Needles, on the river. But the river is a stranger in this place. Up from Needles and over a burned range, and there's the desert. And 66 goes on over the terrible desert, where the distance shimmers[4] and the black centre mountains hang unbearably in the distance. At last there's Barstow, and more desert until at last the mountains rise up again, the good mountains, and 66 winds through them. Then suddenly a pass, and below the beautiful valley, below orchards[5] and vineyards and little houses, and in the distance a city. And, oh, my God, it's over.

The people in flight streamed out on 66, sometimes a single car, sometimes a little caravan. All day they rolled slowly along the road, and at night they stopped near water. In the day ancient leaky radiators sent up columns of steam [...]. And the men driving the trucks and the overloaded cars listened apprehensively. How far between towns? It is a terror between towns. If something breaks – well, if something breaks we camp right here while Jim walks to town and gets a part and walks back and – how much food we got?

John Steinbeck, *The Grapes of Wrath* (1939)

1. the Continental Divide (i.e. the line that divides the flow of water between the Pacific Ocean and the Atlantic Ocean) running along the crest of the Rocky Mountains to New Mexico.

2. getting smaller

3. an area bordered by the state of New Mexico to the west and the state of Oklahoma to the north and east.

4. *miroiter*

5. /ˈɔːtʃəd/ pieces of land where fruit trees are grown.

← Dust Bowl refugee family, Texas, 1936.

The Dust Bowl refers to a series of dust storms which devastated American prairie lands from 1930 to 1940.

1. **Look at the photograph**. **Read the introduction** to the text. Discuss what you have understood about the time, the events and the people represented. Imagine their feelings.
2. **Read the text** to find more information about these people. List your findings.
3. Read the first two paragraphs again (lines 1 to 12). Explain why Route 66 is referred to as "the migrant road" (line 1) and "the road of flight" (line 12).
4. **a. In groups**, read line 13 to 40 again. Focus on:
   - Route 66 *(group 1)*;
   - the people's situation, trip and destination *(group 2)*.

   b. Discuss your findings and complete the people's itinerary.
   pages 28-29 or www.didierpassword.fr
5. **a.** Explain why "It is a terror between towns" (line 38).
   b. Many different places are mentioned in this passage. What is the impact on the reader?

Recap → Explain what Route 66 represented for some people during the Great Depression.

LANGUAGE TOOLS

★ WORDS → p. 64

Dreams

- a hope, a wish, expec**ta**tions
- dream of = hope for
- look **for**ward to = be **ea**ger to

→ I look forward to reaching California.
→ I am eager to start a new life.

- **stru**ggle for = fight for

Landscapes

- a **pla**teau, a **de**sert, a **moun**tain, a hill, a pass, a gorge, a **can**yon, a **val**ley, a **vine**yard /ˈvɪnjəːd/

★ GRAMMAR → p. 65

Past - present - present perfect

→ I have been to Arizona several times. The last time I went there was last year.

TRAINING TASK

Creative writing

A teenager from Oklahoma fleeing the Dust Bowl in the 1930s with his/her family has just arrived in California. He/she writes a letter back to friends in Oklahoma about:

the journey | hopes of a new life | regrets about the past | etc.

Dear ...

At last the journey's over.

★ WORDS

❶ Place and direction

a. **Read this passage from a travel blog.**

Last time we were in Normandy, we drove towards a magical place, through old villages along the coast, past Honfleur. At the end of our first day, we stopped at Colleville which is somewhere between Caen and Cabourg, not far from Ouistreham. We stopped at a hotel which was perfectly located, right behind a gorgeous restaurant, opposite the beach. The next day we headed off southwards, to Mount St Michael, an amazing abbey that is built on a hill in the middle of a bay. We stood just outside the wall of the medieval village to admire the sight, it was fantastic! Then we walked around the village up to a creperie for lunch. We sat on the terrace in the sun, we had the sea below us and the sky above. What a glorious time!

b. **Prepositions have been highlighted in the text: some of them indicate a direction or a movement, others indicate a position. Classify them in a grid similar to the one below:**

Position ×	Direction/movement →
...	through

c. **Imagine travelling on Route 66. Write a postcard to a friend of yours using some of these prepositions (80 words).**

❷ Describing landscapes

a. **Link adjectives to nouns in order to find as many expressions as possible.**
→ *windings roads*

Adjectives	Nouns
barren - winding - scenic - rocky - dusty - dense - wooded - steep - concrete - lush - dark - tarred - baked - deserted	forest - deserts - hills - valleys - roads - mountains

b. **Choose some of these expressions to depict a landscape you like (50 words).**

More exercises in your **Workbook** ▶ p. 34-36

★ PRONUNCIATION

❸ Place names

track 24

Here are the place names which you can hear in the song *Route 66*:

- Chicago, Los Angeles, Saint Louis, Joplin, Missouri, Oklahoma, Amarillo, Gallup, San Bernardino, Flagstaff, Arizona, Winona, Kingman, Barstow, New Mexico, California

a. **Pinpoint them on a map.** pages 28-29

b. **Listen to them and underline the stressed syllable. Check with your classmates.**

c. **Practise pronouncing them.**

❹ Intonation and point of view

track 25

"...it's gone from superhighway to the road less travelled..."

Une intonation montante ou descendante nous permet de connaître le sentiment du locuteur.

a. **Listen to this extract from *A Date With Route 66* p. 59 where the presenter is comparing Route 66 in the past and in the present.**

b. **From what you have understood and by discussing it with your classmates, say what the expressions *superhighway* and *the road less travelled* refer to: the past or the present?**

c. **Listen again to the presenter of the documentary and say what you notice about the intonation (rising or falling) which accompanies this comparison of the past and present.**

More exercises in your **Workbook** ▶ p. 36-37

GRAMMAR

Comparing

Observe

Route 66 is more famous than all the other American highways. Indeed, it's the most famous highway in America, even if it isn't the longest. Nowadays there are fewer travellers than before and there are not so many road side attractions as there used to be.

Identifiez les différents types de comparaison exprimés dans les formes surlignées.

→ Précis grammatical ⑥ p. 189-190

Practise

5 Compare the three road side attractions on Route 66 below. The following adjectives will be helpful:

- tall, gigantic, new, impressive, remarkable, interesting, funny, attractive, kitschy, tacky, amazing...

→ *If you want to see the tallest, most gigantic ... visit ...*

→ ...

1 Ed Galloway's Totem Pole, Okl.

Very large concrete Totem Pole, 66 feet tall, completed in 1948.

2 Wilmington Gemini Giant, Illinois

A 28 foot-tall spaceman. Built in the 1960s.

3 Giant soda bottle, Arcadia, Okl.

A 66 foot-tall soda bottle, 2007.

Past - Present - Present Perfect

Observe

The birth of the Interstate in the 1950s marked the beginning of the end for Route 66: it has gone from superhighway to the road less travelled. The petrol stations have long since dried up, the motels that once provided a haven for travellers are now nothing more than rusty artefacts.

Identifiez les formes verbales surlignées. Dites quand elles sont employées.

→ Précis grammatical ⑨ ⑩ p. 192-193

Practise

6 Use the appropriate verbal forms for the verbs between brackets.

I *(drive)* all of 66 twice, and I *(be)* on 66 west of Flagstaff quite often. Last time I *(go)* there, I *(have)* the fright of my life. I *(run)* out of gas and I *(can)* not find any gas station to fill up. Since then I *(decide)* that whenever I *(go)* on a road trip I'll always carry a spare can of gas.

7 Write a short paragraph about Route 66 in the 1950s and nowadays describing the changes.

More exercises in your Workbook ▶ p. 37-38

Stratégies

Comprendre un message oral (2)

Les premières étapes d'une écoute vous permettent de saisir un certain nombre d'éléments que vous pouvez lier afin de résumer brièvement ce que vous avez compris.

Lors d'écoutes supplémentaires, vous pourrez alors émettre de nouvelles hypothèses de sens puis procéder à des repérages plus précis.

1 Faites des repérages

Voici un certain nombre de repérages qui peuvent vous aider à comprendre un document sonore :

Repères	Aides	→ À vous
1. Les mots	**Les liaisons systématiques** en anglais oral rendent parfois la compréhension difficile. S'entraîner régulièrement à lire un texte à haute voix en respectant les liaisons vous aidera, à l'écoute, à mieux **détacher les mots** et à repérer les mots porteurs de sens.	• Entraînez-vous à lire la phrase suivante en faisant les liaisons : *"They didn't‿even turn‿around‿and look‿out‿of the window‿at the‿open countryside‿or‿at the monastery!"* • Écoutez et détachez les mots. track 28
2. Formes négatives	**Les formes négatives** sont aisément repérables car elles sont **toujours accentuées**.	Écoutez et repérez les formes négatives. track 29
3. Formes non accentuées	**Peu audibles, elles donnent pourtant des indications importantes :** • sur les temps (verbes et auxiliaires), • sur les intentions et les relations des locuteurs (modaux), • sur les éléments mis en relief (voix active/voix passive). S'appuyer sur l'**entourage immédiat** de ces formes vous permettra de mieux les saisir.	Écoutez et repérez les formes non accentuées. track 30
4. Les mots de liaison	**Ils organisent le discours** et lui donnent sa cohérence. → *so, and, but, first, last, then...*	

2 Soyez actif pendant l'écoute : anticipez/déduisez

Comme vous le faites inconsciemment dans votre langue maternelle, entraînez-vous à :

1. Comprendre l'après	2. Comprendre l'avant
Anticipez, faites des prédictions sur ce qui va suivre au fur et à mesure de l'écoute.	**Ne vous laissez pas décourager** si vous ne comprenez pas un mot, continuez à écouter ; le locuteur va peut-être : - l'expliquer plus loin, - donner des synonymes, ou des antonymes, - développer le champ lexical autour de ce mot. Rappelez-vous que répétitions et redondances font partie des messages oraux.

→ À vous

track 37

Écoutez deux extraits de l'émission *Global trends* et faites des hypothèses sur ce qui a été dit avant et/ou ce qui pourra suivre.

3 Organisez votre prise de notes

Si le document est long, il vous sera peut être difficile de tout mémoriser.

Vous pourrez prendre des notes :
- soit de manière linéaire, au fil de l'écoute, et les organiser après ;
- soit les organiser au fur et à mesure des écoutes dans des cercles concentriques.

→ À vous

Global Trends radio phone-in programme track 9 part 2

Écoutez 3 fois la deuxième partie de l'émission et organisez votre prise de notes.

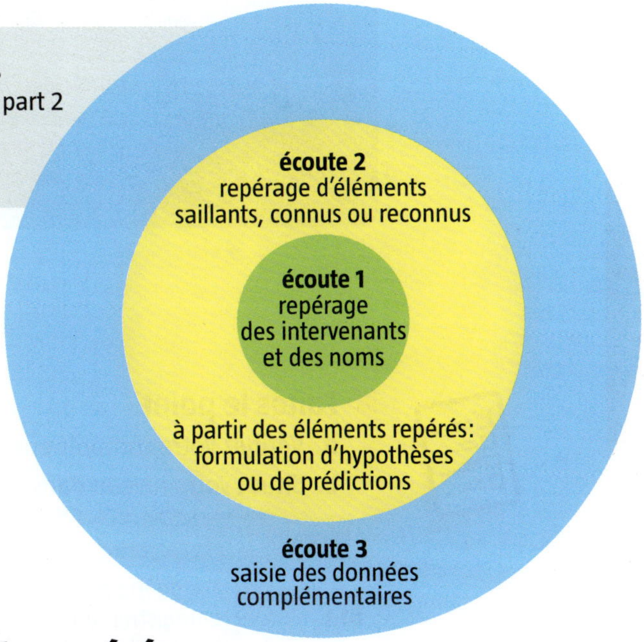

4 Mettez en relation les éléments repérés pour construire le sens

a. Confirmez ou non vos hypothèses à partir des repérages effectués.

b. Dégagez une ou deux idées clés dans le message que vous avez écouté.

c. Recherchez dans le texte tous les éléments qui explicitent cette ou ces idées clés.

Comprendre un message oral (2)

■ **Vous allez écouter un extrait d'une émission radiophonique.**

track 32

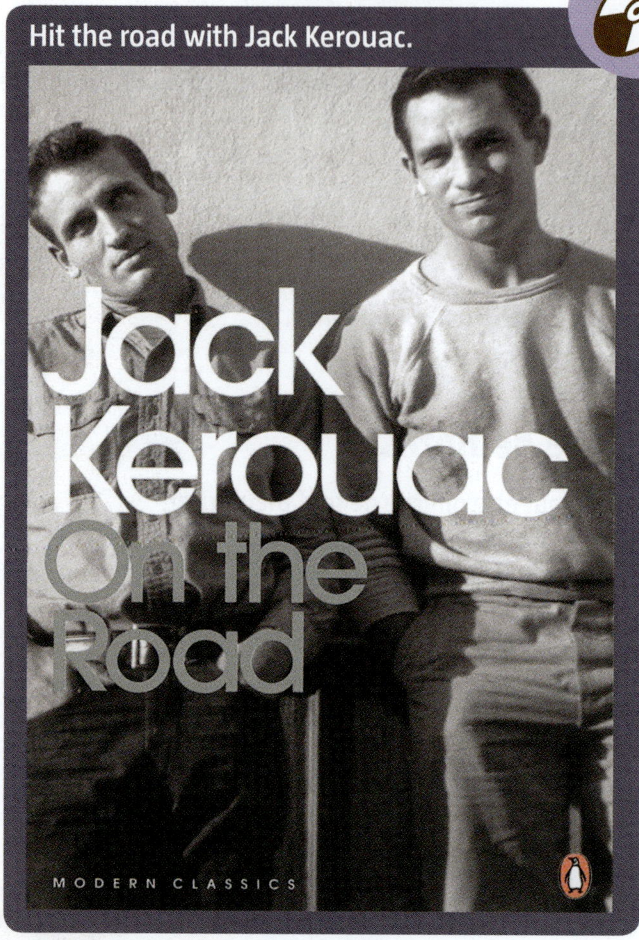

a. Préparez-vous à l'écoute.
b. Écoutez l'extrait (3 fois) : qu'avez-vous repéré et compris ?

■ **Faites le point**

a. Vérifiez votre compréhension. **Auto-corrigé** ▶ www.didierpassword.fr
b. Situez votre niveau dans le tableau ci-dessous.

Niveaux	Mes compétences
B1-1	J'ai pu me préparer et faire des repérages pour comprendre l'essentiel d'un enregistrement audio, sur un sujet familier ou que j'ai étudié (thème, point de vue du locuteur).
B1-2	J'ai pu comprendre différents aspects du thème abordé.
B1-3	J'ai pu repérer et suivre certaines explications données.
B2	J'ai pu comprendre l'ensemble des explications données en m'appuyant sur le plan général de l'exposé.

FINAL TASKS

Slide show

A

task 1

Speaking

Present a slide

Present the picture of a place that particularly appeals to you on Route 66.

B

1. Get ready

Select a place you have discovered in this chapter or that you have heard of. Collect and organize information about it. Choose a picture that you find particularly attractive.

- Prepare clear, concise notes.
- Be ready to explain why you have selected the place.

C

2. Action!

- Present the place to the class and explain your choice.
- Maintain eye contact with your listeners; don't hesitate to point out specific details in the photograph or to write key information on the board to keep your audience's attention.

D

task 2

Listening

Match slides with commentaries

You are going to listen to a presentation about four different places on Route 66.

- Match each presentation with one of the pictures on this page.
- Pick out two or three details to justify your choice.

E

Listening test

- Listen to a radio programme, then answer the questions your teacher will give you.

Culture File 1

PERSONAL JOURNEYS

Pick out one of the documents on these pages.

In groups

1. Read it or listen to it. Try to figure out what type of personal journey the document evokes.
2. Jot down a few notes to share your findings and reflections with the class.

Whole class

3. Compare the different journeys and say which one most appeals to you.

1 The road not taken

Two roads diverged in a yellow wood,
And sorry I could not travel both
And be one traveler, long I stood
And looked down one as far as I could
To where it bent in the undergrowth;

Then took the other, as just as fair,
And having perhaps the better claim,
Because it was grassy and wanted wear;
Though as for that the passing there
Had worn them really about the same,

And both that morning equally lay
In leaves no step had trodden black.
Oh, I kept the first for another day!
Yet knowing how way leads on to way,
I doubted if I should ever come back.

I shall be telling this with a sigh
Somewhere ages and ages hence:
Two roads diverged in a wood, and I—
I took the one less traveled by,
And that has made all the difference.

Robert Frost (1874-1963) *American poet*

2 Me & Bobby McGee

track 33

A song **by Kris Kristofferson.**

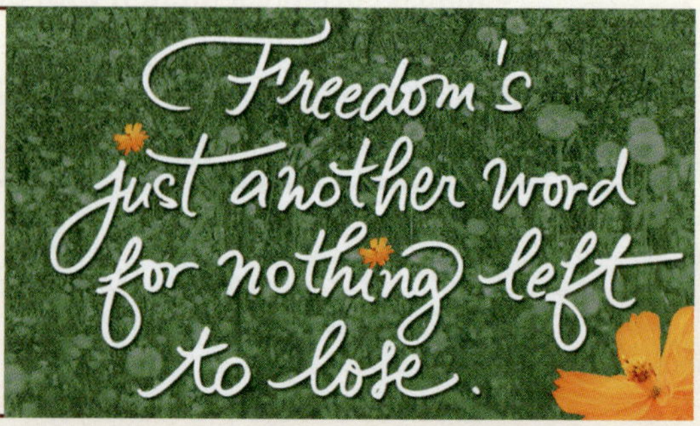

3 My trip out West

In the month of July 1947, having saved about fifty dollars from old veteran benefits, I was ready to go to the West Coast. My friend Remi Boncoeur had written me a letter from San Francisco, saying I should come and ship out with him on an around-the-world liner. [...] I left with my canvas bag in which a few fundamental things were packed and took off for the Pacific Ocean with the fifty dollars in my pocket. [...]

It was a warm and beautiful day for hitchhiking. To get out of the impossible complexities of Chicago traffic I took a bus to Joliet, Illinois, went by the Joliet pen, stationed myself just outside town after a walk through its leafy rickety streets behind, and pointed my way. [...]

My first ride was a dynamite truck with a red flag, about thirty miles into great green Illinois, the truckdriver pointing out the place where Route 6, which we were on, intersects Route 66 before they shoot west for incredible distances. Along about three in the afternoon, after an apple pie and an ice cream in a roadside stand, a woman stopped for me in a little coupé. I had a twinge of hard joy as I ran after the car. But she was a middle-aged woman, actually the mother of sons my age, and wanted somebody to help her drive to Iowa. I was all for it. Iowa! Not so far from Denver, and once I got to Denver I could relax. She drove the first few hours, at one point insisted on visiting an old church somewhere, as if we were tourists, and then I took over the wheel and, though I'm not too much of a driver, drove clear through the rest of Illinois to Davenport, Iowa, via Rock Island. And here for the first time in my life I saw my beloved Mississippi River, dry in the summer haze, low water, with its big rank smell that smells like the raw body of America itself because it washes it up. Rock Island – railroad tracks, shacks, small downtown section; and over the bridge to Davenport, same kind of town, all smelling of sawdust in the warm Midwest sun. Here the lady had to go on to her Iowa hometown by another route, and I got out.

The sun was going down. I walked, [...] to the edge of town, and it was a long walk. All the men were driving home from work, wearing railroad hats, baseball hats, all kinds of hats, just like after work in any town anywhere. One of them gave me a ride up the hill and left me at a lonely crossroads, on the edge of the prairie. It was beautiful there. The only cars that came by were farmer-cars; they gave me suspicious looks, they clanked along, the cows were coming home. Not a truck. A few cars zipped by. [...] The sun went all the way down and I was standing in the purple darkness.

Jack Kerouac,
***On the Road* (1957)**

Jack Kerouac (1922-1969)
American novelist and poet of Canadian origin. His most famous book, On the Road, *launched and inspired the "Beat generation", a phrase which he coined to characterize America's anti-conformist youth culture in the 1950s.*

UNIT 5 Culture shock

"***Culture, in its broadest sense***, is what makes you a stranger when you are away from home."

How do you adapt to culture shock?

← **Look** at the film poster and **read** the statement. **Discuss** the link between the two.

FINAL TASKS

P. 87

Different perceptions

Writing
Rewrite a story from a different point of view

Reading
Culture shock diagnosis

CULTURE	COMMUNICATION	TOOLS
• Learning about culture shock and its different stages. • Discovering cultural differences. • Literary works: - G. Jen, *The Love Wife* - J. Lahiri, *Interpreter of Maladies* - C. Hove, *"Letter to my Mother"*	Relating experiences in detail and describing feelings and reactions. • Understanding the main points in a narrative or a letter as well as the description of feelings. • Understanding explicit and implicit information in a piece of fiction. Understanding the account of a personal experience. Asking and answering questions about personal experiences.	★ **Words** • Impressions and reactions • Doubt and uncertainty • Fear and apprehension • Incident • Habits • Integration ★ **Pronunciation** • Stress on negatives ★ **Grammar** • Be + V-*ing* • Reported speech **Stratégies** → *Écrire un récit en adoptant un point de vue*

What is culture shock?

1 Experiencing culture shock

track 34

David, an American student living in Paris, talks about his experience in France.

1. **Before listening**, list the questions you would like to ask David.
2. **Listen** to David: did you get any answers to your questions? Would you say that David experienced culture shock?
3. Listen again and identify different stages in David's experience. Discuss your findings.

2 Discovering new ways of life

❶ http://www.cultureshocksblog.us

Where is the restroom?

When I moved to the United States, I got a job as an assistant waiter at a Holiday Inn. One day a customer asked me where the restroom was.
I didn't know this word very well so I tried to guess its meaning."Rest" means "sit" so I thought that this person was tired and needed a quiet area to sit in. So I took him out to the lobby and I showed him a big sofa. I thought he could sit there. It soon became obvious that I had not guessed correctly! After that, when I didn't know the answer, I would ask my boss.
It is puzzling, however, why Americans call the bathroom **a restroom** in a public place and **a bathroom** in one's home.

Victor, from France

❷ http://www.cultureshocksblog.us

Speak up, or you're fired!

When I first started working in the US, I was very quiet. I never said anything to my colleagues and I never spoke at meetings.
One day my boss called me to his office. He was very upset with me. He told me that I would lose my job if I didn't change my behavior. I should talk with my co-workers during break time and I should speak up at meetings. I explained to him that I didn't know that I was behaving improperly. In my native culture, one gained respect from his co-workers by being quiet. I learned that this was not the case in the US. I had to change my ways immediately. It was not easy at first but I got used to it. Now I feel very comfortable talking with everyone.

Haile, from Ethiopia

3

http://www.cultureshocksblog.us

Where are you going, my Siberian friend?

I am from Siberia and I am currently living in the US. My old friend Valentina came to visit me last week, and I decided to take her to visit the Big Apple.
We stayed with Jonathan, the son of a dear American friend of mine. As Valentina and I were leaving his apartment to go sightseeing the first morning, our host asked us where we were going. I told him that we were going to see the Statue of Liberty.
He asked me if I knew how to get there. I said that I didn't. Silence. He seemed surprised.
Then he asked me if I had a map. I told him that I didn't. Silence. He seemed bewildered.
He then invited us back inside. He offered to draw us a map and to give us directions. We went into the living room. He carefully drew us a map and gave us very precise directions. He was intrigued but completely baffled by our lack of preparedness. But, we explained to him, in Siberia we do not prepare for our outings in advance the way Americans do with maps, directions, etc. We simply ask people along the way until we arrive at our destination. That's what we were planning to do in New York. Just ask people until we got to the Statue of Liberty! That is obviously not the American Way!

Larissa, from Siberia

LANGUAGE TOOLS

★ WORDS → p. 82

Impressions	Reactions
• **puz**zling, in**trigu**ing	• **puz**zled, sur**prised**
• as**ton**ishing, unex**pec**ted = very sur**pri**sing	• as**ton**ished = sur**prised**
• em**bar**rassing	• em**bar**rassed
• **baf**fling ≈ inex**pli**cable	• **baf**fled = per**plex**, be**wil**dered

→ His answer was really baffling.
→ I was baffled by his answer.

★ PRONUNCIATION → p. 82

Stress on negatives

→ I had no idea what this voice was saying.

★ GRAMMAR → p. 83

Be* + V-*ing

→ I was behaving improperly.

1. **In groups**, **read** these posts by foreigners visiting or living in the US. Choose one of the three anecdotes and identify:
   - the problem;
   - the person's idea or attitude before the incident;
   - what the incident helped him/her understand.
   Organise your findings and report to the other groups.

2. **Discuss** why these incidents can be considered examples of culture shock.

Recap → How would you define culture shock? Illustrate your point with examples.

TRAINING TASK

Post a comment

1. In groups, discuss what you understand from the cartoon.

2. You are the man or the woman at the front of the queue. Write an account of the incident to be posted on a culture shock forum.

And I say you're *not* properly dressed!

Comparing perceptions

How amazing!

Lan (nicknamed Lanlan), 45, has just arrived in Boston from China. She is visiting her new surroundings with Lizzy and Wendy, the two teenage daughters of the family she is staying with.
Lan's perceptions are expressed through Wendy's comments and through her own thoughts (in italics).

Wendy / And how everyone crosses the street in the crosswalk downtown. —Lanlan thinks that's amazing, that people don't just walk all over. Though how fast people walk here! Everyone in a hurry all the time.

Lan / *Chinese people were much more relaxed. Everything was so easy in America, so convenient. And yet people were tense.*

Wendy / And the bicyclists all wear helmets and how many cars people had! —In China, many people have cars now, she says.
But still, she is amazed that some families have two or three, that even some kids have cars. And will Lizzy really be learning to drive soon? She is surprised that people drive one-handed, some of them, and talk on their cell-phones at the same time, she thinks everybody in America talks, especially the children are so curious. In China, kids do not ask *why why why*, she says. Then make everyone listen to them, as if they have something to say.
—At school, people say American children are very easy, she says. People say you ask them one question and they will talk, talk, talk. You ask them three questions, they will love you.
— Like you ask us questions! I say.
She smiles her funny smile.

Lan / *At school, people say that when you talk to American children you have to ask,* You want this one or that one? The blue one or the red one? *Then they will be happy. If you simply say* Here is the red one, I know you like red, *the children will not be happy. They don't want you to know what they like, they want to choose for themselves.* [...]

Wendy / And the way they sit, she says. The women not even covered with clothes some of them, and as big as mountains and all over their chairs. She's surprised American chairs are not bigger. And she stares at the black people with their hair braided all different ways [...]. She's amazed at how different people look from each other, she knew it from the movies but still, she's shocked by that, and by how complete strangers say hello on the street, even if they never saw you before. She says the first time that happened, she ran away.

Lan / *Sometimes I saw men let women walk in front of them. Even open doors for them, as if they were important! Just like in the movies. I was amazed to see that. And nobody ate the squirrels*, even in the countryside, that's what the girls said. There was so much food. People let whole trees full of fruit just fall to the ground.*

Gish Jen, *The Love Wife* (2004)

* *écureuils*

1. **Read the title and the introduction** and explain the situation. Imagine what Lan, as a Chinese woman, might have figured out about America before she arrived.
2. **Skim-read the text** and identify what subjects or issues are mentioned.
3. Read the text again. Highlight:
   - what the characters see;
   - what they say;
   - what they think.

   pages 39-40
4. Share your conclusions with your classmates.

LANGUAGE TOOLS

★ **WORDS** → p. 82

Reactions: doubt and uncertainty
- a **quiz**zical/**puz**zled ex**pres**sion
- be **skep**tical a**bout** sth/**crit**ical of sth/ **doubt**ful a**bout** sth

Recap → Compare the characters' perceptions.

TRAINING TASK

Writing workshop

Read two other comments by Wendy. Choose one and write Lan's corresponding thoughts.

❶ Lanlan is amazed by how much people throw out, like how many napkins they use in restaurants, and how they take ketchup packets they don't even use.

❷ Lanlan is amazed that people in America drive and eat at the same time, eating in cars makes her shake her head. [...]. She says she doesn't know how Americans can eat without stopping to eat, although obviously they do because look how many fat people there are! Many more than in the movies.

Adjusting

Reunion in America

After leaving India to study in England, the narrator has found work and settled in the USA. He has just received a letter from his wife, Mala, who is about to join him. Mala has never travelled outside India.

A few days after receiving the letter, as I was walking to work, I saw an Indian woman on the other side of Massachusetts Avenue, wearing a sari with its free end nearly dragging on the footpath and pushing a child in a stroller. An American woman with a small black dog on a leash was walking to one side of her. Suddenly the dog began barking. From the other side of the street I watched as the Indian woman, startled, stopped in her path, at which point the dog leapt up and seized the end of the sari between its teeth. The American woman scolded the dog, appeared to apologize, and walked quickly away, leaving the Indian woman to fix her sari in the middle of the footpath and quiet her crying child. Such a mishap, I realized that morning, would soon be my concern. It was my duty to take care of Mala, to welcome her and protect her. I would have to buy her her first pair of snow boots, her first winter coat. I would have to tell her which streets to avoid, which way the traffic came, tell her to wear her sari so that the free end does not drag on the footpath. [...]

At the airport I recognized Mala immediately. The free end of her sari did not drag on the floor, but was draped in a sign of bridal modesty over her head, just as it had draped my mother until my father died. Her thin brown arms were stacked with gold bracelets, a small red circle was painted on her forehead, and the edges of her feet were tinted with a decorative red dye. I did not embrace her, or kiss her, or take her hand. Instead I asked her, speaking Bengali for the first time in America, if she was hungry.

She hesitated, then nodded yes.

I told her I had prepared some egg and curry at home. "What did they give you to eat on the plane?"

"I didn't eat."
"All the way from Calcutta?"
"The menu said oxtail[1] soup."
"But surely there were other items."
"The thought of eating an ox's tail made me lose my appetite."

When we arrived home, Mala opened up one of her suitcases, and presented me with two pullover sweaters, both made with bright blue wool, which she had knitted in the course of our separation, one with a V neck, the other covered with cables[2]. She had also brought me two new pairs of drawstring pajamas, a letter from my brother, and a packet of loose Darjeeling tea. I had no present for her apart from the egg curry. We sat at a bare table, each of us staring at our plates. We ate with our hands, another thing I had not yet done in America.

"The house is nice," she said. "Also the egg curry." With her free left hand she held the end of her sari to her chest, so it would not slip off her head.

"I don't know many recipes."

She nodded, peeling the skin off each of her potatoes before eating them. At one point her sari slipped to her shoulders. She readjusted it at once.

1. *soupe de queue de bœuf*
2. *torsades*

"There is no need to cover your head," I said. "I don't mind. It doesn't matter here."

She kept it covered anyway. [...]

At the end of our first week, on Friday, I suggested going out. Mala set down her knitting and disappeared into the bathroom. When she emerged I regretted the suggestion; she had put on a clean silk sari and extra bracelets, and coiled her hair with a flattering side part on top of her head. She was prepared as if for a party, or at the very least for the cinema, but I had no such destination in mind.

Jhumpa Lahiri, "The Third and Final Continent", in *Interpreter of Maladies* (1999)

1. a. Read the introduction and the first paragraph (lines 1 to 14). Discuss what you have understood about:
- the incident;
- the narrator's reactions.

pages 41-42

b. Explain line 10-11: "Such a mishap, I realized that morning, would soon be my concern."

2. Read from line 15 to the end of the text:
a. Identify the three different moments in the story. Explain what you have understood.
b. Highlight references to:
- food and eating;
- clothing. pages 41-42

c. What can you guess about cultural differences between India and America?

3. Read lines 20 to 21, 36, 42 to 43 and 52 to 53. Explain what they show about the narrator.

4. Look at the photograph: do you find it a suitable illustration for the text? Why or why not?

Recap → List examples of problems Mala might encounter as she adjusts to life in America.

LANGUAGE TOOLS

★ WORDS → p. 82

Fear and apprehension
- fear = anx**ie**ty
- **ir**ritated = an**noyed**
- **sca**red, in**tim**idated, ill-at-**ease**

Incident
- a **mis**hap /ˈmɪshæp/ = a misad**ven**ture, mis**for**tune, an incon**ven**ience

★ GRAMMAR → p. 83

Reported speech
→ I told her I had prepared some egg and curry at home.

TRAINING TASK

Write a dialogue

Starting from the examples you have listed, imagine and write a dialogue between the narrator and his wife.

Looking back and moving on

Writing home

In 2002, writer and poet Chenjerai Hove was forced to leave his country, Zimbabwe, for political reasons. He first went to France and then to Norway. He currently resides in the USA. Here are extracts from a letter he wrote to his mother while living in Norway.

Dear Mother,

Remember the day I arrived in my new town, one of my many stops on this journey that is life. The rains at the airport in Stavanger[1] brought me memories of you working in the fields, not shielding yourself from the warm raindrops. I remembered you then, way back in February, 2005. For, I knew you would have composed an instant poem to celebrate first raindrops, those songs about the fish eagle up in the sky, the harbinger[2] of rain, giving life to people, animals and plants.

Here they still have not stopped cursing[3] the rain. I always remind them that one who curses the rain is a witch who wishes that life should not be brought to this earth. But no, they still curse at their gentle, thunderless rain. They prefer the sun instead. Or the white snow which paints the street white as if cotton wool had embraced the whole earth. My fear of snow still persists, especially when it hardens and becomes slippery ice.

For me, a step on ice is a potential disaster. Ice is more slippery than the muddy clay soils of your maize fields. Norwegians hardly fall on ice. They float on it like Arabs walking on sand, never sinking, never falling. They even run races on the ice and win competitions! Can you imagine? [...]

Normally, Norwegians are deep in silence. Forget about the noise you hear in the streets of Harare[4], or in the village in Gotami's country down there in Chireya. Here they are silent, and it is the silence which explodes into your ears as soon as you arrive in their lands. No, they are not afraid of strangers. They are too shy to venture into the life space of anyone, including their own people. It takes time for them to remove that veil of silence which sometimes shields them so much from the possibility of laughter and the good humour which enkindles the human spirit in times of sorrow and despair. [...]

Maybe your attacks of malaria will already be haunting you. There is no malaria in this country. The little mosquitoes they have are as harmless as pieces of flying paper. No one bothers much about them. But this is not to say there are no diseases here. They have different kinds of illnesses, some to do with the mind, others to do with eating too much wrong food, and maybe others to do with a life controlled too much by watches and clocks. You should see how they walk in the street. They rush to everywhere as if in a permanent state of emergency. Slowing down might help reduce some of their tensions.

So, mother, you can see how complex life is here, with its ups and downs. As I yearn for the voices of home, I begin to think there are more downs here than ups. The voices of home, the music of our birds and the beauty of our setting sun, they weave patterns in my dreams as live as this never-ending desire to be home one day.

I hope the thunderous rains have come by now. Maybe the maize you planted is already the height of a small child. Every sun which rises gives me fresh

1. the 4th largest city in Norway, about 350 miles west of Oslo

2. a sign announcing something

3. *maudire*

4. capital city of Zimbabwe

memories of you, and every early sunset reminds me that I am in other lands. Maybe one day we will sit together, switch off the street lights and gaze at the beauty of that lovely African moon which displays the image of a rabbit with large ears. Maybe I will be older, but I will not have given up the idea of being young.

Now I know that there are so many streams to the river of knowledge, and one of them is to live in other lands.

Your Son, Chenjerai,
www.icorn.org/articles

← A village in Zimbabwe

1. Before reading, concentrate on the title, the introduction and the photo: imagine how Chenjerai Hove may have felt when he arrived in Norway.

2. Read the first line of each paragraph. Identify the different topics.

3. a. Read the text from lines 1 to 34. Pick out the differences between the two countries.
page 43
b. Share your findings.

4. Scan the same passage and underline Hove's comments on those differences. What are his feelings for Norway and Zimbabwe?
page 43

5. Read lines 35 to 55. Share what you have understood. Sum up why Hove's life away from home has "its ups and downs".

6. Discuss the meaning of the last sentence (lines 52 to 55).
pages 43-44

Recap → List positive and negative aspects one may encounter when settling in a new country.

LANGUAGE TOOLS

★ WORDS → p. 82

Habits
- be used to /ˈjuːstə/ = be ac**cus**tomed to, be fa**mi**liar with

→ He is used to living in Norway.
⚠ → He used to live in Zimbabwe. He no longer lives there.

Integration
- ad**just** to
- fit in = blend in
- be **home**sick = miss one's **coun**try

TRAINING TASK

Press conference

While living in France, Chenjerai Hove gives a press conference and shares his impressions of the country.

a. In groups: prepare the journalists' questions and Chenjerai Hove's possible answers.

b. Whole class: act out the press conference.

Chenjerai Hove, ↑ 2009

★ WORDS

❶ Expressing feelings

You are going to read series of words expressing:

apprehension | surprise | anger | sadness | enthusiasm

In each series, identify the feeling expressed and find the odd man out.

1. astonished - dumfounded - unconcerned - amazed - stupefied
2. enlivened - enthralled - sickened - thrilled - enraptured
3. infuriated - elated - furious - outraged - fuming
4. delighted - despondent - sorrowful - disconsolate - devastated
5. worried - anguished - disquieted - carefree - uncomfortable

❷ Deriving words

a. Combine the suffixes below with the nouns or verbs provided, in order to create adjectives.
wonder → wonderful

Sometimes different suffixes can be used with the same words. Check in a dictionary if necessary.

Suffixes	Nouns, verbs
-ful, -less, -y, -ly, -ish	shame - grump - fool - regret - self - hope - help - friend - cheer - mood - fear - child

b. List other words you know with the same endings.

c. Use the adjectives you have created to write about the characters' feelings and reactions in the texts on pp. 74-75, 76 or 78.

❸ Reporting feelings and intentions

a. A couple is discovering New York City from the top of the Empire State Building. Read their conversation and decide which feelings or intentions the speakers express:

admiration | promise | regret | irritation | suggestion | acceptance

1. "**What a fantastic view!**" Helen said.
2. "Yeah sure, the view's awesome," Max said, "**but it's a real shame we didn't come at sunrise...**"
3. "Oh come on, Max!" Helen said. **"Why can't you be more positive?"**
4. "Forget it," Max said. **How about going down and grabbing a sandwich on the way back to the hotel?**"
5. "No, I mean it, really!" Helen said. "**If you carry on like this, I won't travel with you anywhere ever again**, I'm not kidding!"
6. "OK, you're right," Max said, "**I can be a real kill-joy sometimes...** Can we go now?"

b. Which verbs from the list below do you associate with each feeling? Use them to replace "said" in the conversation.

- marvel - regret - complain - swear/promise - admit/acknowledge - suggest

c. Now use these verbs or other verbs you know to report the conversation and the speakers' feelings (see *Stratégies* pp. 50-51).
→ Helen marvelled at the view but Max regretted that...

★ PRONUNCIATION

❹ Stress on negatives

track 34

"I had no idea what this voice was saying..."

La forme négative est toujours accentuée parce qu'elle coupe le lien entre le sujet et la proposition qui suit. L'accentuation apporte une information importante.

a. Listen to David's experiences of living in another country.

b. By paying attention to the stress on negatives, make a list of some of the things he didn't find or couldn't do.

c. Discuss them with your classmates.

d. Practise doing the same by saying what you didn't find and what you couldn't do in a place you visited.

→ Précis de prononciation ⑩ p. 213

More exercises in your Workbook ▶ p. 44

★ GRAMMAR

Reported speech

Observe

A. "I don't understand why I decided to start working here in the first place," he said. "I will go back to London as soon as the job is over." Then he paused and he asked his wife: "Do you think I'm exaggerating?"
"A decision like this needs time," she answered. "You don't have to make it now."

B. He said that he didn't understand why he had decided to start working there in the first place. He said he would go back to London as soon as the job was over. Then he paused and asked his wife if she thought he was exaggerating.
She answered that a decision like that needed time and that he didn't have to make it then.

Décrivez les différences entre les énoncés au discours direct et les énoncés au discours rapporté.

g → Précis grammatical ⑰ **p. 199**

Practise

5 **Rephrase the following sentences using reported speech.**

a. "I have made a terrible mistake," he said.
b. "Are you sure you want to go out dressed like this?" he asked her.
c. "I can't remember the last time I saw him," she said.
d. "It's no use thinking about it now, we will consider that later," I said.

6 **Before leaving India, Mala had the following conversation with her mother. Now she reports it to her husband. Write down what she tells him.**

"I'm so scared, mom," Mala said. "Of course I want to be with my husband, but America is so far! I belong here!"
"Mala, honey," her mom said, "remember when you were a child, you always dreamt of going to America. It's time for you to fulfil this dream. As long as you believe in yourself and your dreams, you will be fine."

Be + V-*ing*

Observe

I always read on the bus home. It makes the journey shorter. Many people just stare out the window. Some play video games and others make phone calls. Last week, I noticed an elderly old lady who was staring at me: "I can't believe you're actually reading a book!" she said. "People say youngsters don't read anymore – and that's true, they're always playing with their digital gadgets!"

Comparez les formes verbales soulignées :
- lesquelles sont employées pour présenter des faits, à simple titre d'information ?
- lesquelles attirent l'attention sur l'activité du sujet (pour réagir : approuver/désapprouver...) ?

g → Précis grammatical ⑪ **p. 193-194**

Practise

7 **Choose the correct verbal form.**

People generally *(think – are thinking)* that the British are phlegmatic people who *(always hide – are always hiding)* their feelings and *(never give away – are never giving away)* their emotions. Well I *(saw – was seeing)* something quite different the first time I *(went – was going)* to a football stadium! The supporters *(screamed – were screaming)* constantly, most of them *(hugged – were hugging)* every time a goal was scored, and some of them *(fought – were fighting)* for no reason!

8 **Read again the text *Speak up, or you're fired!* p. 74. As one of Haile's colleagues, write about Haile's behaviour before the boss talked to him.**

More exercises in your Workbook ▶ p. 45-46

Stratégies

Écrire un récit en adoptant un point de vue

Qu'il s'agisse d'une lettre, d'une œuvre de fiction ou d'un article de presse, écrire un récit ne se limite pas à raconter des faits. Lorsqu'on réécrit un récit en changeant de narrateur (et donc de point de vue) cela a une incidence sur le contenu.

1 Le narrateur

Il y a deux types de narrateurs :

Identité du narrateur	Implications dans la narration
Le narrateur n'est pas un personnage de l'histoire : il ne prend pas part aux événements et ne s'exprime à la 1re personne que s'il donne ouvertement son point de vue.	• L'histoire est racontée à la 3e personne. • Le narrateur sait généralement ce que pensent les personnages.
Le narrateur est un personnage de l'histoire : il peut présenter les événements comme s'il en faisait l'expérience en temps réel, ou bien les présenter avec du recul.	• Le narrateur s'exprime à la 1re personne *(I/me)* et peut donner son sentiment au fur et à mesure du récit. • Il a accès à ce que les autres personnages font et disent, mais pas à ce qu'ils pensent (il ne peut qu'interpréter).

→ À vous

Lisez l'extrait suivant et réécrivez-le du point de vue du personnage principal :

Sayuki was standing in the middle of the airport, looking around. She seemed to be lost in the crowd. She recognized some of the other passengers of the Seoul-Seattle flight. One of them, a 20-year-old dark-haired girl, suddenly screamed with joy and threw herself in the arms of a tall young man who had been waiting for her. The couple started kissing. This kind of thing was not done back in Korea.

2 La cohérence du récit

Elle relève principalement du temps du récit et de sa structuration.

Temps du récit	Exemples
Le récit est raconté d'un point de vue présent : il donne l'impression que les événements se déroulent en temps réel.	→ *I rush to the luggage area, grab my suitcase and head to the customs. The agent takes a look at my passport and lets me pass. I'm thrilled: soon I will be visiting the Empire State Building!*
Le récit est raconté d'un point de vue passé : les événements sont présentés comme sans lien avec le présent.	→ *I rushed to the luggage area, grabbed my suitcase and headed to the customs. The agent took a look at my passport and let me pass. I was thrilled: soon I would be visiting the Empire State Building!*

Éléments de structuration	Exemples
Utilisez les **marqueurs chronologiques** pour organiser les événements.	→ ***After*** *the movie, I decided to take Sandra to an Italian restaurant in Soho. But* ***as soon as*** *we arrived, she said she'd rather eat Chinese.*
Adaptez les **marqueurs de temps et de lieu** au temps du récit.	→ **Récit au present** : *I don't want to leave, but I have to. So I tell her that I will come back here tomorrow.* → **Récit au passé** : *I didn't want to leave, but I had to. So I told her that I would come back there the next day.*
Alternez les phases de narration du récit et les phases de dialogue.	→ *"Could you tell me the way to Times Square?" I asked a passer-by.* → *But the man just looked at me as if I had been speaking Greek. "I'm sorry?" he said. "What did you just say?"*

Remarque : ne pas confondre le **temps du récit**, et le temps utilisé dans les dialogues.
→ *"I have always done my best for my family!" Tom* ***cried out****. "And now you're saying I don't do enough for you? That's it, I'm leaving!" And he* ***stomped*** *out of the room.*

→ À vous

À partir des notes suivantes, écrivez la scène :
- choisissez les temps à adopter (point de vue présent ou au passé) ;
- distinguez dialogue et narration ;
- ajoutez la cohérence chronologique.

Mala and I *(walk)* down Park Lane. / Mala *(wear)* one of her favourite saris. / We *(stop)* in front of the State capitol. / Mala *(look)* fascinated. / So beautiful. / It *(remind)* me of the Taj Mahal. / Three kids *(come)* our way. / They *(run)*. / They *(hold)* ice creams. / One of them *(drop)* his ice cream on the Sari. / He *(apologize)*. / Mala *(look)* confused and embarrassed. / She nearly *(reprimand)* the kid. / Instead she *(tell)* him there *(be)* no problem. / Back at home, she *(laugh)*. / This is just like India! / Kids are just as wild!

3 La richesse du récit

On peut étoffer son récit en développant des informations :

Stratégies d'enrichissement	Exemples
Ajoutez des informations pour expliciter votre propos.	→ *Norwegians hardly fall on ice. [...] They even run races on the ice and win competitions!*
Ajoutez un élément de comparaison.	→ *There is no malaria in this country. The little mosquitoes they have are as harmless as pieces of flying paper.*
Ajoutez un commentaire, une réaction, un sentiment... **Remarque** : dans le cas d'une réécriture, faites réagir les personnages en accord avec ce que vous savez d'eux.	→ *I was so lonely I was beginning to feel depressed, until I met Jorge. I was so happy to meet another person from Peru, to finally speak Spanish again, though he had lost some of his accent.* → Hove and a Norwegian friend are watching an ice-skating competition. The Norwegian friend: *"Maybe this will encourage Hove to try ice-skating from time to time. He might like it in the end."* Hove: *"Sure it's beautiful to watch, but there's no way I'm ever going to try this. I don't want to end up in hospital."*

→ À vous

Développez le récit suivant :

Last time I was in London, something really funny happened to me. I was waiting for the bus...

Auto-évaluation

Écrire un récit en adoptant un point de vue

Lisez la bande dessinée ci-dessous.

Racontez l'histoire en adoptant le point de vue de l'un des trois personnages suivants :

- Pierre
- Lily
- le père de Lily

Glasgow, Scotland. Lily introduces Pierre, her French boyfriend, to her father.

Faites le point

a. Vérifiez votre production.

Auto-corrigé ▶ www.didierpassword.fr

b. Situez votre niveau dans le tableau ci-dessous.

Niveaux	Mes compétences
B1-1	J'ai pu raconter un événement réel ou imaginé.
B1-2	J'ai pu rendre compte d'expériences en décrivant le point de vue d'un personnage.
B1-3	J'ai pu raconter une histoire en mettant en relief la succession et la cohérence des événements et des comportements.
B2	J'ai pu écrire un texte articulé décrivant des événements et des expériences réels, en donnant des détails et en mettant en valeur un point de vue par rapport aux événements ou expériences.

FINAL TASKS

Different perceptions

task 1

Writing

Rewrite a story from a different point of view

Rewrite a text you have studied from another person's point of view (200-250 words).

1. Get ready

- Remember the themes mentioned in the story you read.
- Invent other elements.

2. Action!

- Keep the reader interested: develop the events and give details.
- Do not forget your strategies (p. 84-85).

task 2

Reading

Culture shock diagnosis

Read the definitions of the four major stages in culture shock. Then read the six testimonies your teacher will give you and decide which phase they correspond to.

Honeymoon	Rejection/distress	Flight	Recovery
A positive, even euphoric stage, often shortly after arrival, when the newcomer finds everything exciting.	A negative phase when the newcomer loses his/her initial excitement, feels disoriented and lonely.	The most difficult stage, when the newcomer's feelings of depression, impatience or anger towards the new country make him/her long to escape.	When the newcomer begins to integrate and adjust to the new culture, feeling more at ease with his/her environment.

Reading test

- Your teacher will give you a text: read it carefully, then answer the questions.

UNIT 6 Stand up for your rights

16 October, 1968 – Olympic Stadium in Mexico City.
Tommie Smith (centre), John Carlos (right) and Peter Norman (left).

How can individuals change the course of history?

Look at the photograph. What is your first reaction?

Find a link between the theme of this chapter and the photo.

FINAL TASKS

P. 103

Press article

Writing
Write a short article

Reading
Match headlines and press articles

CULTURE

- Learning about the Civil Rights Movement in the USA:
  - personal acts of defiance and resistance,
  - desegregation.
- Literary works

  Autobiographies:
  - Melba Pattillo Beals, *Warriors Don't Cry*
  - Tommie Smith with David Steele, *Silent Gesture*
  - Carlotta Walls LaNier, *A Mighty Long Way: My Journey to Justice at Little Rock Central High School*

  Fiction:
  Toni Morrison, *Sula*

COMMUNICATION

- Understanding newspaper headlines as well as information and opinions in press articles.
- Understanding facts and feelings in personal testimonies and fictitious narratives.

Writing an account of events and explaining them.

Presenting an event, its issues and the reactions to it.

TOOLS

★ Words
- Defiance
- Violence and heroism
- Fear and resistance
- Tribute and legacy

★ Pronunciation
- Stress and subjective meaning
- Words ending in *-ate*

★ Grammar
- Passive forms
- *Make/have/get*: causative structures

Stratégies

→ *Lire et comprendre un article de presse*

Acts of defiance

1 Protest on the victory stand

Black Power Advocates Ousted[1] From Olympics

U.S. Team Drops Smith and Carlos for Clenched-Fist Display on Victory Stand
By JOSEPH M. SHEEHAN
Special to *The New York Times* - October 19, 1968

Mexico City, Oct. 18, 1968
The United States Olympic Committee suspended Tommie Smith and John Carlos today for having used last Wednesday's victory ceremony for the 200-meter dash at the Olympic Games as the vehicle for a black power demonstration. The two Negro sprinters were told by Douglas F. Roby, the president of the committee, that they must leave the Olympic Village. Their credentials also were taken away, which made it mandatory[2] for them to leave Mexico within 48 hours.

↑ 1968 Olympic Games, men's 200 metres final

Clenched Fists Raised
At Wednesday's 200-meter victory ceremony, Smith, the winner, and Carlos, who finished third, wore black scarves around their necks and black gloves (Smith on his right hand and Carlos on his left).

After receiving their medals from the Marquis of Exeter the president of the International Amateur Athletic Federation, who was an Olympic 400-meter hurdles champion in 1928, Smith and Carlos raised their gloved hands with fists clenched and kept their heads deeply bowed during the playing of the national anthem and raising of the United States flag in their honor.

This demonstration produced a mixed reaction among United States officials and members of the United States squad, black and white. Some hailed[3] it as a gesture of independence and a move in support of a worthy cause. Many others said they were offended and embarrassed. A few were vehemently indignant. ■

1. /aʊstɪd/: ejected by force **2.** obligatory **3.** hail: describe something as being good

1. Before reading, study the photo, headline, sub-headline and dates. Then say:
- how the article relates to the photo p. 88;
- what information you expect to find.

2. Read the article and discuss what you have understood.

3. Read again and find out about:
- the athletes' gesture and how it was interpreted;
- the consequences for the athletes;
- the different reactions to their demonstration.

4. Share your findings with the class and give a chronology of events. Fill in a time line: page 47 or www.didierpassword.fr

5. a. Say whether the journalist appears biased (subjective) or not to you.
b. He writes "The two Negro sprinters". Judging from the tone of the article, would you say that at that time, the word "Negro" was offensive or not?

2 Standing up alone

video 9

A video about Claudette Colvin.

↑ New York City street art: mural paying tribute to Claudette Colvin.

LANGUAGE TOOLS

★ **WORDS** → p. 98

Defiance

- **bold**ness, diso**be**dience, oppo**si**tion
- dare, de**fy**, speak out ag**ainst**
- speak in **pro**test about sth
- stand up for, stand up to

→ They stood up for their rights.

→ She stood up to the Montgomery authorities.

- pro**vo**cative, bold, **chal**lenging

★ **PRONUNCIATION** → p. 98

Stress and subjective meaning

1. **Before watching**, look at the mural. Why do you think it was painted? What would you like to know about Claudette Colvin?

2. **a. In groups. Pick out** information about:
- segregation in the USA in the 1950s;
- Claudette Colvin's personal story;
- her situation and goal today.

Group 1: watch the documentary with the sound muted;
Group 2: listen to the soundtrack without watching the images.

b. Summarise your findings and compare them with the other group.

3. **Whole class**: according to you, what is Claudette's message to today's teenagers?

4. **Watch and listen** to the end of the documentary.

a. Summarise Claudette's advice and say what you think about it.

b. Fill in the time line:
page 47 or www.didierpassword.fr

Recap → Mention different ways of protesting publicly.

TRAINING TASK

News story: the Montgomery Bus Boycott

Using these headlines from the *Montgomery Adviser*, recount this episode. page 48

On December 1, 1955, Rosa Parks refused to give up her seat to a white man on a segregated bus, sparkling the Montgomery, Alabama bus boycott.

NEGRO GROUPS READY TO BOYCOTT CITY LINES
December 4, 1955

NEGRESS DRAWS FINE SEGREGATION CASE INVOLVING BUS RIDE
December 5, 1955

THE MECHANICS OF THE BUS BOYCOTT
January 10, 1956

BOMB ROCKS RESIDENCE OF BUS BOYCOTT LEADER
- None Injured After Bombing Of King's Home
January 31, 1956

SUPREME COURT OUTLAWS BUS SEGREGATION
November 14, 1956

The battle for school integration

1957 The Little Rock Crisis

A look back at one of the key events of the civil rights era. Ninety-two years after the abolition of slavery, the public schools in the Southern States of America were still segregated. President Dwight D. Eisenhower had to send in federal troops to ensure that nine black students made it to an all-white school.

Unexpected heroes

I hadn't intended anything heroic when I signed up to attend Little Rock Central High School which was less than a mile from my home and, at the time, all white. The school system had come up with a plan to phase in the desegregation order issued by the U.S Supreme Court in its 1954 *Brown v Board of Education* decision. So when the homeroom teacher in my ninth-grade class at the all-black Dunbar Junior High School in spring 1957 instructed those of us who lived in the boundaries to sign if we would be interested in attending Central the following fall, I did so without hesitation. I didn't ask my parents' permission or even mention it to them right away. It was just a given fact that I would pursue the top-quality education that Mother and Daddy had always preached about at home. But that simple declaration changed the course of my life, of my family's, and that of countless black students for generations to come. The change would have to be forced though. Arkansas governor Orval Faubus and staunch segregationists* throughout Little Rock resisted with all their might. In a show of federal force, President Dwight D. Eisenhower ultimately sent the U.S. military to escort the nine of us, who came to be known to the world as the Little Rock Nine, to integrate Central High School for the first time. White students ostracized and harassed us daily, and many teachers looked the other way. My father lost jobs and had to travel cross country, sometimes for weeks, to find work. [...] Three months before my graduation, my home was mysteriously bombed and my father and childhood friend were targeted as suspects by an unjust legal system. But I persevered through it all and became the first black girl ever to receive a diploma from Little Rock Central High School.

Carlotta Walls LaNier, *A Mighty Long Way: My Journey to Justice at Little Rock Nine Central High School* (2009)

* strong supporters of segregation

1. a. Skim-read the document and discuss what it may be about.
b. Read the introduction and explain the photograph.

2. Read "Unexpected heroes"
a. Discuss what you have understood about Carlotta and the US school system in the 1950s.
b. Pick out and discuss:
- the reasons for Carlotta's decision;
- the consequences of her decision.

3. a. Read the *New York Times* article: collect information about the place, the time, and what happened. Discuss your findings.
b. Read the article again and pick out references to:
- the crowd;
- the city authorities;
- the white students;
- the black students.
Explain what you have understood about their behaviours.

pages 49-50

President Threatens to Use U.S. Troops, Orders Rioters in Little Rock to Desist; Mob Compels 9 Negroes to Leave School

Students Unhurt Return Today Unlikely – City Authorities Yield to Crowd

By BENJAMIN FINE SPECIAL TO *THE NEW YORK TIMES* **September 24, 1957**

Little Rock, Ark., Sept. 23 – A mob of belligerent, shrieking and hysterical demonstrators forced the withdrawal today of nine Negro students from Central High School here.

Despite a heavy turnout[1] of local and state police to see that the Negroes were not molested in Little Rock's newest attempt to integrate the high school, city authorities bowed to the fury of about 1,000 white supremacists. They ordered the Negro students to leave the school about noon. The integration attempt had lasted 3 hours 13 minutes.

While fringe[2] fights broke out, and several persons were "roughed up"[3] by irate segregationists, the mob shouted insults and obscenities against the "niggers" and "nigger lovers." Groups of white students who had walked out of the school after the nine Negroes entered chanted: "Two, four, six, eight, we ain't gonna integrate."

The Little Rock Nine
Front right: Carlotta Walls LaNier.

1. a large number **2.** less important **3.** treated violently, beaten up

c. In your opinion, what is the journalist's point of view? Point out the devices he uses to make his point.

4. Fill in the time line:
page 47 or www.didierpassword.fr

Recap → React to what you have read about the battle for school integration.

LANGUAGE TOOLS

★ WORDS → p. 98

Violence

- a mob, a **rio**ter
- a violent demon**stra**tion = a **riot**, a re**volt** ≠ a **pea**ceful march, a **ra**lly
- at**tack**, **per**secute, **ha**rass, **bu**lly, in**sult**
- **threa**ten, in**ti**midate

→ They threatened to kill him if he tried to integrate.

Heroism

- brave, cou**ra**geous, bold ≠ **fear**ful
- **figh**ter, **wa**rrior
- **strug**gle for, fight for, ≠ fight a**gainst**

→ They fought for equality and against discrimination.

★ GRAMMAR → p. 99

Passive forms

→ My home was bombed.

TRAINING TASK

A tribute

A speech was delivered by a school official when the Little Rock Nine monument was unveiled.

↑ *Testament* (2005), Arkansas

Discuss:

a. what the school official may have evoked in his speech;

b. how he explained the monument's name.

Defending oneself

1 "Thank you"

This is what Melba Pattillo Beals, one of the nine black students chosen to integrate Little Rock Central High School, wrote in her diary in 1958.

February 19.

Andy again. He's really beginning to frighten me. As I emerged from the cafeteria today, he walked right up, face to face, stepping on my toes so I couldn't move for a long moment. He shoved me backward and then held a wrench up to my face. He waved it around and shouted all sorts of threats that he could do a lot of awful things to my face with it. My knees were shaking and I didn't know what to do. I said "Thank you". His eyes grew huge. Quicker than the speed of light, I jumped away from him and ran. "Just think all night about what I'm gonna do to you tomorrow," he shouted after me.

February 20.

I got hit across the back with a tennis racquet. I managed to smile and say "Thank you". Andy said, "what did you say nigger?" I repeated "Thank you very much". I spit up blood in the rest room. I felt as though someone had stuck a hot poker* through my back, into my insides. I saw him several times during the afternoon, but I never let him see me cry, and I didn't report it to anybody.

I think only the warrior exists in me now. Melba went away to hide. She was too frightened to stay here.

Melba Patillo Beals, *Warriors don't cry* (1994)

*un tisonnier

1. a. Focus on the title "Defending oneself" and the illustration. What springs to your mind?
b. You are going to read a passage from an autobiography and a passage from a novel: read their titles and discuss what you expect to read.

2. a. In groups. Read one of the two extracts. Discuss what you have understood. pages 50-52
b. Read the extract again and highlight:
- the victims' feelings and behaviour;
- the attackers' feelings and behaviour. pages 50-52

c. Discuss your findings and organise them. Report them back to the other group. pages 50-52

3. Whole class. Read and compare the two extracts. Discuss the reasons for the protagonists' behaviours.

Recap → List different ways of defending oneself. Discuss the most effective ones.

LANGUAGE TOOLS

★ WORDS → p. 98

Fear
- a**frai**d, **fea**rful, **frigh**tened, scared, **ter**rified

→ I'm afraid of going out alone.
→ I'm terrified by his threats.

Resistance
- re**sis**t, stand firm = not sub**mit** ≠ give way, yield, sur**ren**der
- con**front**, op**pose**, fight back, kick back,
- **pas**sive re**sis**tance ≠ sub**mi**ssion
- re**sis**ting, un**yiel**ding ≠ sub**mis**sive

★ GRAMMAR → p. 99

***Make/have/get*: causative structures**

→ He made her cry.

2 Fighting back

Four white boys in their early teens, sons of some newly arrived Irish people, occasionally entertained themselves in the afternoon by harassing black schoolchildren. [...]

These particular boys caught Nel once, and pushed her from hand to hand until they grew tired of the frightened helpless face. Because of that incident, Nel's route home from school became elaborate. She, and then Sula, managed to duck[1] them for weeks until a chilly day in November when Sula said, "Let's us go on home the shortest way."

Nel blinked, but acquiesced. They walked up the street until they got to the bend of Carpenter's Road where the boys lounged on a disused well[2]. Spotting their prey, the boys sauntered forward as though there were nothing in the world on their minds but the grey sky. Hardly able to control their grins[3], they stood like a gate blocking the path. When the girls were three feet in front of the boys, Sula reached into her coat pocket and pulled out Eva's paring knife. The boys stopped short, exchanged looks and dropped all pretence of innocence. This was going to be better than they thought. They were going to try and fight back, and with a knife. Maybe they could get an arm around one of their waists, or tear...

Sula squatted down in the dirt road and put everything down on the ground: her lunchpail, her reader, her mittens, her slate[4]. Holding the knife in her right hand, she pulled the slate toward her and pressed her left forefinger down hard on its edge. Her aim was determined but inaccurate. She slashed off only the tip of her finger. The four boys stared open-mouthed at the wound and the scrap of flesh, like a button mushroom, curling in the cherry blood that ran into the corners of the slate.

Sula raised her eyes to them. Her voice was quiet. "If I can do that to myself, what you suppose I'll do to you?"

Toni Morrison, *Sula* (1973)

1. *éviter*
2. *un puits*
3. *larges sourires*
4. *une ardoise d'école*

TRAINING TASK

Breaking news

As a journalist, you have been informed of what happened to Melba or Sula. Write a short article giving facts and opinions. Give your article a headline.

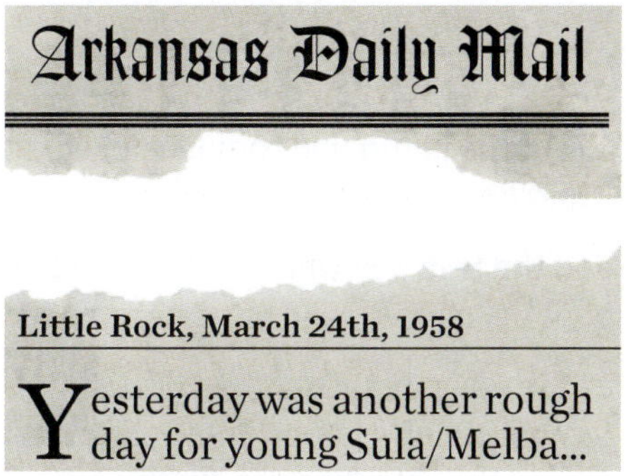
Arkansas Daily Mail

Little Rock, March 24th, 1958

Yesterday was another rough day for young Sula/Melba...

Four decades later

1 Recognition

↑ Statue constructed by political artist Rico 23. San Jose State University

On October 16, 2003, Smith and Carlos were on the campus of San Jose State University where a ceremony was held to honor their protest on the medal stand.

"I had truly believed that I would be six feet under before something like this took place. But I had lived long enough to see it, and to be part of it. My alma mater* was welcoming me back. It was embracing me as one of its own, as a part of its history and of its legacy and of its contribution to American society. And it was going to immortalize me with a statue right on the campus grounds I once walked. [...]

Thirty-five years earlier, I had thought I would never see the city of San Jose, the campus of San Jose State College, my home on the west edge of campus, or my wife and son ever again. On the night of October 16, 1968, I had stood on a platform on the infield of the Olympic Stadium in Mexico City [...] and I knew there were people, a lot of people, who wanted to kill me [...] because I had dared to make my presence- as a black man, as a representative of oppressed people all over America, as a spokesman for the ambitious goals of the Olympic Project for Human Rights known to the world. [...]

That was my victory stand. Not only because I had won the gold medal in the 200-meter final a half hour earlier, in world-record time. This was my platform, the one I had earned by years of training my body and my mind for the ultimate achievement. The athletic achievement paved a road toward my quest for a social victory, where everyone would be listening to and watching my statement about the conditions in which my people and I were living in the greatest country in the world. I never said a word as the national anthem was playing. My silent gesture was designed to speak volumes. As hard as I had worked to climb the victory stand, I had worked just as hard to earn the platform that the stand provided. For me, and for all of those who had participated in the struggle to bring me there and to put that platform to its best use, this victory stand represented more than just a place to accept a medal. [...] And I lived long enough to step onto campus again, [...] to see and hear San Jose State university honor what we had done [...]. Now the school was saying I was, and am, part of it. More specifically the students were saying I was part of it.

I realized that today's students and I probably had similar thoughts - about society and change and what America really represents and what it ought to represent - but these students likely were thinking of these things because of Carlos and me, because this day was dedicated to us, because we had done what these students ought to be doing today, nearly four decades after we opened the door for them and showed them the way.

Tommie Smith with David Steele, *Silent gesture* (2007)

* *université dont on est issu*

1. **Look at the photo** and compare it with the picture on p. 88.
2. **Read the text.** Say what you have understood about the narrator and his state of mind.
3. Read it again. Highlight then discuss:
   - Tommie Smith's double motivation for winning the gold medal in 1968;
   - what he expected to happen then;
   - the actual consequences over the years.

   pages 53-54
4. **Comment** on line 35: "My silent gesture was designed to speak volumes" and line 55: "We had done what these students ought to be doing today". Fill in the time line:

   page 47 or ▶ www.didierpassword.fr

2 The legacy of the Little Rock Nine

track 37

A 2007 NPR radio programme.

← 50 years later: planning the city to reconnect long-separated black and white neighbourhoods, New Haven, USA, 2010.

1. **Before listening**: judging from the title above, what do you expect the programme to be about?
2. **Listen to the whole programme**. Does it correspond to what you expected?
3. **a. Listen to the journalist's introduction** and summarise his main points about the past and present situations.
   b. Listen again, focusing on today's situation:
   - list different examples of "separation";
   - explain the difference between separation and segregation.
4. **Listen to Matthew Lassiter** and summarise his main points.

Recap → Using what you have learnt, illustrate Carlos's quote: "We still have a way to go but we can see some distance from where we were."

LANGUAGE TOOLS

★ WORDS → p. 98

Tribute
- **ho**mage = tri**bu**te
- praise, **ho**nour, **ce**lebrate, ac**know**ledge, hail, pay tribute to sb

Legacy
- **her**itage, contri**bu**tion
- em**brace** o**pi**nions

★ PRONUNCIATION → p. 98

Words ending in *-ate*
→ integrate, educate, demonstrate

TRAINING TASK

Paving the way

Tommie Smith wrote: "We opened the door for them [i.e. today's students] and showed them the way."

Discuss to what extent individuals can show the way to others. Back up your opinion with examples from history.

Language Tools

★ WORDS

❶ Derived words

a. Read the following sentences and pick out one derived word in each of them:
→ *The demonstration started at 3 o'clock.*

1. Claudette's story is unbelievable.
2. The mob addressed the students disrespectfully.
3. Tommie Smith had trained for the ultimate achievement.
4. The students would have liked to enjoy the freedom to go to school.
5. They had their share of daily abuse.
6. President Eisenhower ultimately sent the US military to escort the students.
7. The friends she had made in her childhood were targeted as suspects.
8. The rioters threatened the nine teenagers.
9. The demonstrators advocated civil disobedience.
10. The Arkansas governor resisted with all his might.

b. Fill in a grid like the one below with the derived words you have picked out.

Derived word	Root word	Prefix or suffix used (changes)
demonstration (noun)	demonstrate (verb)	-ion (changes verb into noun)
...	...	...

c. Find other examples of derived words with the above suffixes and prefixes.

More exercises in your **Workbook** ▶ p. 55-56

★ PRONUNCIATION

❷ Stress and subjective meaning

track 38

*"...that **really** intrigued me..."*

Pour souligner ses sentiments ou convictions, le locuteur peut choisir de placer une forte accentuation sur certains mots.

a. Listen again to Philip Hoose's introduction (*Standing up alone*, p. 91) and pick out the words which he chooses to stress more heavily:
"...hearing this one story that really intrigued me was the story of a girl in Montgomery, Alabama, who refused to surrender her public bus seat to a white passenger almost a year before Rosa Parks did it and I felt I've got to find this person..."

b. Discuss the stressed words with your classmates to make sure you agree.

c. Try to explain why Philip Hoose decided to write about Claudette Colvin's experience.

d. Practise reading out loud the following account in two different ways:

1. as it would be read on the news (objective meaning);
2. to convey your personal opinion (subjective meaning).

A 42-year-old black female worker took a seat in the front row of the black section of a city bus in Montgomery, Alabama. The bus filled up, and the bus driver demanded that she move so a white male passenger could have her seat...

❸ Verbs ending in *-ate*

track 39

Here are some words from this unit. They all have three or more syllables and end in *-ate*.

- integrate, participate, dedicate, segregate, graduate, hesitate, educate, demonstrate, elaborate

a. Listen to them and find the stressed syllable. Thinking about this stressed syllable, say what they have in common.

b. Practise pronouncing them.

→ Précis de prononciation ⑧ p. 212

More exercises in your **Workbook** ▶ p.56

★ GRAMMAR

Passive forms

Observe

A. Hysterical demonstrators forced the withdrawal of nine black students.
B. The nine black students were not molested by the angry mob but they were told to leave the school.
C. White students ostracised and harassed the Little Rock Nine daily.
D. The change would have to be forced.
E. Carlotta's father was targeted by an unjust legal system.
F. Rosa Parks is often believed to have been the first black woman to stand up for her rights.
G. Segregation in American public schools was declared unconstitutional in 1954.

- **Dites ce qui différencie et caractérise les formes verbales surlignées en vert et celles en jaune. Que pouvez-vous dire du sujet de l'action et du sujet du verbe ?**
- **Dans chaque cas, pourquoi l'énonciateur a-t-il choisi une forme plutôt que l'autre ? Qu'a-t-il voulu souligner ?**

Practise

↑ Rosa Parks' arrest after bus boycott. Montgomery, February 1956.

4 **Look at the photo and write what happened to Rosa Parks.**
You may use some of the following verbs:
- arrest, take to the police station, ask/answer questions, fingerprint, jail...

g → Précis grammatical ⑱ p. 200

Make/have/get: causative structures

Observe

A. The USA Olympic Committee made the athletes leave the Olympic Village.
B. The rioters had the authorities yield.
C. Hysterical demonstrators made the black students withdraw.
D. Some journalists got their readers to realise segregation existed.
E. Smith and Carlos got American citizens to understand the situation of black people.

- **Observez les formes soulignées. Quelle idée générale expriment-elles ?**
- **D'après vous, quelle nuance de sens la présence de *to* indique-t-elle ?**

g → Précis grammatical ㉑ p. 202

Practise

5 **Use the verbs *make, have, get* to talk about slaves and slave owners.**
Start from the photo below.
→ *Slave owners made their slaves obey. They had them live in terrible conditions.*

↑ Slave family in cotton field near Savannah, circa 1860.

More exercises in your **Workbook** ▶ p. 57-58

Stratégies

Lire et comprendre un article de presse

Pour lire efficacement un article de presse, vous pouvez suivre les étapes suivantes.

"Little Rock Nine" prepare to celebrate day of victory

The president-elect has invited as inauguration guests the nine black people who as children defied racist mobs in Arkansas over 50 years ago.

Joanna Walters in New York

***The Observer*, Sunday 28 December 2008**

When Barack Obama is inaugurated next month, thousands of African Americans who risked their lives in the civil rights movement will flock to Washington to witness the moment.

Among the vast crowds, none will feel more proud than a small group of black pioneers who faced down violent mobs more than 50 years ago when they struggled to end racial segregation in schools.

Beaten, kicked, spat at, threatened with death and abused daily for months after enrolling in a white high school in Arkansas, the "Little Rock Nine" have been invited as honoured guests to perhaps the most eagerly awaited inauguration in American history.

Melba Patillo, one of the nine, said: "I'm honoured that Barack Obama saw fit to invite me. He has said that he aspired to climb the steps of the White House because the Little Rock Nine climbed the steps of Central High School." [...]

The civil rights leader Martin Luther King met the nine and encouraged them not to give up. Patillo said: "I had eggs thrown all over me and I was whining to Dr King about it. He said 'Melba, you are not doing this for yourself, you are doing this for generations yet unborn'. Now when I look at what Nelson Mandela did and slaves who revolted, and Rosa Parks, and Gandhi, we are all one." [...]

The nine were awarded the Congressional Gold Medal by President Bill Clinton in 1999. But the crowning confirmation of their battle for civil rights will come on 20 January in Washington DC. ■

1 Anticipez le contenu de l'article avant de le lire

a. Étudiez les éléments autres que l'article lui-même (mise en page, documents visuels, date de publication, lieu, etc.).

b. Repérez le sujet principal grâce aux titre et sous-titre.

c. Identifiez le journal, le journaliste et à qui il s'adresse.

→ À vous

Étudiez tous ces éléments dans l'article ci-dessus.

a. Déduisez qui est *The president-elect* dont il est question ;

b. Déduisez de quelle « victoire » il s'agit dans le titre ;

c. Quel mot clé du sous-titre reprend l'idée de *celebrate* ?

d. Dans quel pays le journal est-il publié ? Vérifiez dans une encyclopédie si nécessaire.

2 Lisez attentivement le premier paragraphe

Il fournit en général les **informations essentielles** en développant titre et sous-titre.
Il vous permettra de découvrir :
- de qui on parle ;
- de quoi on parle (événements, problème avec ses causes et conséquences...) ;
- où et quand les faits ont eu lieu.

→ À vous

a. Lisez le titre et le sous-titre et trouvez les informations essentielles.

b. Le premier paragraphe (lignes 1-8) développe ce qui a été annoncé dans le titre et le sous-titre ; **trouvez les correspondances** en les notant à droite dans un tableau comme celui-ci.

Dans le titre et le sous-titre	Dans le premier paragraphe
the president-elect →	...
to celebrate day of victory →	...
black people who... defied racist mobs →	...

3 Lisez la suite de l'article

a. La première (et/ou la dernière) phrase donne souvent l'**idée clé** du paragraphe. Si celui-ci ne contient qu'une phrase, concentrez-vous sur la **proposition principale** : le verbe conjugué, son sujet, son complément direct.

b. Repérez les mots de liaison pour mieux comprendre la logique de l'article, pointez des détails significatifs, et cherchez si des exemples sont donnés.

c. Faites la différence entre faits bruts et opinion du journaliste : c'est essentiel. Le point de vue du journaliste s'exprime au travers d'adjectifs, d'adverbes ou du choix des personnes auxquelles il donne la parole. Il peut aussi bien sûr parler en son nom propre et utiliser la première personne « *I* ».

→ À vous

a. Pour chaque paragraphe, relevez la phrase clé ou les éléments essentiels. Proposez ensuite un résumé de l'article.

b. Étudiez l'évolution du lexique utilisé:
- *thousands of African Americans who risked their lives in the civil rights movement:* **§ 1**
- *a small group of black pioneers:* **§ 2**
- *the "Little Rock Nine":* **§ 3**
- *Melba Patillo:* **§ 4**

Expliquez ces changements. Quel est l'effet induit ?

c. Dans le paragraphe 4, vous avez repéré *because*. Expliquez le rapport de cause à conséquence.

d. Dans le paragraphe 6, vous avez repéré *but*. Quelle est sa signification ici ?

e. Quels éléments dans l'article indiquent que le journaliste n'est pas neutre ?

Lire et comprendre un article de presse

Lisez l'article ci-dessous et répondez aux questions :

a. Quel est l'événement majeur dont parle l'article ? Quand et où a-t-il eu lieu ?
b. Quelles sont les autres informations importantes contenues dans l'article ?
c. Quel est le point de vue du journaliste ?
d. Dans quel but l'article a-t-il été écrit ?

Sports of The Times; Vilified* to Glorified

By WILLIAM C. RHODEN ***THE NEW YORK TIMES*** **– October 17, 2005**

PEOPLE often ask about my sports heroes – specifically, whether I have any. The standing answer is that I know too much about too many athletes to have heroes. There were, however, two icons who made an indelible mark on my life at an early age: John Carlos and Tommie Smith. They are the closest I've come to having sports heroes.

In 1968, Smith and Carlos made one of the most courageous and enduring acts of sports demonstration in my lifetime, possibly in modern athletic history, when they raised black-gloved fists and bowed their heads on the victory stand at the Mexico City Olympic Games. The act was a profound gesture against oppression.

Today at San Jose State University, their message will come full circle, 37 years later, with a day long celebration that will end with the unveiling of a 24-foot bronze statue commemorating their Mexico City demonstration. [...]

In October 1968, Smith and Carlos were two of the world's greatest sprinters. In Mexico City, they punctuated the United States' domination of the Olympics: Smith won the gold medal in the 200 meters and Carlos won the bronze. Peter Norman of Australia won the silver.

I don't remember whether the Games were live on television or shown on a tape delay. But I remember being stunned as I watched Smith and Carlos climb the podium and, as the national anthem played, raise clenched fists and bow their heads. Smith raised his right fist as a symbol of black power, and Carlos raised his left to represent unity in black America. Norman wore a badge in support of an organization that Smith had co-founded, the Olympic Project for Human Rights.

In my mind, the demonstration became the perfect symbol of protest, and illuminated the power of a silent but well-timed demonstration. [...]

Thirty-seven years later, their demonstration is being memorialized at their alma mater as part of a movement to encourage and recognize student activism.

* vilify: say bad things about someone or something

Faites le point

a. Vérifiez votre compréhension. **Auto-corrigé** ▶ www.didierpassword.fr
b. Situez votre niveau dans le tableau ci-dessous.

Niveaux	Mes compétences
B1-1	J'ai pu anticiper et reconnaître une information importante dans un article de journal, sur un sujet qui m'est familier ou que j'ai étudié.
B1-2	J'ai pu identifier les points significatifs d'un article de journal bien structuré sur un sujet familier.
B1-3	J'ai pu reconnaître le point du vue du journaliste.
B2	J'ai pu comprendre dans le détail un article relatif à un domaine familier en distinguant faits et opinions.

FINAL TASKS

Press article

One of the "Little Rock Nine" braves a jeering crowd.

↑ Elizabeth Eckford attempting to enter Little Rock School on 4th September, 1957.

task 1

Writing

Write a short article

Start from a headline and a photo your teacher will give you.

1. Get ready

In groups

- Make sure you understand the headline and the photograph.
- Find out about the events and the people if necessary.

On your own

- List the points you are going to develop (Who? What? Where? When? Why? How?).
- Don't forget to express your opinion.

2. Action!

- Provide a clear and concise overview of the main points in the first paragraph.
- Choose your words carefully to make the account of events clear and interesting to your reader.

task 2

Reading

Match headlines and press articles

Read the headlines below and match them with the press articles your teacher will give you.

The Long March
Jun. 21, 1963

"To All on Equal Terms"
May. 24, 1954

The End of Integration
By James S. Kunen
Apr. 29, 1996

Integration on the Rails
Dec. 5, 1955

Reading test

- Your teacher will give you a text: read it carefully, then answer the questions.

Culture File 2

CIVIL RIGHTS MOVEMENT

Pick out one of the documents on these pages.

In groups

1. Identify the speaker or writer and the circumstances.
Discuss this person's views on the civil rights movement.

2. Jot down a few notes to share your ideas with the class.

Whole class

3. Compare these people's views and contributions to the civil rights movement. Then comment on document 5.

1 We shall overcome!

track 41

A speech by Martin Luther King, Jr (June, 1966).
M.L. King, Jr (1929-1968) was a Baptist minister and a prominent civil rights leader.
He was assassinated in Memphis in 1968.

Martin Luther King Day, 2010 →

2 The Ballot or the Bullet

"Mr. Moderator, Brother Lomax, brothers and sisters, friends and enemies: I just can't believe everyone in here is a friend, and I don't want to leave anybody out. The question tonight, as I understand it, is "The Negro Revolt, and Where Do We Go From Here? or What Next?" In my little humble way of understanding it, it points toward either the ballot or the bullet. [...]

All of us have suffered here, in this country, political oppression at the hands of the white man, economic exploitation at the hands of the white man, and social degradation at the hands of the white man.

Now in speaking like this, it doesn't mean that we're anti-white, but it does mean we're anti-exploitation, we're anti-degradation, we're anti-oppression. And if the white man doesn't want us to be anti-him, let him stop oppressing and exploiting and degrading us.

Whether we are Christians or Muslims or nationalists or agnostics or atheists, we must first learn to forget our differences. If we have differences, let us differ in the closet; when we come out in front, let us not have anything to argue about until we get finished arguing with the man.

If we don't do something real soon, I think you'll have to agree that we're going to be forced either to use the ballot or the bullet. It's one or the other in 1964. It isn't that time is running out – time has run out!"

Speech delivered by Malcolm X on April 3, 1964

Malcolm X (1925-1965)
Influential civil rights leader, assassinated while giving a speech in New York.

3 Tired of giving in

On December 1, 1955, Rosa Parks refused to give up her seat to a white man on a segregated bus. She recalls how it happened.

The next stop was the Empire Theater, and some whites got on. They filled up the white seats, and one man was left standing. The driver looked back and noticed the man standing. Then he looked back at us. He said, "let me have those front seats", because they were the front seats of the black section. [...]

People always say that I didn't give up my seat because I was tired, but that isn't true. I was not physically, or no more tired than I usually was at the end of a working day. I was not old, although some people have an image of me as being old then. I was forty-two. No, the only tired I was, was tired of giving in.

The driver of the bus saw me still sitting there, and he asked was I going to stand up. I said, "No". He said, "Well, I'm going to have you arrested." Then I said, "You may do that." These were the only words we said to each other. I didn't even know his name, which was James Black, until we were in court together. He got out of the bus and stayed outside for a few minutes, waiting for the police.

As I sat there, I tried not to think about what might happen. I knew that anything was possible.

Rosa Parks with Jim Haskins, *My Story* (1992)

4 We shall overcome

track 42

A protest song by Joan Baez.

In August 1963, folksinger Joan Baez memorably led a crowd of 300,000 in singing *We Shall Overcome* at the Lincoln Memorial during a freedom ride on Washington.

↑ Lincoln Memorial, August 28, 1963

5 Historic win

WWW.TUSCALOOSANEWS.COM

OBAMA OVERCOMES

TURNOUT Record number of voters crowd polls in Tuscaloosa

SENATE Democrats fall short of winning 60-seat control

LOCAL RACES Incumbents on County Commission keep their seats

REACTION Local blacks inspired by historic presidential election

Barriers fall as U.S. elects black president

Democrats in power

Dems expand control of Senate

Obama wins election

← *The Tuscaloosa News*, Nov. 5, 2008

UNIT 7 Utopia

"Here we are in some world which is nowhere. Or if you prefer the Greek of it, we are in Utopia."

H. G. Wells, *Men Like Gods* (1923)

How do people imagine the ideal society?

← **Look** at the picture, **read** Wells's sentence and **state** your first reactions. **Discuss** the meaning of the word "Utopia". What images or thoughts do you associate with "Utopia"?

FINAL TASKS

P. 121

My Utopia

Writing
Imagine your ideal society

Reading
Draw the map of a utopian city

CULTURE

- Discovering alternative societies:
  - Auroville, an experimental township,
  - The Amish: an American community.
- Literary works:
  - William Morris, *News from Nowhere*
  - Lois Lowry, *The Giver*

COMMUNICATION

- Writing short descriptions presenting facts and giving explanations.
- Reading literary texts and understanding the main facts, the characters, their actions and motives.
- Describing and explaining different aspects of a society.

TOOLS

★ Words
- Dreams and aspirations
- Modernity and tradition
- Values
- Surprise/astonishment
- Gloom and pleasure

★ Pronunciation
- Intonation and opinions

★ Grammar
- Expressing purpose and aim
- Simple present

Stratégies
→ *Écrire un texte descriptif et explicatif*

Auroville: an ideal city?

1 City of the Dawn*

video 10

A trailer for a documentary about Auroville, 2009.

← Auroville is a township in South India. Its founders conceived it as "an alternative exercise in ecological and spiritual living".

* *aurore, aube*

1. **Before watching the trailer**, focus on the photograph and the caption. What is your first reaction?
   Tell the class who the inhabitants of Auroville might be and how they might live.
2. **Watch the trailer** and focus on the people, the places and the captions.
   Discuss your findings. How would you define "wishful thinking"?
3. **Watch again** and focus on what the Aurovilians say. Find out about:
   a. the state of today's world, as they see it;
   b. the kind of world they want to live in.
4. **Share** your findings. Summarise the Aurovilians' positive and negative arguments.

2 The township

1. **a. Look at the document** on p. 109. In the text, the names of the different zones in the city have been replaced by numbers.
   Read each paragraph and find the name of the corresponding zone:
   Industrial Zone | Cultural Zone | Residential Zone
   Peace Area | International Zone | Green Belt
   b. Complete the plan: page 59 or www.didierpassword.fr
2. **a.** Read again and highlight the characteristics of each zone. pages 59-60
   b. Share your findings with the class.
3. **Compare** Auroville to other cities you know.
4. **React:** would you like to live in Auroville? Why or why not?

Recap → Give some possible reasons why the founders of Auroville named it the "City of the Dawn".

http://www.auroville.org

At the centre of the township lies the ❶ ..., comprising the Matrimandir ("Temple of the Mother" in Sanskrit) and its gardens, the amphitheatre with the Urn of Human Unity that contains the soil of 121 nations and 23 Indian states, and a lake to help create an atmosphere of calm and serenity and to serve as a groundwater recharge area.

A 109-hectare area to the north of the Peace Area, the ❷ ..., a zone for "green" industries, is focused on Auroville's efforts towards a self-supporting township. It will contain small and medium-scale industries, training centres, art and craft studios, and the city's administrative offices.

The largest of the four city zones, the ❸ ..., is bordered by parks. The aim of this zone is to provide a living-area that successfully balances collective and individual needs. 55% of the area will be green and only 45% built surface, thereby creating an urban zone counter-balanced by nature.

The ❹ ..., a 74-hectare zone to the west of the Peace Area, will host national and cultural pavilions, grouped by continents. Its central focus is to create a living demonstration of human unity in diversity through the expression of the genius and contribution of each nation to humanity.

Planned on a 93-hectare area situated to the east of the Peace Area, the ❺ ... will be a site for applied research in education and artistic expression. Facilities for cultural, educational, artistic and sporting activities will be located in this zone.

The city area will be surrounded by a ❻ .... As a zone for organic farms, dairies, orchards, forests and wildlife areas, this belt will act as a barrier against urban encroachment*, provide a variety of habitats for wildlife, and serve as a source for food, timber, medicines etc. and as a place for recreation. It stands as an example of successful transformation of wasteland into a vibrant eco-system.

Adapted from www.auroville.org

* *invasion*

Overview of the city plan

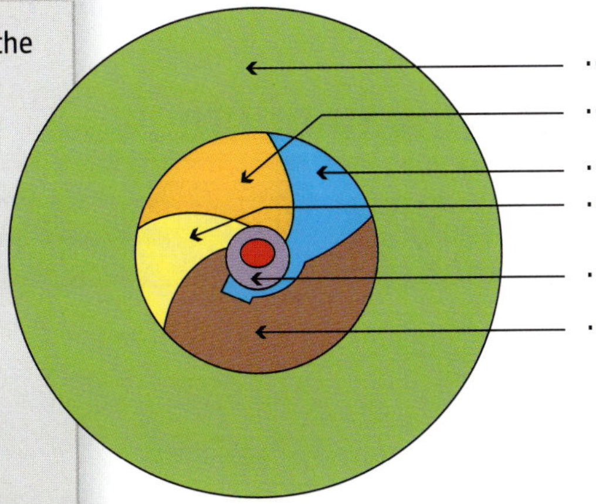

LANGUAGE TOOLS

★ **WORDS** → p. 116

Dreams and aspirations

- crave for, long to, yearn for
  = have a strong de**sire** for

→ He's craving/yearning for peace.

→ I long to take a walk in the Green Belt.

- look **for**ward to + *-ing*

→ He looks forward to living in Auroville.

- **hope**ful

→ She is hopeful that Auroville will exist forever.

★ **PRONUNCIATION** → p. 116

Intonation and opinions

★ **GRAMMAR** → p. 117

Expressing purpose and aim

→ want to, so as to, in order to

Simple present

→ The Green Belt surrounds the city.

TRAINING TASK

Guided tour of Auroville

video 11

1. In groups, watch a few seconds of a video about Auroville.

2. Supply the missing commentary: describe and explain what you see.

↑ Aurovilians building the Matrimandir, 1986.

The Amish: an ideal society?

1 The Amish way of life

video 12

In this documentary from 1975, historian John Ruth states the ancestral principles on which the Amish communities were established.

An Amish family in 2009

1. **Before watching**, look at the photograph.
   a. Tell the class what you know or can guess about the Amish.
   b. List questions you could ask John Ruth to find out more about them.
2. **Watch the video** and tell your classmates what you have understood.
3. Watch the first part once more. Make a note of what you have understood about the Amish's ancestors and their religious beliefs.
4. **In groups**. Watch the second part again.
   - find out about Amish culture: family, links with modern technology, etc. *(goup 1)*.
   - pick out the arguments which explain their attitudes *(goup 2)*.
   Paying attention to strongly stressed words, verbal forms, repeated words and vocabulary networks will help.
5. **Discuss** your findings with the class.

2 Leaving the community

The following testimonies were made by people who chose to leave the Amish community.

❶ http://www.mapministry.org

I grew up Amish; I found it extremely frustrating and left home when I was 18 and moved to Montana. I worked for an outfitter for 7 years and now I am in the University of Montana becoming a high-school teacher in English and History.

Duane S., December 16, 2009

❷ http://www.mapministry.org

While I was Amish, many of my Amish friends, including me, were hiding some of the things we did that were not Amish—like listening to the radio, calling someone on the phone, and other things. I always wondered why God made some people to be allowed to have cars and we were in this little Amish community—having to work hard with our hands alone.

Mattie S., May 15, 2009

❸ http://www.mapministry.org

I left the Amish in 1968 and I did not want any part of any religion, not even a wedding or a funeral. I was very vulnerable; I got into drugs, partying, and that kind of lifestyle. When I look back, I realize it was because I did not know how to live outside of the boundaries and "protection" of the Amish community. I did not know how to manage money, how to have normal relationships with people, especially of the opposite sex.

Henry B., September 25, 2009

❹ http://www.mapministry.org

I was born a typical Amish boy in central Michigan. Growing up, my brothers and I did what normal Amish boys do. Since my dad did construction, and we only had a 1½ acre farm, we got bored a lot. I have 2 brothers, one just older than me and one just younger than me. I'm sure we caused Mom some gray hair as she tried to keep up with us mischievous little guys. We had goats for milk, so oftentimes we rode goats, led them around, hitched them to sleds in the wintertime, chased cats, climbed trees, rode wagons.

Monroe R., August 12, 2010

1. **Before reading** the testimonies, look at the title and discuss what you may learn.
2. **Read** and discuss what you have understood.
3. Read again and pick out information about:
   - the Amish way of life as seen by these people;
   - the reasons why they left the Amish community.

   page 61
4. **Discuss** your findings.

LANGUAGE TOOLS

★ **WORDS** → p. 116

Modernity and tradition

- **pro**gress, speed, tech**no**logy
- **an**cestors
- change ≠ keep, main**tain**, pre**serve**, save
- **mo**dern, **up**-to-**date**, **state**-of-the-**art** ≠ **ob**solete, out**mo**ded
- pro**gres**sive ≠ tra**di**tional

Recap → Write a short paragraph summing up the positive and negative aspects of the Amish community.

TRAINING TASK

A brochure for visitors

In groups

1. Use the Internet to gather information about a modern-day Amish community:

location, settlements, clothes, technology, food, family, languages, education, beliefs, etc.

2. Create a brochure for people visiting an Amish community. Include illustrations to depict the information presented. pages 62-63

Trading in a utopian world

How much?

One day the narrator, William Guest, falls asleep and awakes to find himself in a future society (shortly after 2003). In this extract, he is in a small boat on the Thames with a waterman[1].

"Please take me ashore now: I want to get my breakfast". He nodded, [...] and we were at the landing-stage again. He jumped out and I followed him; and of course I was not surprised to see him wait, as if for the inevitable after-piece[2] that follows the doing of a service to a fellow-citizen. So I put my hand into my waistcoat-pocket, and said, "How much?" though still with the uncomfortable feeling that perhaps I was offering money to a gentleman.

He looked puzzled, and said, "How much? I don't quite understand what you are asking about. Do you mean the tide[3]? If so, it is close on the turn now".

I blushed, and said, stammering[4], "Please, don't take it amiss if I ask you; I mean no offence: but what ought I to pay you? You see I am a stranger, and don't know your customs – or your coins."

And therewith I took a handful of money out of my pocket, as one does in a foreign country. [...]

He still seemed puzzled, but not at all offended; and he looked at the coins with some curiosity. I thought, Well after all, he is a waterman, and is considering what he may venture to take. He seems such a nice fellow that I'm sure I don't grudge him a little over-payment. I wonder, by the way, whether I couldn't hire him as a guide for a day or two, since he is so intelligent.

Therewith my new friend said thoughtfully:

"I think I know what you mean. You think that I have done you a service; so you feel yourself bound to give me something which I am not to give to a neighbour, unless he has done something special for me. I have heard of this kind of thing; but pardon me for saying, that it seems to us a troublesome and roundabout custom; and we don't know how to manage it. And you see this ferrying and giving people casts about the water[5] is my business, which I would do for anybody; so to take gifts in connection with it would look very queer[6]. Besides, if one person gave me something, then another might, and another, and so on; and I hope you won't think me rude if I say that I shouldn't know where to stow away[7] so many mementos of friendship".

And he laughed loud and merrily, as if the idea of being paid for his work was a very funny joke. I confess I began to be afraid that the man was mad, though he looked sane enough.

William Morris, *News from Nowhere* (1890)

1. boatman (someone who works on a boat)
2. payment
3. *marée*
4. *bégayer*
5. helping people
6. strange
7. put away

LANGUAGE TOOLS

★ **WORDS** → p. 116

Values
- an in**cen**tive = a moti**va**tion
- con**sid**er, pass **judge**ment on, re**gard**
- **self**less = un**self**ish
- **gree**dy, **grasp**ing ≈ **mo**tivated by **mo**ney

Surprise/astonishment
- unex**pec**ted
- as**ton**ish = be**wil**der
- odd = weird /ˈwɪəd/, strange

1. **Read the source and the introduction** and try to predict what the narrator may find most striking about life at the beginning of the 21st century.
2. **Read the titles and the text** and discuss what you have understood.
3. a. **In groups**, read the text again. Pick out information about:
   - the narrator's attitude and reactions *(group 1)*;
   - the waterman's attitude and reactions *(group 2)*.

   Paying attention to adjectives and verbs will help.

   b. Discuss your findings.
4. **Read the last sentence** (lines 33-34) and explain what the narrator may be feeling.

Recap → Explain in what way the waterman's world is a utopia.

TRAINING TASK

Drama workshop

Imagine another episode from the narrator's utopian experience. Use one of the situations below or imagine another incident:

shopping | having dinner | travelling | etc.

1. Write down the dialogue.
2. Perform the scene.

Elsewhere

Leaving Sameness

Jonas lives in a world under control where all problems have been solved. The Giver alone holds the memories of the true pain and pleasure of life, and he must pass them on to someone. When he turns 12, Jonas is singled out to be that person. After several months of training, Jonas decides to leave the community, taking with him Gabriel, a very young child.

"Plane! Plane!" Gabriel called, and Jonas turned swiftly into the trees, though he had not seen planes in days, and he did not hear an aircraft engine now. When he stopped the bicycle in the shrubbery and turned to grab Gabe, he saw the small chubby arm pointing towards the sky.

Terrified, he looked up, but it was not a plane at all. Though he had never seen one before, he identified it from his fading memories, for The Giver had given them to him often. It was a bird.

Soon there were many birds along the way, soaring overhead, calling. They saw deer[1]; and once, beside the road, looking at them curious and unafraid, a small reddish-brown creature with a thick tail, whose name Jonas did not know. He slowed the bike and they stared at one another until the creature turned away and disappeared into the woods.

All of it was new to him. After a life of Sameness and Predictability, he was awed[2] by the surprises that lay beyond each curve of the road. He slowed the bike again and again to look with wonder at wildflowers, to enjoy the throaty warble[3] of a new bird nearby, or merely to watch the way wind shifted the leaves in the trees. During his twelve years in the community, he had never felt such simple moments of exquisite happiness.

But there were desperate fears building in him now as well. The most relentless of his new fears was that they would starve. Now that they had left the cultivated fields behind them, it was almost impossible to find food. They finished the meager store of potatoes and carrots they had saved from the last agricultural area, and now they were always hungry. [...]

At night, while Gabriel slept beside him, Jonas lay awake, tortured by hunger, and remembered his life in the community where meals were delivered to each dwelling[4] every day.

He tried to use the flagging power of his memory to recreate meals, and managed brief, tantalizing[5] fragments: banquets with huge roasted meats; birthday parties with thick-frosted cakes; and lush fruits picked and eaten, sun-warmed and dripping, from trees.

1. *cerfs*
2. impressed and slightly afraid
3. high continuous song
4. home
5. *alléchant*

But when the memory glimpses subsided[6], he was left with the gnawing, painful emptiness. Jonas remembered, suddenly and grimly, the time in his chilhood when he had been chastised[7] for misusing a word. The word had been "starving". You have never been starving, he had been told. You will never be starving.

Now he was. If he had stayed in the community, he would not be. It was as simple as that. Once he had yearned for choice. Then, when he had had a choice, he had made the wrong one: the choice to leave. And now he was starving.

But if he had stayed...

His thoughts continued. If he had stayed, he would have starved in other ways. He would have lived a life hungry for feelings, for color, for love.

Lois Lowry, *The Giver* (1993)

6. die down
7. physically punished

1. **Read the introduction** and look at the book cover. React.
2. **Read the title and the text** and discuss what you have understood.
3. Read the text again and highlight:
   - elements characterising the community that Jonas is leaving;
   - what he discovers on the way that he did not know before;
   - his feelings, expectations and fears.

   pages 64-65
4. Share your findings with the class and comment on Jonas's feelings.
5. **Summarise** Jonas's dilemma.

LANGUAGE TOOLS

★ **WORDS** → p. 116

Gloom
- **bor**ing, dull
- de**press**ing = bleak, **gloo**my
- be bored

Pleasure
- **hap**piness = **cheer**fulness, de**light**, **won**der
- ap**pre**ciate = **re**vel
- lush /ˈlʌʃ/ = a**bun**dant

Recap → State the main reason(s) why Jonas has decided to leave his community.

TRAINING TASK

Creative writing

In her novel *The Giver*, Lois Lowry imagines a future society in which everyone is happy.
Here are some characteristics of this society:
- it has chosen to be happily ignorant of its past,
- it has given up individuality and free will,
- extreme "sameness" guides daily life,
- it is a society without diseases, but also without weather or colours.

You have spent some time in this society.
Write a short article presenting one of its aspects.

★ WORDS

❶ Dreams and aspirations

a. Among these words, which ones can be both verbs and nouns?
• achieve, ambition, aspire, demand, desire, dream, goal, hope, deal, will, wish

Use a monolingual dictionary if necessary. Do not forget to check the structures of the verbal forms.

b. Match the two columns to write meaningful and correct sentences:

1. I demand...	a. to peace
2. He desires...	b. to lead a new life
3. She dreams...	c. that you follow our rules
4. They look forward...	d. they managed to build a utopian city
5. I hope...	e. for a better future
6. They aspire...	f. to achieving unity
7. I wish...	g. of preserving the past

c. Choose some words from *a* and *b* to explain what people usually expect from an ideal society. Write down a few lines.
→ *When people imagine a utopian world, they usually look forward to living in a place where they can fulfil their dreams of happiness.*

❷ Traditional and modern ways of life

a. Consider the nouns, verbs and adjectives below and place them in two lists:

Tradition   Modernity

• ***n***: ancestors, progress, speed, technology
• ***vb***: change, keep, maintain, preserve
• ***adj***: modern, obsolete, outmoded, progressive, state-of-the-art, up-to-date

b. Choose five of those words and use each one in a sentence to describe the Amish way of life.

❸ Values

Match the following words to their definitions:

Words	Definitions
1. incentive *(n)*	a. think about something carefully specially in order to make a decision
2. selflessness *(n)*	b. something that induces action or motivates effort.
3. consider *(vb)*	c. think about something in a particular way
4. pass judgment on *(vb)*	d. the quality of unselfish concern for the others.
5. regard *(vb)*	e. eager to get money and unwilling to give any of it away or spend it
6. free *(adj)*	f. express a strong opinion.
7. grasping *(adj)*	g. that does not cost anything.

More exercises in your **Workbook** ▶ p. 66-67

★ PRONUNCIATION

❹ Intonation and opinions

track 43

"...a carefree existence..." "...no queues..." "...no computers..."

Un locuteur utilise l'intonation, montante ou descendante, pour exprimer ses sentiments : enthousiasme (↗), désapprobation (↘), etc.

a. Listen to these two people talking about what life might be like on a desert island.

b. By paying attention to the rising and falling intonation, try and decide whether they are for or against moving to a desert island.

c. Listen again, take some notes and practise repeating what you have heard.

More exercises in your **Workbook** ▶ p. 67-68

★ GRAMMAR

Expressing purpose and aim

Observe

A. He wants to go to Auroville so as to start a new life.
B. The purpose/aim of these people is to create a different society.
C. The Amish resist technology in order to prevent their old people from becoming obsolete.
D. Jonas left with Gabriel so that they could live in a world full of colors and love.

a. Dans chacune des phrases ci-dessus, relevez les mots ou groupes de mots qui expriment le but.

b. Classez-les dans un tableau en fonction de leur nature :

Verbes	Mots de liaison	Noms
....	....	....

g → Précis grammatical ⑳ p. 202

Practise

5 What did the Amish and the Aurovilians create their society for? Write down your answers.
→ *The Aurovilians created their society in order to live in harmony with nature.*
→ *The Amish want to preserve a certain way of life also linked with nature.*
→ ...

Simple present

Observe

A. In my utopia, things change everyday, there is not a day like any other: people are never bored. The inhabitants of my utopia are happy as everyone has a job. As a reward for working, people's needs are met by the society they serve. They all own a house or a flat, they have the food and clothing they need. Working also guarantees free health care.

B. In my utopia, things will change everyday, there will not be a day like any other: people will never be bored. The inhabitants of my utopia will be happy as everyone will have a job. As a reward for working, people's needs will be met by the society they serve. They will all own a house or a flat, they will have the food and clothing they need. Working will also guarantee free health care.

a. Étudiez les formes verbales surlignées. En quoi diffèrent-elles dans les deux paragraphes ?

b. Dans quel texte le narrateur décrit-il :
- un monde qui n'existe pas encore ?
- un monde utopique comme s'il existait déjà en donnant ses caractéristiques ?

c. Concluez en disant à l'aide de vos propres mots quand on peut utiliser le présent simple.

g → Précis grammatical ⑨ p. 192

Practise

6 Write down a paragraph (35-40 words) to describe your utopian society.

More exercises in your Workbook ▶ p.68

Stratégies

Écrire un texte descriptif et explicatif

Lorsque vous écrivez un texte descriptif et explicatif, votre objectif est de permettre au lecteur de comprendre un sujet qu'il ne connaît pas et d'avoir une vision précise de ce dont vous parlez. Voici quelques conseils pour vous y aider.

1 Décrivez pour permettre de visualiser

Étapes	Exemples
1. Utilisez des verbes de perception	→ *see, look (at), hear, listen to, feel, seem, notice, sound...* → *You can notice the industrial zone is very busy.*
2. Donnez des repères spatiaux en précisant où se situent les différents éléments.	→ *The cultural zone is situated to the east of the Peace Area.*
3. Fournissez des exemples pour aider à visualiser.	→ *Among the sporting facilities, there are tennis courts.*

→ *À vous*

Écrivez un paragraphe décrivant la photo ci-contre à l'intention de quelqu'un qui ne l'a pas vue.

2 Expliquez pour enrichir et mieux faire comprendre

Étapes	Exemples
1. Donnez des détails (à l'aide d'adjectifs, d'adverbes, de relatives, de nouvelles idées, etc.).	→ *People in the educational and artistic fields work hand in hand for the children's benefit.*
2. Ajoutez des impressions personnelles.	→ *I think this zone is what young people need most.*

→ **À vous**

Reprenez le texte de *The township*, page 109.
Choisissez l'une des 6 zones et ajoutez des éléments pour enrichir le paragraphe.

Exemple :

Texte de base
The city area will be surrounded by a Green Belt. Its further planned extension will make it into a demonstration site for soil and water conservation. It will be the lungs* of the township.

Texte enrichi
The city area will be surrounded by a Green Belt of 1.25 km width. Its further planned extension, with an additional 800 hectares, will make it into a remarkable demonstration site for soil and water conservation. To my mind, it will be the lungs of the entire township.

* *poumons*

3 Mettez en valeur la cohérence de votre texte

a. Prévoyez une introduction, une conclusion et plusieurs paragraphes.

Introduction	Conclusion
• **Captez l'attention du lecteur** avec une première phrase. • **Présentez le sujet.** • **Annoncez le plan**, donc les paragraphes du développement.	• **Synthétisez** ce qui précède. • Éventuellement, ajoutez une **prise de position personnelle**.

b. Utilisez correctement les pronoms afin d'éviter les répétitions.
→ *The city area will be surrounded by a Green Belt. The Green Belt will be a vibrant eco-system.*
→ *The city area will be surrounded by a Green Belt which will be a vibrant eco-system.*

c. Marquez les étapes de l'explication avec des repères chronologiques et **logiques** :

Our Farm is a community of families and friends in Ireland. First, a group of five people decided to start it in 1969 to establish a cohesive community. Then other families joined them **because** they were fed up with living in cities. We want to protect nature **by** using alternative technologies and we share everything.

→ **À vous**

1. Remplacez les mots soulignés par un mot de substitution pour éviter des répétitions ou **ajoutez ce qui manque** dans les espaces prévus.

→ Précis grammatical ⑧ **p. 191**

Faites des phrases complexes lorsque c'est possible.

Auroville is not really a tourist place. Although Auroville is referred to in travel and tourist literature, visitors are sometimes disappointed to find no Ashram* in Auroville. Auroville is quite different from an Ashram, ... people are considered to have consecrated their lives to integral yoga. When visitors arrive, visitors are encouraged to go first to the Visitors Centre. The Visitors centre is open daily. The people ... actually want to visit one of Auroville's projects should make an appointment.

Adapted from http://www.auroville.org

* a kind of religious retreat

→ **À vous**

2. Réordonnez ces phrases puis ajoutez des connecteurs pour souligner les étapes de l'explication et obtenir un paragraphe cohérent. Vous pouvez choisir parmi les mots proposés *(first, then, now, last, before, after, before, afterwards, finally)* et aussi en utiliser d'autres.

a. The concept was ... put before the Government of India.
b. ... in 1966 UNESCO passed a unanimous resolution commending it as a project of importance to the future of humanity.
c. ..., in the mid 1960s the Sri Aurobindo Society in Pondicherry proposed that the township, devoted to an experiment in human unity, should be started.
d. Auroville is ... concerned with sustainable living and the future cultural, environmental, social and spiritual needs of mankind.
e. ... they took it to the General Assembly of UNESCO.

Écrire un texte descriptif et explicatif

Lisez les deux sujets ci-dessous :

Sujet 1

In Auroville, another extension has been planned with a new zone. Imagine which one and write two paragraphs about it, without forgetting an introduction and a conclusion.

Sujet 2

Imagine a society in which money does not exist anymore.

"It's a deal! I give you a complete overhaul in exchange for a thorough checkup!"

a. Choisissez un sujet.

b. Faites le brouillon par groupes de 3 ou 4.
Vous pouvez organiser votre brouillon de cette façon :

Sujet 1

nom de la zone	ce qu'on y trouve	pourquoi/dans quel but

Sujet 2

pourquoi l'argent a-t-il disparu ?	quelles sont les conséquences ?

c. Rédigez seul deux paragraphes, avec une introduction et une conclusion (au moins 150 mots).

Faites le point

a. Vérifiez votre production. **Auto-corrigé** ▸ www.didierpassword.fr

b. Situez votre niveau dans le tableau ci-dessous.

Niveaux	Mes compétences
B1-1	J'ai pu écrire un texte simple en décrivant mes rêves pour une société idéale.
B1-2	J'ai pu mettre en relief la cohérence des éléments en utilisant des phrases complexes et des mots de liaison.
B1-3	J'ai pu expliquer mes idées en faisant plusieurs paragraphes.
B2	J'ai pu décrire en donnant des détails à l'aide d'un vocabulaire varié, et en articulant clairement pourquoi et comment.

FINAL TASKS

My Utopia

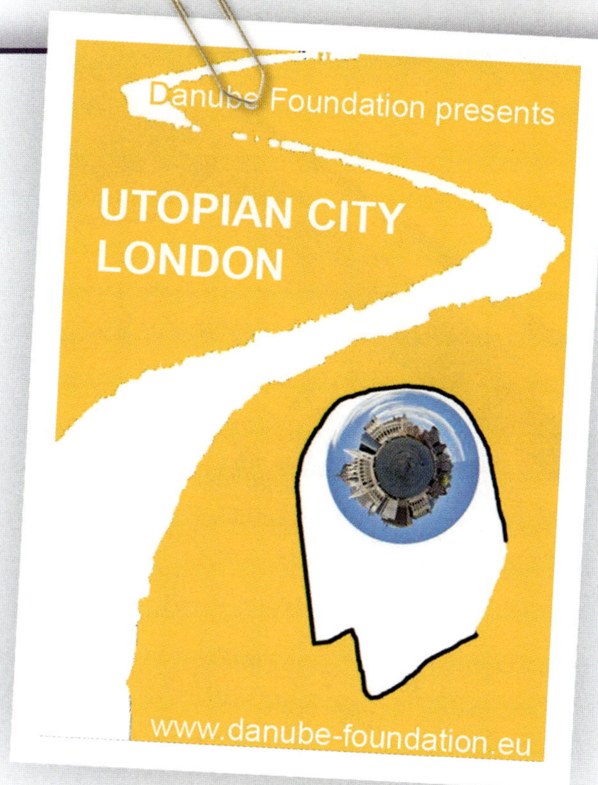

task 1

Writing

Imagine your ideal society

The Danube Foundation is organising a Utopian City workshop in London.

- With a group of friends, you have decided to join the workshop to work on your ideal city or society.

1. Get ready

- **In groups**, choose several aspects:

architecture | housing | education | rules | women's rights | etc.

- Make notes.
- Elaborate on them.

2. Action!

On your own, write about one aspect of your utopian city or society. Your teacher will tell you which aspect you have to develop.

task 2

Reading

Draw the map of a utopian city

- Your teacher will give you a written description of an ideal city.
- Read this description carefully and draw a plan of the city.

Reading test

- Your teacher will give you a text: read it carefully, then answer the questions.

UNIT 8 Art and peace

↑ **Belfast, 2008.** Dylan Wilson plays in front of the mural that shows him with the grand-daughter of a former Republican. The poem was written by Dylan's grandfather, Jim Wilson, a former Loyalist.

Art as testimony in Northern Ireland

Read the title of the chapter and **look** at the photograph. **Discuss** their meanings. In pairs, **list** what you already know or would like to know about the history of Northern Ireland.

FINAL TASKS

P. 135

Art show

Speaking
Present a mural

Listening
Picture dictation

CULTURE

- Learning about the "Troubles" and the peace process in Northern Ireland.
- Discovering street art in Northern Ireland: the murals.
- Literary works:
  - Fiona Barr, "The Wall-Reader"
  - Seamus Heaney, *The Cure at Troy*

COMMUNICATION

- Giving a brief presentation of a mural, explaining what it means.
- Understanding key facts and personal comments in documentaries.
- Understanding the characters' feelings and opinions in a narrative.
- Reading and interpreting a poem.

TOOLS

★ Words
- Description
- Conflict, betrayal and loyalty
- Desire, dilemma and reproach
- Pain, hope and despair
- Peace

★ Pronunciation
- Reading a text out loud
- Rhythm and meaning

★ Grammar
- Supposition and probability
- *What I know is that...*

Stratégies
→ *Faire un exposé sur un document iconographique*

Depicting a nation at war

1 The Troubles

video 13

A 2010 documentary about the Troubles in Northern Ireland.

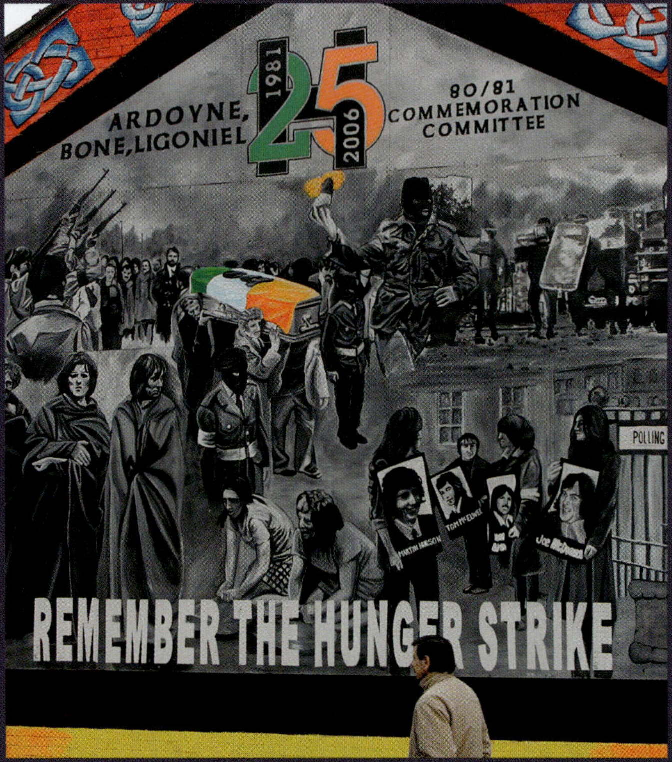

1. **Before watching**, look at the map and read the chronology below. Discuss what may have happened during the Troubles.
2. **Watch the documentary** and discuss what you have understood about the Troubles. Focusing on the pictures and dates will help.
3. Watch again and pick out more information about:
   a. why the Troubles started;
   b. the key events during the Troubles.
4. **Complete the chronology** of Northern Ireland's history, using what you have learnt.
   page 69 or www.didierpassword.fr
5. **Recap** the most significant events, using the chronology as a starting point.

- **1905** Foundation of Sinn Fein, a political party. Its aim is to gain independence for the whole of Ireland by political means.
- **1916** Foundation of the IRA (Irish Republican Army), a military organisation advocating armed resistance to British Rule.
- **1921** Partition of Ireland. The South becomes an independent Republic, the North remains in the "Union", i.e. part of the UK.
- **1969** The Troubles start in Northern Ireland between the Republicans (mainly Catholics) and the Unionists or Loyalists (mainly Protestants).
- **1971-1976** Peak of violence
- **1972** "Bloody Sunday"
- **1980-81** Hunger Strikes
- **1996** Peace talks
- **1998** Good Friday Agreement

2 "This painting thing should carry on"

video 14

A documentary about Belfast murals presented by Scottish comedian Billy Connolly, 2008.

↑ Mural paintings, a form of street art in Northern Ireland, have existed for more than a century.

1. **Before watching**, discuss what you know about street art and murals. What is their purpose?
2. **Watch** the documentary, focusing on the pictures only (murals and flags). Discuss what you have seen and understood.
3. **a.** Watch again, focusing on the sound, and pick out:
   - more information about the murals;
   - Billy Connolly's opinions and feelings.

   b. Share and discuss your findings with your classmates.
4. What might the people of Belfast think about these murals?

LANGUAGE TOOLS

★ WORDS → p. 130

Description
- a **tes**timony

→ Murals are testimonies to Northern Ireland's history.
- repre**sent**, show, de**pict**, de**scribe**, **ill**ustrate, **tes**tify

Conflict
- war, oppo**si**tion, a di**vi**sion, an **e**nemy, a **sol**dier, troops, **mil**itary **for**ces
- a demon**stra**tion = a **pro**test
- pro**test**, **de**monstrate, strike

★ PRONUNCIATION → p. 131

Reading a text out loud

Rhythm and meaning

Recap → Why could we say that murals depict Northern Ireland's history?

↑ *Bobby Sands*, Falls Road, West Belfast.

TRAINING TASK

One-minute talk

1. Choose one of the murals on these pages.

2. In groups of 2 or 3, recall what you have learnt about the event or the person depicted. Search the Internet to find out more if necessary. Make notes.

3. Give the class a brief and clear talk about the person or the event.

Personal dilemmas

"Hopes and desires"

The story is set in Belfast during the Troubles. The main character is a young Catholic mother who likes reading the murals she sees when walking with her young child. She has befriended an Englishman and they regularly meet in a park.

One day–it was, perhaps, the last day in April–her husband returned home panting and trembling a little. He asked if she had been to the park, and she replied that she had. Taking her by the hand, he led her to the wall on the left of their driveway. She felt her heart sink and thud[1]. She felt her face redden. Her mouth was suddenly dry. She could not speak. In huge angry letters the message spat itself out,

TOUT[2]

The four-letter word covered the whole wall. It clanged in her brain, its venom[3] rushed through her body. Suspicion was enough to condemn. What creature had skulked to paint the word? Whose arm, dismembered and independent, had swung from tin to wall to deliver judgement? The job itself was not well done, she had seen better. The letters were uneven, paint splattered down from the crossed T, the U looked a misshapen O. The workmanship was poor, the impact perfect.

Her husband led her back into the kitchen. The baby was crying loudly but the woman did not seem to hear. Like sleepwalkers, they sat down on the settee. The woman began to sob. Her shoulders heaved in bursts as she gasped hysterically. Her husband took her in his arms gently and tried to make her sorrow his. Already he shared her fear.

"What did you talk about? Did you not realise how dangerous it was? We must leave." He spoke quickly, making plans. Selling the house and car, finding a job in London or Dublin, far away from Belfast, mortgages, removals, savings, the tawdry[4] affairs of normal living stunned her, making her more confused.

"I told him nothing," she sobbed, "what could I tell? We talked about life, everything, but not about here." She trembled, trying to control herself.

"We just chatted about reading walls, families, anything at all. Oh Seán, it was as innocent as that. A meeting of minds we called it, for it was little else."

She looked into her husband's face and saw he did not fully understand. There was a hint of jealousy, of resentment at not being part of their communion. Her hands fell on her lap, resting in resignation. What was the point of explanation? She lifted her baby from the floor. Pressing the tiny face and body to her breast, she felt all her hopes and desires for a better life become one with the child's struggle for freedom. How could she invite the trauma of war into this new pure soul? Belfast and innocence. The two seemed incongruous and yet it must be done. The child's hands wandered over her face, their eyes met. At once that moment of maternal and filial love eclipsed her fear, gave her the impetus to escape.

Fiona Barr, "The Wall-Reader" (1979)

1. beat hard
2. In Northern Ireland: a traitor; a police informer. To be named a "tout" was a death sentence.
3. poison
4. /ˈtɔːdrɪ/: sordid

↑ A loyalist mural in Northern Ireland, 2001.

1. **Read the titles and the introduction** on p. 126. Imagine how the story may continue.

2. **Read lines 1 to 14** and discuss what you have understood about the characters and the situation.

3. **a.** **Read the whole text** and highlight:
- the husband's reactions and feelings;
- the woman's reactions and feelings.

pages 70-71

b. **Share** your findings with your classmates and compare the characters' reactions.

LANGUAGE TOOLS

★ WORDS → p. 130

betrayal/loyalty
- **trea**son ≠ **loy**alty
- be a **trai**tor ≠ be **loy**al = be **faith**ful
- **won**der

→ I'm wondering whether I should stay or not.

Desire/dilemma
- want, wish, hope
- **hes**itate, **wa**ver

→ I'm wavering between staying and leaving.

Reproach
- blame/**cri**ticise for + V-*ing*
- ac**cuse** of + V-*ing*

★ GRAMMAR → p. 131

Supposition and probability

→ A bomb may have gone off.

→ She must be wondering what to do.

Recap → Discuss why this extract can be seen as a testimony of the Troubles.

TRAINING TASK

Chain speaking

1. In groups.
Look at the picture and guess:
- what has happened;
- what the people are feeling and why;
- etc.

2. Whole class. Chain speaking activity: one person starts a description of the situation with one sentence. The next person goes on with a further sentence, and so on.

→ *They must have heard gunshots...*

→ *...and the young girl may have come out of her house to see what is happening.*

→ ...

Belfast, 1981 ↑

A poet's wish for peace

"And hope and history rhyme"

← *The Wave*, C. R. Wynne Nevinson, 1917

track 45

Human beings suffer,
They torture one another,
They get hurt and get hard.
No poem or play or song
Can fully right a wrong
Inflicted or endured.

The innocent in gaols[1]
Beat on their bars together.
A hunger-striker's father
Stands in the graveyard[2] dumb[3].
The police widow[4] in veils
Faints at the funeral home.

History says, Don't hope
On this side of the grave.
But then, once in a lifetime
The longed for tidal wave[5]
Of justice can rise up,
And hope and history rhyme.

So hope for a great sea-change
On the far side of revenge.
Believe that a further shore[6]
Is reachable from here.
Believe in miracles
And cures and healing wells[7].

Call the miracle self-healing:
The utter self-revealing
Double-take[8] of feeling.
If there's fire on the mountain
Or lightning and storm
And a god speaks from the sky

That means someone is hearing
The outcry and the birth-cry
Of new life at its term.
It means once in a lifetime
That justice can rise up
And hope and history rhyme.

Seamus Heaney, *The Cure at Troy*, 1990

1. /ˈdʒeɪlz/ jails, prisons
2. cemetery
3. silent
4. *veuve*
5. *raz-de-marée*
6. coast, land near the sea
7. *puits.* In Celtic folklore, a healing well is a well whose water is said to be miraculous.
8. looking twice at something because it is remarkable

Born in Northern Ireland in 1939 and currently living in Dublin, poet and playwright Seamus Heaney was awarded the Nobel Prize in Literature in 1995. The text above is an excerpt from his play The Cure at Troy, *a modern version of a Greek tragedy.*

1. a. **Before reading the poem**, focus on the title and think about:
- what "hope and history" may refer to;
- why they may "rhyme".

b. Read the information about Seamus Heaney. Look at the photo of the statue on the right and discuss its meaning. Say what you expect the poem to be about.

2. **Listen to the poem** and share your first reactions.

3. **Read the poem** and highlight:
a. what you understand;
b. the words with positive connotations and those with a negative meaning.
pages 71-73

4. a. **Discuss** where most of the negative words are in the poem and what they refer to. What about the positive words?
b. Discuss the role of the word "but" in stanza 3 (line 15).

5. **Match** the following titles with the right stanzas and briefly explain your choice:

Miracle Signs | Hope | Rage and Grief | Remedies | Pain and Despair | Belief

Going further: pages 71-73

↑ *Reconciliation/Hands Across the Divide*, Derry City.

Recap → Discuss the poet's intentions and your personal interpretation of this text.

LANGUAGE TOOLS

★ WORDS → p. 130

Pain
- **suff**er = en**dure**
- **tor**ture = in**flict** = hurt

Hope and despair
- faith ≠ disbe**lief**
- opti**mis**tic ≠ **des**perate, pessi**mis**tic

Peace
- a**gree**ment, reconci**lia**tion, under**stan**ding
- a**gree** on, come to an a**gree**ment

★ GRAMMAR → p. 131

What I know is that...
→ What is surprising is that he is optimistic.

TRAINING TASK

Creating your work of art

In groups

1. Discuss what should be illustrated in the poem (what struck you, positive or negative images, etc.).

2. Discuss how you could illustrate those elements.

3. Create your work of art (it can be either a collage, or a drawing, a painting...).

4. Present your work to the class: explain it and answer the other groups' questions.

★ WORDS

← Children from a local school painting a new mural in the lower Shankill area, Belfast.

❶ Describe and give your impressions

a. Describe the photo above to someone who can't see it.
→ *in the foreground, we can see...*
→ *in the background...*

b. Here is a list of verbs used to describe or give impressions:
look, look like, look as if, seem, appear, give the impression that, show, suggest, convey the impression of, strike

Sort them out under one of these two headings:
describe | give impressions

c. Give your impressions about the photo orally, using some of the verbs above.

❷ Commemoration

a. These words are used to commemorate an event. Check their meanings if necessary.
- commemorate, pay tribute to, celebrate, honor, glorify, be dedicated to the memory of, remind
- a memorial, a memento, a reminder

b. Most of the pictures in the chapter are testimonies. Choose one and, orally, explain what it commemorates.

❸ Feelings and reactions

a. Here is a list of adjectives referring to fear, grief, anger or courage:
fearful, brave, determined, sad, afraid, frightened, courageous, scared, outraged, tenacious, miserable, infuriated, sorrowful, alarmed, resentful, apprehensive, fearless

Sort them out under one of these four headings:
fear | grief | anger | courage

b. Write a personal anecdote, emphasising your feelings (80 words).
→ *The last time I was really afraid was when...*
→ *Once I was really sad because...*

❹ Cause and consequence

a. Here is a list of words expressing cause or consequence:
- **Cause:** because, as, since...
- **Consequence:** so, therefore, that's why, consequently...

Read the following examples:
→ *British troops were sent to Northern Ireland* ***because*** *there were many acts of rebellion.*
→ *There were many acts of rebellion* ***so*** *British troops were sent to Northern Ireland.*
→ ***As*** *there were many acts of rebellion, British troops were sent to Northern Ireland.*

b. Connect the following pairs of sentences using words from the list above. Try to use different link-words.
1. Some Irish prisoners wanted to rebel. / They started a hunger-strike.
2. During Bloody Sunday, innocent civilians were killed. / The British troops opened fire on them.
3. The Irish wanted to express their opinions and feelings. / They started painting murals.
4. A wall was built to separate the Catholics from the Protestants. / The two communities couldn't get on well.

★ PRONUNCIATION

5 Reading a text out loud

track 46

Here is part of the script for the video p. 124:

In 1969 | a peaceful civil rights group | protesting these and other injustices | marched from Belfast to Derry | where the police just watched on | as a violent mob created havoc for the marchers ||

|: pause between tone units

red text: stressed syllable green text: reduced syllable.

Listen to the recording and then practise reading.

6 Rhythm and meaning

track 47

Le locuteur accentue les mots qu'il juge essentiels à son message, ce qui ralentit le rythme. Plus le rythme ralentit, plus les propos sont importants.

a. Listen to a person talking after a visit to an art gallery.

"I've seen a lot of portraits and paintings in the gallery but what I find the most attractive, in fact, really striking, is this self-portrait. Everyone has an idea of the image he projects to the world but it's quite incredible to see how totally different someone can appear to himself, as opposed to the human being other people see."

b. Pick out the stressed words which slow down the rhythm.

c. Listen again and practise repeating the extract.

d. Now practise doing the same: talk about one of the murals in the chapter.

More exercises in your Workbook ▶ p. 74

★ GRAMMAR

Supposition and probability

Observe

A. I am not sure but **perhaps** she fought for peace.
→ *She **may/might** have fought for peace.*
B. He was **certainly** her first English friend.
→ *He **must** have been her first English friend.*
C. Judging by the look on her face, I think she is **probably** wondering what is going on.
→ *Judging by the look on her face, she may **be wondering** what is going on.*

Qu'expriment *may* et *must* ? Expliquez l'emploi des formes verbales qui suivent *may* et *must*.

→ Précis grammatical ⑫ p. 194-195

Practise

7 Rephrase the following sentences using either *may* or *must*.

a. I'm not sure but I think they left Ireland during the Troubles.
b. They certainly feared for their lives.
c. Perhaps they emigrated to the United States. Perhaps they had relatives there.
d. No doubt it was difficult for them to leave their homeland.

8 Look at the photo on page 132 and make hypotheses to explain the situation.
→ *The two girls may...*

What I know is that...

Observe

A. Tourists mostly want to see the murals.
B. → *What tourists mostly want to see are the murals.*
C. This sculpture symbolizes hope.
D. → *What this sculpture symbolizes is hope.*

Comparez les phrases A et B, puis C et D. Quel est le but du locuteur dans les phrases en italique ?

→ Précis grammatical ⑱ p. 200

Practise

9 Present the following information differently.

a. I first noticed that this mural was not signed.
b. The absence of colours in this painting makes it sad.
c. I find it really interesting to discover a country's history through paintings.

10 Look at the sculpture on page 129 and express your reactions.
→ *What I find striking is that...*

More exercises in your Workbook ▶ p. 75

Stratégies

Faire un exposé sur un document iconographique

Une présentation orale se prépare et s'organise afin de favoriser l'écoute et la compréhension.

The Troubles, 1973: British troops stand by armoured cars on routine patrol in Belfast.

1 Listez et structurez vos idées

Lors d'une présentation, un certain nombre d'étapes sont à respecter :

Étapes	Exemples
1. Présentation générale du document (type de document, titre, date, auteur)	→ *This is a mural painted in... by... The scene takes place in...*
2. Événement, personne ou thème décrit	→ *It represents/illustrates/depicts...*
3. Détails descriptifs pertinents	→ *"Armoured cars" = war; child = innocence*
4. Impressions personnelles	→ *I find it scary/beautiful/sad/colourful...*
5. Idées et exemples en lien avec le document	→ *It makes me think about.../ It reminds me of...*

→ À vous

a. Choisissez l'une des deux photos sur ces pages. Listez toutes les idées qui vous viennent à l'esprit sans vous soucier de les organiser dans un premier temps.
b. Ordonnez-les en vous inspirant du tableau ci-dessus.

2 Développez vos idées avec précision

Illustrez vos idées avec des exemples concrets tirés du document.
Apprendre le vocabulaire par champ lexical peut être une aide efficace.
army protection → we can see armoured cars, troops, soldiers...

→ À vous

Pour chacune des idées que vous avez listées, trouvez dans le document des éléments qui vous permettront de la préciser.

3 Décrivez vos réactions et étayez votre propos

- Ce que le document vous inspire a autant d'importance que ce qu'il représente : faites part de vos sentiments et réactions.
- Si vous avez des connaissances culturelles en lien avec le document, évoquez-les.
- Si vous vous interrogez sur un élément du document, faites une petite recherche pour enrichir votre exposé.

→ À vous

Listez les réactions et les idées que vous inspire l'image choisie.
Appuyez-vous sur ce que vous savez du sujet pour enrichir votre exposé.

4 Mettez oralement en valeur les points importants

Pour que votre auditoire soit attentif, accentuez les mots importants et significatifs, articulez et ne parlez pas trop vite.

→ À vous

Faites une brève description du document que vous avez choisi en insistant bien sur les mots porteurs de sens. **Parlez clairement** et regardez votre auditoire pour vous assurer de son attention et de son intérêt.

"Hope this finds you well" (Belfast) by Steve Powers.

Auto-évaluation

Faire un exposé sur un document iconographique

← *Bloody Sunday*
by the Bogside Artists (1997).

Observez le document ci-contre :

a. Notez les éléments significatifs (voir étape 1 p. 132) et vos réactions.

b. Vérifiez au besoin les faits auxquels se rapporte le document.

c. Organisez et structurez vos notes pour un exposé oral de 1 à 2 minutes.

d. « Répétez » à voix haute votre intervention avant votre présentation.

Faites le point

a. Vérifiez votre production.

Auto-corrigé ▶ www.didierpassword.fr

b. Situez votre niveau dans le tableau ci-dessous.

Niveaux	Mes compétences
B1-1	J'ai pu faire un exposé simple, bref et structuré, préparé à l'avance sur un sujet que je connais bien. J'ai dû faire quelques pauses pour chercher mes mots.
B1-2	J'ai pu faire un exposé simple et structuré, préparé à l'avance, sur un sujet familier. J'ai pu développer les points importants avec précision et revenir sur certaines choses pour les corriger.
B1-3	J'ai pu décrire mes sentiments et réactions. J'ai su revenir sur certains points pour exprimer mes idées plus précisément.
B2	J'ai pu faire un exposé en insistant sur les points importants et sur les éléments significatifs. J'ai pu illustrer mon propos par des exemples pertinents et parler sans trop d'hésitations.

Final tasks

Art show

task 1

Speaking

Present a mural

Your teacher will suggest some murals.
You may choose one of them or find a different one.

1. Get ready

- Briefly research the mural and what it refers to.
- Jot down your ideas (descriptive elements, impressions, feelings...) and organise them.
- Develop your ideas.
- Make a few notes to help you during your talk.

2. Action!

- Do not read your notes!
- Be ready to slow down, repeat, rephrase and explain if you see the audience is not following you.

task 2

Listening

Picture dictation

- Listen to the description of a mural.
- Draw a sketch of the mural as you visualise it.

Listening test

- Listen to a recording, then answer the questions your teacher will give you.

UNIT 9 Gene ethics

↑ ***Time Magazine*, 10 March 1997.** Dolly the sheep was the first animal to be cloned in 1996.

What are the promises and perils of biotechnology?

← **Look** at the *Time* cover, **read** its legend and the title of the chapter.
List other examples of genetic engineering you know and **share your opinions** on them.

FINAL TASKS

P. 151

TV debate

Speaking
Debate and have your say

Reading
Find out the debaters' opinions

CULTURE

- Learning about the biotechnological revolution: key dates and discoveries.
- Genetic engineering: breakthroughs and ethical concerns.
- Literary works:
  - Kazuo Ishiguro, *Never Let Me Go*
  - Aldous Huxley, *Brave New World*

COMMUNICATION

- Understanding headlines, facts and comments in press articles.
- Understanding opinions and arguments in literary fiction.

Explaining why certain issues can be controversial, exchanging impressions and discussing pros and cons.

Identifying the main points and opinions in a TV documentary.

TOOLS

★ Words
- Body and health
- Scientific progress
- Genetic engineering
- Respect and disrespect
- Similarities and differences

★ Pronunciation
- Real questions and rhetorical questions
- Subjective intonation

★ Grammar
- Meanings of *can*
- *If... will/would*

Stratégies
→ *Identifier les opinions exprimées dans un texte argumentatif*

The biotechnological revolution

1 "The age of scientific mastery?"

video 15

A BBC Four documentary on the biotechnological revolution, 2007.

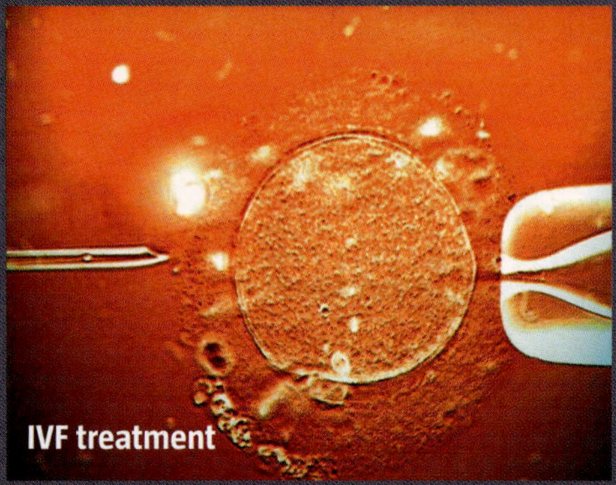

IVF treatment

Michia Kaku

1. **Before watching**, say what the word "biotechnological" brings to mind.
2. **Watch** the video and discuss what you have understood.
3. Watch the video again and find out information about:
   a. scientific possibilities;
   b. their consequences.
4. **Discuss** your findings and explain why the scientist talks about a "revolution".
5. Discuss the atmosphere, focusing on the music and visual effects.
6. **Give your impression and opinions** on what you have learnt.

2 Breaking news

1

Organ Grown From Stem Cells In Lab Successfully Transplanted

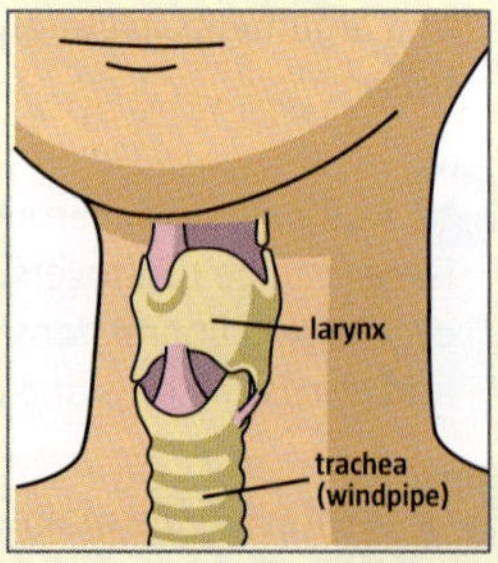

Surgeons replaced the damaged windpipe of Claudia Castillo, a 30-year-old mother of two, with one created from stem cells* grown in a laboratory at Bristol University.

Because the new windpipe was made from cells taken from Ms Castillo's own body, using a process called "tissue engineering", she has not needed powerful drugs to prevent her body rejecting the organ.

The Telegraph, November 2008

* nonspecialised cells that have the capacity to self-renew and become various types of cells. In French: *cellule souche*

2

A lab mouse

Scientists use skincells to create fertile mice which go on to have their own babies

A new cloning technique has passed the ultimate scientific test, showing that it is possible to generate healthy animals from single skin cells without the need for sexual reproduction. Scientists have shown that these clones grow into healthy adults capable of producing their own offspring by normal breeding.

www.independent.co.uk, July 2009

3

Bionic Cat

When Oscar the cat was hit by a combine harvester, he lost his two hind feet. That should have been the end of his mobility and maybe even his life.

Noel Fitzpatrick, a high-tech vet in Eashing, near London, fitted metal implants to the bottom of Oscar's legs and attached two flexible pegs to act as feet. Now Oscar is walking, jumping and chasing like a normal cat.

The breakthrough was being able to bond the metal implants into Oscar's leg. Fitzpatrick added a substance to encourage the bone and skin to grow over the metal. This skin grew around the metal and formed a natural seal.

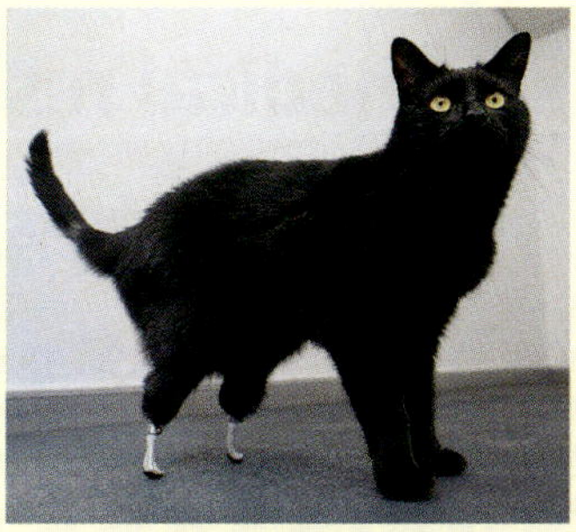

"It's just a miracle," Fitzpatrick told the BBC. "If you had metal sticking out of your leg, you would just get an infection."

AOL News, June 2010

LANGUAGE TOOLS

★ WORDS → p. 146

Body and health

- an **or**gan, a cell, a gene /dʒiːn/
- a di**sease**, an **ill**ness
- cure, treat, heal: *soigner*
- **heal**thy, in good health ≠ in poor/bad health

Scientific progress

- an ex**pe**riment: *une expérience scientifique*
- a **break**through: an im**por**tant dis**co**very
- suc**ceed**, en**able**

→ The doctor succeeded in treating the patient's disease.

→ It will enable us to change our genetic heritage.

★ GRAMMAR → p. 147

Meanings of *can*

→ Scientists can now create organs in labs.

→ Can this be done?

1. **Read the headlines** of these three articles and look at the photos. Discuss what you think the three articles deal with.
2. **In groups**, choose one article. Discuss what you have understood about the experiment.
3. **Whole class**: tell the other groups about your findings and exchange your reactions about these scientific experiments.
4. **Read the headline of article 1 again**. Use the information in the article to turn it into a complete sentence.

Recap → Give your opinion on the experiments you have studied.

TRAINING TASK

The story behind the headline

In groups, choose one of these headlines and guess what the corresponding article probably deals with. Report to the class.

Genetic engineering gives mouse human intelligence

Beating heart created in laboratory

Dentistry breakthrough: French scientists develop a gel that helps decayed teeth grow back

Young forever: stem cells in anti-age beauty cream

Shaping life in the lab

1 Recent breakthroughs in medical research

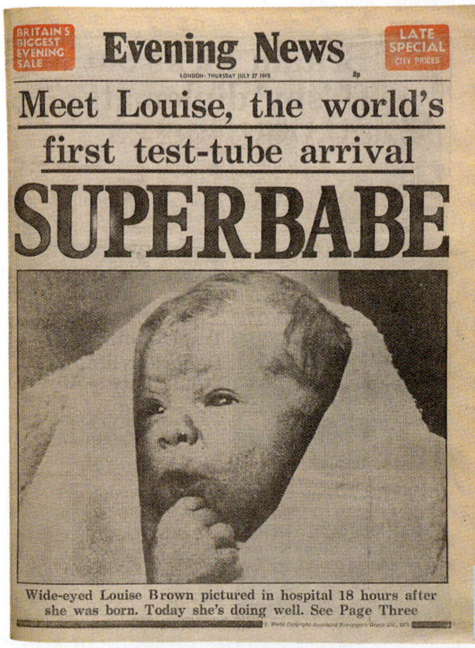

BRITAIN'S BIGGEST EVENING SALE

Evening News

LATE SPECIAL CITY PRICES

Meet Louise, the world's first test-tube arrival

SUPERBABE

Wide-eyed Louise Brown pictured in hospital 18 hours after she was born. Today she's doing well. See Page Three

Evening News, 27 July, 1978 →

Dr. J. Craig Venter conducts an experiment, April 2007. →

- **1950:** first human organ transplant: a 44-year-old woman receives a kidney from a dead donor.
- **1967:** first human heart transplant.

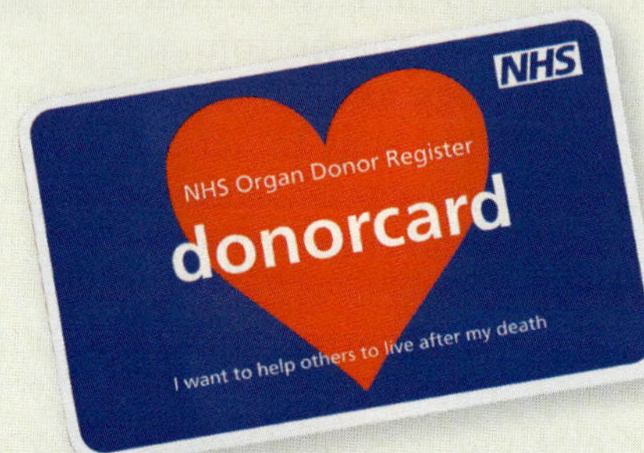

- **1968:** bone marrow[1] transplant between two siblings successfully treats severe genetic disease.
- **1978:** Louise Brown, the world's first test-tube baby, is born in England.
  (**October 2010**: Nobel Prize in Medicine awarded to Robert Edwards for the development of human in vitro fertilization (IVF) therapy. (Professor Edwards is the "father" of Louise Brown.)
- **1982:** Amandine, first French test-tube baby.
- **1996:** Dolly the sheep, first mammal to be cloned.
- **2003:** the 20,000–25,000 genes of the human genome[2] are identified.
- **2010:** researchers at the J. Craig Venter Institute create the first synthetic cell.

1. *moelle osseuse*
2. /ˈdʒiːnəʊm/: the complete set of genes or genetic material present in a cell or organism

1. **Look at the front page** of the *Evening News* and comment on it.
2. **Split into two groups:**
   - *Group 1* will read and present medical advances **before** the world's first test-tube baby;
   - *Group 2* will read and present medical advances **after** the first test-tube baby.
3. **Discuss your reactions** to those medical breakthroughs.

2 A real-life story

Family Uses Genetic Selection to Have a Baby to Save Their Other Child's Life

When Elisabeth Hartmann was 10 years old, she got a baby brother named Michael who literally saved her from death. Elisabeth was dying of a disease called Fanconi anemia that wasn't letting her body make healthy blood. "She had very little time left," her father, John, told ABC News.

Elisabeth needed a bone marrow transplant. "Without treatment she would have died," Elisabeth's mom, Martina, said. The best option for Elisabeth's survival were stem cells from a close genetic match. And that's what Michael delivered just in time by being born.

"I held the umbilical cord, and we could gather this 1 or 2 ounces of precious blood," John said.

But the fact that the blood from Michael's cord was able to save his sister is no accident because Michael was no accident.

He was genetically selected for birth from more than 40 embryos his parents conceived outside the womb using a process called preimplantation genetic diagnosis. Michael was chosen for life over more than 40 other potential siblings[1] because he had what his family needed. The "unchosen" remain in deep freeze[2] or were donated for research.

John Hartmann acknowledges the ethics[3] of choosing which embryo will be born can be debated.

"If you have a dying child, I'm not saying it's OK to do anything, but I think it's OK to use reasonable ethical measures to save your child's life," he said of his family's decision.

But Michael is loved just for being Michael, though his parents know that if they hadn't had Michael, they'd no longer have Elisabeth.

abcnews.go.com

1. brothers and sisters **2.** very cold temperature **3.** morals

1. **Before reading**, discuss what you may learn from the article.
2. **Read** the article and discuss what you have understood.
3. a. **Read again** and pick out information about:
   - Elisabeth's health problem;
   - how the problem was solved;
   - the questions her parents' decision raises.

   b. Discuss your findings.
4. **Comment on line 40**: "The ethics of choosing which embryo will be born can be debated."

Recap → Explain how life can be shaped in the lab.

LANGUAGE TOOLS

★ WORDS → p. 146

Genetic engineering

- an **em**bryo, a test-tube baby
- a **do**nor; a **trans**plant: *une greffe*
- ge**ne**tics (n.)/ge**ne**tic (adj.)

→ genetic selection, a genetic disease

★ GRAMMAR → p. 147

If...

→ If test-tube babies become the norm, society will be changed forever.

→ If genetic selection was generally allowed, we would all be in danger.

TRAINING TASK

A radio phone-in programme

track 50

1. Listen to five people reacting to the *abcnews* article above and identify their opinions.

2. Join the programme and have your say about one of the listeners' reactions.

How far can we go?

"Your futures have been decided"

Kathy, the narrator, recalls her childhood in Hailsham, a boarding school where she was brought up and educated. One day Miss Lucy, one of the teachers or "guardians", overhears a conversation between some students.

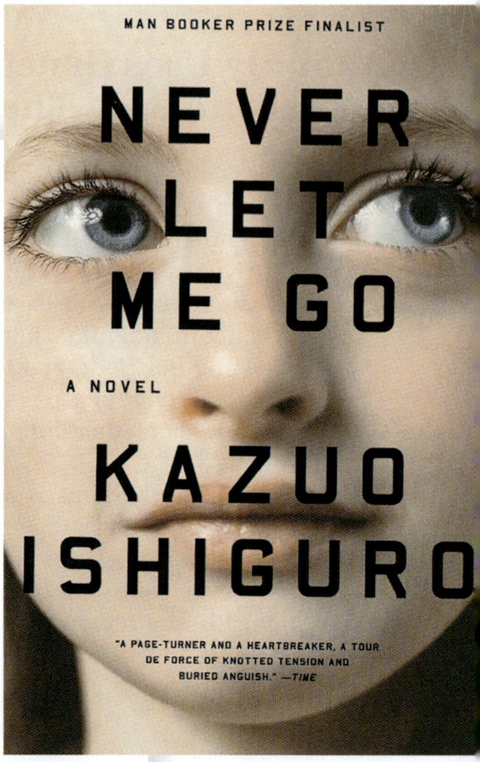

"Boys, you must forgive me for listening. But you were right behind me, so I couldn"t help it. Peter, why don't you tell the others what you were saying to Gordon just now?"

Peter J. looked bewildered[1] and I could see him getting ready his injured innocent face. But then Miss Lucy said again, this time much more gently:

"Peter, go on. Please tell the others what you were just saying."

Peter shrugged[2]. "We were just talking about what it would feel like if we became actors. What sort of life it would be."

"Yes," Miss Lucy said,"and you were saying to Gordon you'd have to go to America to stand the best chance."

Peter J. shrugged again and muttered quietly: "Yes, Miss Lucy."

But Miss Lucy was now moving her gaze over the lot of us. "I know you don't mean any harm. But there's just too much talk like this. I hear it all the time, it's been allowed to go on, and it's not right." I could see more drops coming off the gutter and landing on her shoulder, but she didn't seem to notice. "If no one else will talk to you," she continued, "then I will. The problem, as I see it, is that you've been told and not told. You've been told, but none of you really understand, and I dare say, some people are quite happy to leave it that way. But I'm not. If you're going to have decent lives, then you've got to know and know properly. None of you will go to America, none of you will be film stars. And none of you will be working in supermarkets as I heard some of you planning the other day. Your lives are set out for you. You'll become adults, then before you're old, before you're even middle-aged, you'll start to donate your vital organs. That's what each of you was created to do. You're not like the actors you watch in your videos, you're not even like me. You were brought into this world for a purpose, and your futures, all of them, have been decided. So you're not to talk that way anymore. You'll be leaving Hailsham before long, and it's not so far off, the day you'll be preparing for your first donations. You need to remember that. If you're to have decent lives, you have to know who you are and what lies ahead of you, every one of you." [...]

I think that was all she said. When I was discussing it with Ruth a few years ago at the centre in Dover, she claimed Miss Lucy had told us a lot more, that she'd explained how before donations we'd all spend some time first as carers[3], about the usual sequence of the donations, the recovery centres and so on – but I'm pretty sure she didn't. Okay, she probably intended to when she began talking. But my guess is once she'd set off, once she'd seen the puzzled, uncomfortable faces in front of her, she realized the impossibility of completing what she'd started.

Kazuo Ishiguro, *Never Let Me Go* (2005)

1. uncertain, confused
2. *hausser les épaules*
3. In the novel, "carers" look after the students when they start donating their organs.

1. **Read the titles on page 142**.
Discuss what the text may deal with.

2. **Read lines 1 to 12**.
a. Highlight what you have understood about the conversation (characters, topic, attitudes).
pages 76-77
b. Discuss your findings.

3. **a. Read lines 13 to 32**.
Does it correspond to what you expected?
b. Read the same passage again and find information about:
- Miss Lucy's reaction to the boys' conversation (l. 13- 21);
- Miss Lucy's opinion on these children's futures. (l. 21-32).
pages 76-77
c. Discuss your findings with your classmates.

4. **Line 25**: "That's what each of you was created to do." Discuss why "created" is used and imagine who these children are.

5. How do you react to the children's situation?

6. **Read the last paragraph** (lines 33 to 40) and discuss Ruth's and the narrator's reactions. Compare their reactions to yours.
pages 76-77

Recap → List some ethical questions raised by genetic engineering.

LANGUAGE TOOLS

★ WORDS → p. 146

Respect
- **dig**nity, in**te**grity
- **mo**ral ≠ im**mo**ral
- con**si**der, re**gard**
- take sth into conside**ra**tion = take sth into ac**count**

Disrespect
- in**dif**ference, dis**dain**
- ig**nore** = pay no at**ten**tion to
- de**ny** = re**fuse**
- ne**glect** = over**look**

★ PRONUNCIATION → p. 146

Intonation and questions
Subjective intonation
→ It's an incredible breakthrough!

"My transplanted heart is 29, my transplanted kidney is 41, my transplanted lung is 38, and the rest of me is 59."

TRAINING TASK

Circular debate

In groups of 3 or 5, identify then discuss the issues raised by these cartoons.
page 78

"The kidney shape was a cool idea. Reminds us what you sold to pay for it."

Tomorrow's society?

"Community, identity, stability"

The story is set in England at a time when humans are created and manufactured in test-tubes. A group of students is visiting the central laboratory, called the "Hatchery[1] and Conditioning Centre". The Director is explaining how the fertilization process works.

"Bokanovsky's Process," repeated the Director, and the students underlined the words in their little notebooks. One egg, one embryo, one adult-normality. But a bokanovskified egg will bud[2], will proliferate, will divide. From eight to ninety-six buds, and every bud will grow into a perfectly formed embryo, and every embryo into a full-sized adult. Making ninety-six human beings grow where only one grew before. Progress.

"Essentially," the D.H.C.[3] concluded, "bokanovskification consists of a series of arrests of development. We check[4] the normal growth and, paradoxically enough, the egg responds by budding."

Responds by budding. The pencils were busy.

He pointed. On a very slowly moving band a rack-full of test-tubes was entering a large metal box, another rack-full was emerging. Machinery faintly purred[5]. It took eight minutes for the tubes to go through, he told them. Eight minutes of hard X-rays being about as much as an egg can stand. A few died; of the rest, the least susceptible divided into two; most put out four buds; some eight; all were returned to the incubators, where the buds began to develop. Two, four, eight, the buds in their turn budded; and having budded were [...] left to develop in peace. By which time the original egg was in a fair way to becoming anything from eight to ninety-six embryos – a prodigious improvement, you will agree, on nature. Identical twins – but not in piddling twos and threes as in the old viviparous days, when an egg would sometimes accidentally divide; actually by dozens, by scores[6] at a time.

"Scores," the Director repeated and flung out his arms, as though he were distributing largesse. "Scores."

But one of the students was fool enough to ask where the advantage lay.

"My good boy!" The Director wheeled sharply round on him. "Can't you see? Can't you see?" He raised a hand; his expression was solemn. "Bokanovsky's Process is one of the major instruments of social stability!"

Major instruments of social stability.

Standard men and women; in uniform batches[7]. The whole of a small factory staffed with the products of a single bokanovskified egg.

"Ninety-six identical twins working ninety-six identical machines!" The voice was almost tremulous with enthusiasm. "You really know where you are. For the first time in history." He quoted the planetary motto. "Community, Identity, Stability."

Aldous Huxley, *Brave New World* (1932)

1. a place where eggs are brought to maturity
2. *bourgeonner*
3. the Director of the Hatchery and Conditioning Centre
4. control
5. (make) a low continuous sound
6. twenty
7. groups

1. Read the introduction.
a. Identify the characters, the places and the time.
b. Briefly state your reactions.

2. Read lines 1 to 7.
a. Discuss what you have understood about the result of the process. Pay particular attention to numbers.
b. Find the sentence which sums up the result of the process.

3. Read lines 8 to 27, look at the notes taken by a student and:
a. in your own words, explain the fertilization process;
b. share your first impressions of it.

4. a. In groups, read the whole text and hightlight:
- the students' attitudes and reactions *(group 1)*;
- the Director's attitude and opinion *(group 2)*.
pages 79-80
b. Discuss your findings.

5. Read the introduction again, as well as lines 33 to 38. Discuss what this "Brave New World" is like politically speaking.
pages 79-80

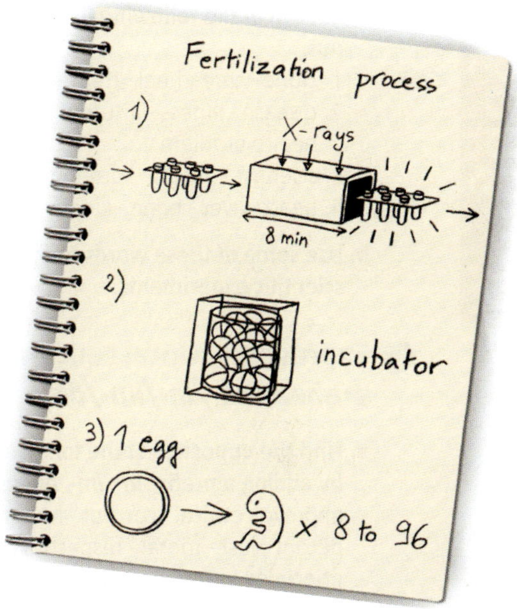

Recap → Discuss the dangers of genetic engineering.

LANGUAGE TOOLS

★ WORDS → p. 146

Difference
- a perso**na**lity
- individu**a**lity, origi**na**lity
- **var**y = **dif**fer
- **sin**gular = **dif**ferent from, dis**tinc**tive

Similarity
- a **rep**lica = a **cop**y/a **du**plicate
- re**sem**ble /rɪ'zembl/, match
- i**den**tical, inter**change**able, **u**niform, **stan**dardised

TRAINING TASK

A letter to the Editor

Write a short letter to *Newsweek*'s Editor (about 10 lines), giving your opinion on cloning humans.

↑ *Newsweek*, March, 10, 1997.

★ WORDS

1 Find the odd one out

a. In each of the following lists, find the odd one out.

1. clone - cure - heal - treat - repair
2. disease - illness - disorder - therapy - health problem
3. scientist - doctor - surgeon - patient - specialist
4. heart - liver - bone - kidney - lung

b. Use some of these words above to talk about scientific experiments.

2 Expressing ethical concerns: prefixes *un-/in-/im-/dis-*

a. Find the opposites of the following words, by adding a prefix: *in-, im-, un- or dis-*.
approve - ethical - corrupt - honorable - fair - decent - just - moral - respectful - honest - principled - humane - tolerable - regard

b. Take part in a bioethics poll and register your opinion about ONE of the following questions:

1. Should selling organs be banned?
2. Should parents be allowed to choose their child's genetic make up (sex, size...)?
3. Should animals be cloned for human medicines?

3 Describe your feelings

a. Read the words in the flower and make sure you understand them.

b. Use some of these words to explain how you feel about genetic engineering.

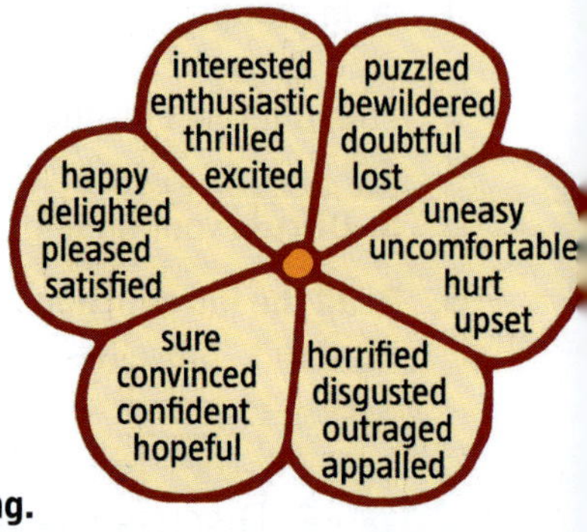

More exercises in your Workbook ▶ p. 80-81

★ PRONUNCIATION

4 Subjective intonation

track 53

↗ ↘
"It's an incredible breakthrough !"

Les mots qui renforcent l'opinion d'un locuteur reçoivent une forte accentuation. La syllabe accentuée de ces mots se trouve au sommet de la courbe intonative et est suivie d'une intonation finale descendante.

a. Listen to the following sentences and pick out the stressed word in each sentence.

1. There was an absolutely amazing atmosphere.
2. The music was really loud.
3. It took ages before the concert actually started.
4. The band looked so incredibly relaxed.
5. It was the most fantastic experience you could ever imagine.

b. Listen again and practise repeating the sentences.

c. Now practise doing the same, talking about a memorable holiday:

- The weather (hot, cold, etc.);
- The sea (rough, blue, calm, etc.);
- The other tourists (vulgar, polite, etc.);
- The food (disgusting, delicious, etc.).

5 Intonation and questions

track 51

a. Listen to the following examples about twin brothers:

1. I've never seen them. Do they look alike? Can you tell them apart? ↗
2. Do they look alike? Can you tell them apart, you might ask yourselves. ↘ Well, I'll tell you.

Dans les questions où une réponse est attendue, l'intonation peut être montante.
Dans les questions rhétoriques, où le locuteur connaît la réponse, l'intonation est toujours descendante.

track 52

b. Now listen to the following questions and decide if they are real questions ↗ or rhetorical ones ↘ :

1. Do you think cloning humans is a good idea? ↗ or ↘ ?
2. Would you be ready to give one of your organs? ↗ or ↘ ?
3. Are you saying genetic manipulation is a good idea? ↗ or ↘ ?

More exercises in your Workbook ▶ p. 81-82

★ GRAMMAR

Meanings of *can*

Observe

A. After years of research and experiments, scientists can now clone cells. They are technically capable of generating new cell types and have the capacity to develop new therapies. A lot of people hope science will soon be able to cure rare genetic diseases.

B. But can scientists pursue their research without any control?
Do they have the right and should they be allowed to do what they want in their labs? Isn't some government permission necessary first?

Quels sont les différents sens de *can* dans les phrases ci-dessus ?

→ Précis grammatical ⑫ p. 195-196

Practise

6 Make sure you understand the meanings of *can*. Rephrase the following sentences:

a. They can go out with their friends. Their parents have agreed.
b. He can speak English fluently. He spent his childhood in London.
c. He can solve difficult problems so quickly. It's amazing!
d. You have been drinking, you can't drive now.
e. Candidates can use a dictionary.

7 You are starting a summer job in a lab. Ask what you are allowed to do.

8 What has medical research made possible? Give a few examples.

If...

Observe

A. Since the first test-tube baby was born in 1978, 4 million babies have been conceived by in vitro fertilisation. If test-tube babies become the norm, the future of mankind will belong to scientists.

B. Most scientists say that human cloning is technically extremely difficult. Many of them think there is no medical evidence that it can be achieved. If it ever became possible, it would mean the end of Man.

Quelles différences de sens peut-on faire entre les phrases où l'on utilise *"if... will"* et celles avec *"if... would"* ?

→ Précis grammatical ⑲ p. 200-201

Practise

9 Use the relevant verbal forms in the following sentences:

a. He really works very hard. If he *(pass)* all his exams, he *(become)* a top scientist.
b. I hope it never happens, but if one day one of my siblings *(need)* a kidney, I *(be ready)* to give one of mine.

10 Complete the following sentences:

a. If I saw a bionic cat...
b. She will become a famous scientist if...
c. I wouldn't like to have a clone of myself even if...

11 Translate into French:

a. If scientists could cure all diseases, we would become immortal.
b. Oscar the cat could never have walked if a veterinary surgeon had not fitted him with metal implants.

More exercises in your Workbook ▶ p.82

Stratégies

Identifier les opinions exprimées dans un texte argumentatif

Dans un texte argumentatif sont exprimés des faits, des opinions et des points de vue sur un sujet donné, dans le but de convaincre ou de persuader.

1 Identifiez la nature du texte et le sujet abordé

On trouve l'argumentatif dans les types d'écrits suivants :

Type d'écrit	Buts
Des écrits qui ne relèvent pas de la fiction : article de presse, discours politique, slogan publicitaire, contribution à un forum de discussion...	• exprimer ce que l'on pense • défendre son point de vue • rallier les lecteurs ou auditeurs à l'opinion exprimée
Des écrits de fiction et des œuvres littéraires : théâtre, roman, poésie...	• exprimer des opinions au travers d'une histoire édifiante (ex. : *Never Let Me Go,* p. 142. *Brave New World* p. 144) • défendre des opinions par la voix des personnages

→ À vous

Lisez les 3 extraits ci-dessous et identifiez :

a. la nature des écrits dont ils sont tirés ;

b. le sujet abordé et le but du texte.

Major, an old pig, is delivering a speech to the other animals on the farm about their living conditions.

"Is it because this land of ours is so poor that it cannot afford a decent life to those who dwell upon it? No, comrades, a thousand times no! The soil of England is fertile, its climate is good, it is capable of affording food in abundance to an enormously greater number of animals than now inhabit it. This single farm of ours would support a dozen horses, twenty cows, hundreds of sheep and all of them living in a comfort and dignity that are now almost beyond our imagining. Why then do we continue in this miserable condition?"

Solutions can be found to help all those who suffer from terrible genetic disorders, give hope to people who cannot have children, and eradicate most diseases. That's why, yes, scientists will be allowed to carry out whatever experiments they think must be carried out and we will finance their work with government funds. But of course we will be very careful who we give money to. Therefore, there will be enquiries, commissions and public consultation. There will be no secret scheme. Do not believe those who say we plan to leave progress in the uncontrolled hands of mad biologists. Do not believe those who claim they can see our future clearly. Do not think [...]

Do you want to keep using face and body creams or lotions that do not give any results? Are mostly made of soap, salt and water? Cost a fortune? May develop allergies? Accelerate aging?
Our incredible techniques were perfected after years of research. For a younger, healthier and completely new *you*, call our Cell Lab 24/7 and discover [...]

2 Distinguez faits et opinions

Appuyez-vous sur le repérage de certains éléments :

Éléments à repérer	Exemples
Les faits objectifs • Ce qui s'est réellement passé ou ce qui est objectivement prouvé	→ *When Oscar the cat was hit by a combine harvester, he lost his two hind feet. That should have been the end of his mobility and maybe even his life.*
Les opinions • Les éléments indiquant clairement que l'on exprime son opinion • Les adjectifs, groupes nominaux, et adverbes « positifs » ou « négatifs » • Les sentiments et réactions	→ *I think, in my opinion, I agree, I disagree,* etc. → *Skilful/untalented, expert/amateur, fortunately/unfortunately,* etc. → *I regret, it is sad to think..., I was so happy to learn,* etc.

→ À vous

Lisez ce courrier de lecteur faisant suite à un article en faveur des OGM. Relevez :

a. les faits objectifs ;
b. les opinions.

Dear Sir,
Thank you for your article on how GMO can improve the lives of many people. It is an excellent article, well written and honest. The information given is all true – at last, a great antidote to the ridiculous ideas defended by Friends of the Earth, Greenpeace or the Soil Association. I have a PhD in agricultural science and many years of professional agronomic experience and know for a fact that Prof Jones's observations are absolutely right.

Dr Smith, Ashford, Kent

3 Cernez l'opinion exprimée

Une opinion peut être exprimée de manière implicite. Pour l'identifier, il s'agira alors de lier tout ce qui est dit explicitement afin de pouvoir en faire la synthèse :

Éléments à repérer	Exemples
Les mots de liaison • cause • concession • conséquence	→ *because, as, since...* → *however, although, even though, and yet...* → *so, that's why, therefore...*
La modalité (auxiliaires ou périphrases)	→ *may, must, should, will* → *no doubt, it is likely to..., I wonder whether..., anyway...*
Distinguer les vraies questions des questions rhétoriques	→ *When was the first test-tube baby born?* (on attend une réponse) → *Don't you think Prof Edwards' achievement gave hope to infertile couples?* (pas de réponse attendue, le locuteur présente une évidence)

→ À vous

Lisez cette contribution à un forum de discussion sur la vivisection et dites quelle opinion est exprimée
(pour ? contre ? ne sait pas ? sous réserves ? etc.)

Firstly the animals that are being tested on are not pets. Although some aspects of vivisection are indeed cruel, I believe testing on animals is acceptable to find ways to cure and prevent cancer, HIV, etc. However, using animals to test cosmetics should not be done.
When the experiments are being carried out, the animals should be treated with the same respect you would give a human. They should be anaesthetised and given pain killers. Over 65% of operations on laboratory animals are carried out without anaesthesia. Is that acceptable?

Rachel, Halifax

Identifier les opinions exprimées dans un texte argumentatif

■ Lisez l'extrait ci-dessous et identifiez :

a. le sujet abordé ;
b. l'opinion exprimée ;
c. les arguments et exemples utilisés.

The aim of (my) book is to argue that the most significant threat posed by contemporary biotechnology is the possibility that it will change human nature and therefore move us into a "posthuman" stage of history. This is important, I will argue, because human nature exists and has provided a stable continuity to our experience as a species. It is, conjointly with religion, what defines our most basic values. Human nature shapes the possible kinds of political regimes so a technology powerful enough to reshape what we are will have possibly malign consequences for liberal democracy...

There may be products of biotechnology that will be obvious in the dangers they pose to mankind – for example superbugs, new viruses, or genetically modified foods that produce toxic reactions. Like nuclear weapons or nanotechnology, they are in a way the easiest to deal with because once we have indentified them as dangerous, we an treat them as a straightforward threat. On the other hand, medical technology offers us in many cases a devil's bargain: longer life but with reduced mental capacity ; freedom from depression together with freedom from creativity; therapies that blur the line between what we achieve on our own and what we achieve because of the levels of various chemicals in our brains [...]

Adapted from Francis Fukuyama, ***Our Posthuman Future. The Consequences of the Bioltechnological Revolution*** (2002)

■ Faites le point

a. Vérifiez votre compréhension. **Auto-corrigé** ▶ www.didierpassword.fr
b. Situez votre niveau dans le tableau ci-dessous.

Niveaux	Mes compétences
B1-1	J'ai pu comprendre suffisamment un texte sur un sujet étudié pour pouvoir reconnaître les informations principales.
B1-2	J'ai pu identifier rapidement les opinions exprimées.
B1-3	J'ai pu reconnaître les arguments et exemples utilisés sans comprendre tous les détails du texte.
B2	J'ai pu comprendre dans le détail un texte relatif à un domaine étudié.

FINAL TASKS

TV debate

task 1

Speaking

Debate and have your say!

Genetic engineering: progress or peril?

1. Get ready

Work in teams

- Jot down arguments
- Don't forget examples
- Anticipate your opponents' arguments

2. Action!

- Don't read your notes
- Take your opponents' remarks into account
- Help your fellow team members if necessary

task 2

Reading

Find out the guests' opinions for a debate on:

"Cloning humans should be allowed"

- Your teacher will give you four texts containing the debaters' opinions on the topic.
- Read them carefully and identify the position of each person.
- Place the debaters around the table according to their opinions.

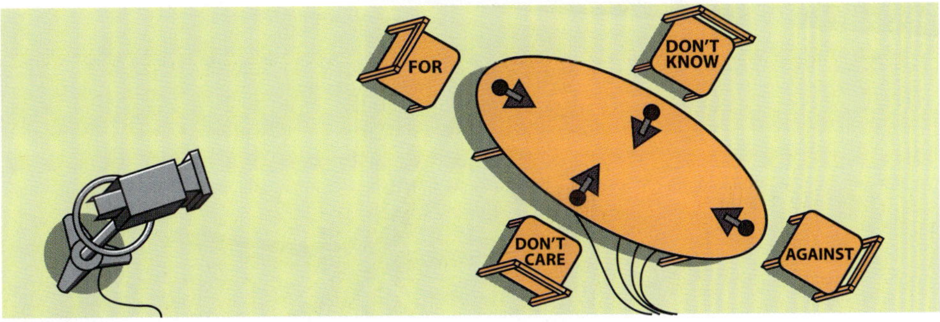

Reading test

- Your teacher will give you a text: read it carefully, then answer the questions.

Culture File 3

IMAGINING THE FUTURE

Pick out one of the documents on these pages.

In groups

1. Figure out what kind of society the document depicts.

2. Say what you think about this kind of society.

3. What would attract you most in this society? What would disturb you? Jot down a few notes.

4. Share your findings and reflexions with the class.

Whole class

5. Discuss your visions of tomorrow's society.

1 Cities of the future

❶ Sketch of the new West Kowloon Terminus in Hong Kong, China, 2010.

❷ The mobile "star city" of the future as imagined by Chinese architects, 2008.

2 Mankind is no longer alone

2057. The narrator, a journalist, is interviewing Doctor Susan Calvin, a 75-year-old scientist about to retire.

↑ *I, Robot*, directed by A. Proyas, 2004.

"Human interest out of robots? A contradiction."

"No, doctor. Out of you."

"Well, I've been called a robot myself. Surely, they've told you I'm not human."

They had, but there was no point in saying so.

She got up from her chair. She wasn't tall and she looked frail. I followed her to the window and we looked out.

The offices and factories of US Robots were a small city; spaced and planned. It was flattened out like an aerial photograph.

"When I first came here," she said, "I had a little room in a building right about there where the fire-house is now." She pointed. "It was torn down before you were born. I shared the room with three others. I had half a desk. We built our robots all in one building. Output – three a week. Now look at us."

"Fifty Years," I hackneyed, "is a long time."

"Not when you're looking back at them," she said. "You wonder how they vanished so quickly."

She went back to her desk and sat down. She didn't need expression on her face to look sad, somehow.

"How old are you?" she wanted to know.

"Thirty-two," I said.

"Then you don't remember a world without robots. There was a time when humanity faced the universe alone and without a friend. Now he has creatures to help him; stronger creatures than himself, more faithful, more useful, and absolutely devoted to him. Mankind is no longer alone. Have you ever thought of it that way?"

"I'm afraid I haven't. May I quote you?"

"You may. To you, a robot is a robot. Gears and metal; electricity and positrons. Mind and iron! Human-made! It necessary, human-destroyed! But you haven't worked with them, so you don't know them. They're a cleaner better breed than we are."

Isaac Asimov, *I Robot* (1950)

Isaac Asimov (1920-1992)

One of America's most famous and prolific science-fiction writers. A professor of biochemistry, he created the word "robotics" which now means the science of engineering robots.

3 Crime prevention

John Anderton, the founder of Precrime, is showing the organization to Dany Witwer, who is to be his assistant.

As they walked along the busy, yellow-lit tiers of offices, Anderton said: "You're acquainted with the theory of precrime, of course. I presume we can take that for granted."

"I have the information publicly available," Witwer replied. "With the aid of your precog mutants[1], you've boldly and successfully abolished the post-crime punitive system of jails and fines. As we all realize, punishment was never much of a deterrent, and could scarcely have afforded comfort to a victim already dead."

They had come to the descent lift. As it carried them swiftly downward, Anderton said: "You've probably grasped the basic legalistic drawback to precrime methodology. We're taking in individuals who have broken no law."

"But they surely will," Witwer affirmed with conviction.

"Happily they don't – because we get them first, before they can commit an act of violence. So the commission of the crime itself is absolute metaphysics. We claim they're culpable. They, on the other hand, eternally claim they're innocent. And, in a sense, they are innocent."

The lift let them out, and they again paced down a yellow corridor. "In our society we have no major crimes," Anderton went on, "but we do have a detention camp full of would-be criminals."

Doors opened and closed, and they were in the analytical wing. Ahead of them rose impressive banks of equipment – the data-receptors, and the computing mechanisms that studied and restructured the incoming material. And beyond the machinery sat the three precogs, almost lost to view in the maze of wiring. [...]

"When was the last time an actual murder was committed?" Witwer asked.

"Five years ago," Anderton said, pride in his voice.

"How did it happen?"

"The criminal escaped our teams. We had his name – in fact, we had all the details of the crime, including the victim's name. We knew the exact moment, the location of the planned act of violence. But in spite of us he was able to carry it out." Anderton shrugged. "After all, we can't get all of them." He riffled the cards[2]. "But we do get most."

"One murder in five years." Witwer's confidence was returning. "Quite an impressive record... something to be proud of."

Quietly Anderton said: "I am proud. Thirty years ago I worked out the theory – back in the days when the self-seekers were thinking in terms of quick raids on the stock market. I saw something legitimate ahead – something of tremendous social value."

He tossed the packet of cards to Wally Page, his subordinate in charge of the monkey block[3]. "See which ones we want," he told him. "Use your own judgment."

As Page disappeared with the cards, Witwer said thoughtfully: "It's a big responsibility."

"Yes, it is," agreed Anderton. "If we let one criminal escape – as we did five years ago – we've got a human life on our conscience. We're solely responsible. If we slip up, somebody dies." Bitterly, he jerked three new cards from the slot. "It's a public trust."

Philip K. Dick,
***The Minority Report* (1956)**

Philip K. Dick (1928-1982)
World famous American science-fiction writer. Described himself as a "fictionalizing philosopher". Many of his stories have been made into films (Blade Runner, Total Recall, The Minority Report).

1. people who can see the future
2. cards bearing the identities of would-be criminals
3. the room where the precog mutants are

4 Futuristic city

The heroine Sophie Bangs, a university student, lives in a present-day New York City similar to our own, but one dominated by science.

Alan Moore, J.H. Wiliams III, Mick Gray, *Promethea, Book 4* (2002)
Alan Moore (born 1953) *British author of popular comic books series such as* The League of Extraordinary Gentlemen.

UNIT 10 Justice in court

↑ *The Verdict*, directed by Sidney Lumet (1982)

What are the different powers in a court of law?

Look at the picture. What thoughts spring to mind?
Explain why the different characters are there and what part they may play in court.

FINAL TASKS

P. 171

In court

Speaking
Stage a trial in class

Reading
Find out who is speaking in court

CULTURE

- Learning about the judicial system in the U.S.
- Discovering aspects of civil lawsuits.
- Literary works:
  - John Grisham, *The Rainmaker*
  - Jonathan Harr, *A Civil Action*
- Cinema:
  - *The Rainmaker*, F. F. Coppola

COMMUNICATION

- Voicing an opinion and justifying it with relevant arguments, counter arguments and explanations.
- Identifying the protagonists, their opinions and arguments in a narrative.
- Delivering a short speech, exposing facts and arguments.

TOOLS

★ Words
- Courtroom vocabulary
- Introducing arguments
- Reparation
- Deliberating
- Responsibility

★ Pronunciation
Intonation in dialogue

★ Grammar
Not only..., hardly..., never...
Do in affirmative sentences

Stratégies
→ *Argumenter pour convaincre*

The case

1 The Rainmaker

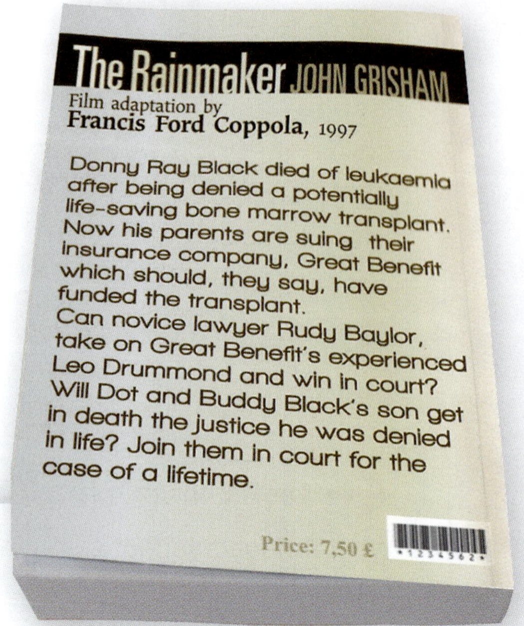

1. **Read** the information on the back cover of the book and state what you have understood about the plot of the novel.
2. **Start filling in** the "Case card" to identify the characters in this lawsuit. page 83 or ▶ www.didierpassword.fr

2 "It's simply not in the policy[1]"

The hearing of the case in court begins with the two lawyers' opening statements. Rudy Baylor has just spoken, it is now Leo Drummond's turn to address the jury.

Drummond strides confidently to the jury box and holds a copy of the policy. He gets off to a dramatic start: "This is the policy purchased by Mr and Mrs Black," he says, holding it up for everyone to see. "And nowhere in this policy does it say that Great Benefit has to pay for transplants." A long pause as this sinks in. The jurors don't like him, but this has their attention. "This policy costs eighteen dollars a week, does not cover bone marrow transplants, yet the plaintiffs expected my client to pay two hundred thousand dollars for, you guessed it, a bone marrow transplant. My client refused to do so, not out of any malice[2] toward Donny Ray Black. It wasn't a matter of life or death to my client, it was a matter of what's covered in this policy." He waves the policy dramatically, and quite effectively. "Not only do they want the two hundred thousand dollars they're not entitled to, they also have sued my client for ten million dollars in extra damages. They call them punitive damages. I call them ridiculous. I call it greed."

This is finding its mark, but it's risky. The policy specifically excludes transplants for every organ transplantable, but doesn't mention bone marrow. Its drafters[3] screwed up and left it out. The new policy given to me by Max Leuberg[4] includes language that excludes bone marrow.

The defense strategy becomes clear. Instead of soft-pedaling by admitting a mistake was made by unknown incompetents deep within a huge company, Drummond is conceding nothing. He'll claim bone marrow transplants are very unreliable, bad medicine, certainly not an accepted and routine method of treating acute leukemia.

He sounds like a doctor talking about the odds[5] against finding a suitable donor, millions to one in some cases, and the odds against a successful transplant. Over and over he repeats himself by saying, "It's simply not in the policy."

He decides to push me. The second time he mentions the word "greed," I leap to my feet and object. The opening statement is not the place for argument. That's saved for last. He's allowed only to tell the jury what he thinks the evidence will prove.

Judge Kipler quickly says, "Sustained."

First blood is mine.

"I'm sorry, Your Honor," Drummond says sincerely.

John Grisham, *The Rainmaker* (1995)

1. *police d'assurance*
2. not out of malice: not to make somebody suffer
3. the person who composes a document
4. Rudy Baylor's former law professor
5. possibility, chance

↑ Rudy Baylor and Donny Ray Black, just before Donny's death.

1. **Read the title of the text.** Imagine what Leo Drummond, the defense attorney, is going to tell the court.

2. **Read the text** and identify the narrator and the main protagonists. Discuss what you have understood and fill in the case card.
page 83 or ▶ www.didierpassword.fr

3. Read the text again.
a. **Concentrate on Leo Drummond** and highlight:
- his position, strategy and arguments;
- his movements.
pages 83-85
b. Share your findings and say what his goal is.

4. **a.** **Now concentrate on Rudy Baylor** and highlight:
- his thoughts;
- what he knows that the jurors still do not know. How important is it?
pages 83-85
b. Share your findings with the class and imagine what strategies Rudy will use to prove his client is right.
c. Read the end of the passage again (lines 27 to 33). Explain Rudy's and the judge's reactions.

Recap → Sum up the arguments used by the defense attorney and what he does to present them efficiently to the jury.

LANGUAGE TOOLS

★ WORDS → p. 166

Courtroom vocabulary
- **ju**ry box, **ju**ror, **law**yer, **plain**tiff, **cli**ent
- **law**suit, **tri**al
- de**fense** at**tor**ney = lawyer for the defense ≠ lawyer for the plaintiff
- Your **Ho**nor (US), sus**tain**ed, ob**jec**tion
- **o**pening **sta**tement ≠ **clo**sing **sta**tement
- **pu**nitive **da**mages
- sue, try, **ar**gue a case, ob**ject**

→ Donny's parents are suing the insurance company.

★ GRAMMAR → p. 167

Not only... also, hardly... when, never...
→ Not only do they want...

TRAINING TASK

Exposing the facts

1. Use Rudy Baylor's notes to imagine what he said in his opening statement.
2. Make your own notes and give a short speech as if you were in court.

√ the company accepted people's premiums*
√ it did not help people when money was needed
√ I have discussed the case with Max Leuberg, he gave me a copy of Great Benefit's new policy that specifically excludes bone marrow transplants.

* *cotisations*

Cross-examination

1 Defense attorney at work

video 16

An extract from *The Rainmaker*, F. F. Coppola, 1997.

Rudy Baylor has asked his client, Mrs Dot Black, to testify in front of the jury. Now Leo Drummond, the defense attorney, is cross-examining her.*

* Questioning a witness already examined by the opposing side.

1. **In pairs: before watching the video**, imagine what questions Leo Drummond may ask Mrs Black.
2. **Watch the scene** and discuss what you have understood about the protagonists. Fill in the case card.
   page 83 or ▶ www.didierpassword.fr
3. Watch again. Find out and discuss:
   - the protagonists' behaviours;
   - Leo Drummond's arguments;
   - the part played by money.

2 Plaintiff's lawyer at work

1. **Read the introduction** to the text on p. 161 and imagine Rudy Baylor's questions to Mr Lufkin.
2. **Read the text** and discuss what you have understood. Complete the case card.
   page 83 or ▶ www.didierpassword.fr
3. **In groups**. Read the text again. Pick out and discuss information about:
   - Rudy Baylor's questions about the claims manual and his attitude *(group 1)*;
   - Mr Lufkin's answers and attitudes *(group 2)*.
4. **Explain** what Rudy Baylor has managed to prove in the scene.

Recap → Explain why attorneys cross-examine witnesses.

LANGUAGE TOOLS

★ **WORDS** → p. 166

Courtroom vocabulary
- cross-exami**na**tion, **e**vidence
- **ques**tion, **tes**tify
- de**fen**dant, **bai**liff, **wit**ness, court re**por**ter

★ **PRONUNCIATION** → p. 166

Intonation in dialogue

"I beg your pardon?"

It is now Rudy Baylor's turn to cross-examine Everett Lufkin, one of the bosses at Great Benefit. Mr Lufkin has just been handed the procedure manual which tells Great Benefit employees how to handle cases.

"Now, Mr Lufkin, is this the entire claims[1] manual?"

He flips through it quickly as if he knows every section, every word.

"Yes."

"Are you certain?"

"Yes." [...]

"Did you personally select this particular copy of the manual to be sent to me?"

"I did."

[...] "Could you take the manual and flip over to Section U, please?"

"I beg your pardon?" Lufkin says, his voice an octave higher. [...] I glance at Kipler, and he's thoroughly enjoying this.

"Section U, Mr Lufkin. Flip over there and find it. I'd like to talk about it."

He actually takes the manual and flips through it again. [...]

"I don't have a Section U," he says, sadly and almost incoherent.

"I beg your pardon," I say loudly. "I didn't hear you."

"Uh, well, this one doesn't have a Section U." He's absolutely stunned, not by the fact that the section is missing, but by the fact that he's been caught. [...]

I make a big production of approaching the witness with Cooper Jackson[2]'s manual. It looks just like the one he's holding. A title page in the front gives the same date for the revised edition: January 1, 1991. They're identical, except that one has a final section called U, and one doesn't.

"Do you recognize this, Mr Lufkin?" I ask, handing him Jackson's copy and retrieving mine.

"Yes."

"Well, what is it?"

"A copy of the claims manual."

"And does this copy contain a Section U?"

He turns pages, then nods his head.

"What was that, Mr Lufkin? The court reporter can't record the movements of your head."

"It has a Section U."

"Thank you. Now, did you personally remove the Section U from my copy; or did you instruct someone else to do it?" [...] Seconds pass, as everyone waits for a response.

"Answer the question," Kipler barks from above.

"I don't know who did it."

"But it was done, wasn't it?" I ask.

"Evidently."

"So you admit that Great Benefit withheld documents."

"I admit nothing. I'm sure it was an oversight[3]."

John Grisham, *The Rainmaker* (1995)

1. *demandes d'indemnisation* **2.** a man who investigated into other lawsuits against Great Benefit **3.** a mistake not done on purpose

TRAINING TASK

The courtroom

You are attending the trial with a friend who does not know anything about the American judicial system. As the trial is temporarily suspended, you tell him/her where the various protagonists are seated and who they are.
First label the plan, then explain it to him/her.

pages 86-87 or ▶ www.didierpassword.fr

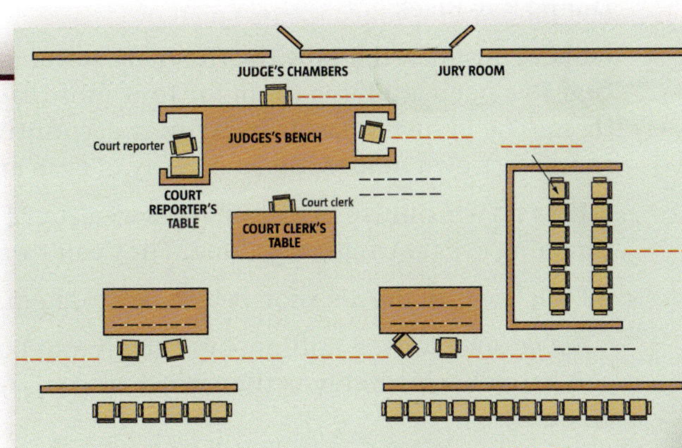

Closing speeches

Rudy Baylor's closing argument

Rudy Baylor is now summing up his arguments before the jury retires to deliberate.

I stand before them, quite tense and frightened, and try to relax. I know what I'll say because I've said it a hundred times. But it's important not to sound rehearsed. I begin by explaining that this is a very important day for my clients because it's their only chance to receive justice from Great Benefit. There's no tomorrow, no second chance in court, no other jury waiting to help them. I ask them to consider Dot and what she's been through. I talk a little about Donny Ray without being overly dramatic. I ask the jurors to imagine what it would be like to be slowly and painfully dying when you know you should be getting the treatment to which you're entitled. My words are slow and measured, very sincere, and they find their mark. I'm talking in a relaxed tone, and looking directly into the faces of twelve people who are ready to roll[1].

I cover the basics of the policy without much detail, and briefly discuss bone marrow transplants. I point out that the defense offered no proof contrary to Dr Kord's testimony. This medical procedure is far from experimental, and quite probably would've saved Donny Ray's life.

My voice picks up a bit as I move to the fun stuff. I cover the hidden documents and the lies that were told by Great Benefit. This played out so dramatically in trial that it would be a mistake to belabor[2] it. The beauty of a four-day trial is that the important testimony is still fresh. I use [...] the statistical data from Great Benefit, and put some figures on a chalkboard: the number of policies in 1991, the number of claims and, most important, the number of denials. I keep it quick and neat so a fifth-grader could grasp it and not forget it. The message is plain and irrefutable. The unknown powers in control of Great Benefit decided to implement a scheme[3] to deny legitimate claims for a twelve-month period. [...] It was an experiment to see how much cash could be generated in one year. It was a cold-blooded decision made out of nothing but greed, with absolutely no thought given to people like Donny Ray Black.

Speaking of cash, I take the financial statements and explain to the jury that I've been studying them for four months and still don't understand them. The industry has its own funny accounting practices. But, using the company's own figures, there's plenty of cash around. [...]

How do you punish a company this wealthy? I ask this question, and I see gleaming eyes staring back at me. They can't wait! [...]

I tell the jury the decision is best left to them.

We've sued for ten million, but they're not bound by that number. They can bring back whatever they want, and it's not my place to suggest an amount.

I close with a smile of thanks, then I tell them that if they don't stop Great Benefit, they could be next.

John Grisham, *The Rainmaker* (1995)

1. start
2. discuss for a long time
3. *exécuter un plan*

↑ A still from *The Rainmaker*, F. F. Coppola 1997.

1. Read the title and the introduction. Comment on the still above.

2. Read the extract and discuss what you have understood about the narrator and the situation. pages 87-88

3. In groups.
a. Read the text again and highlight information about:
- what Rudy Baylor says and how he acts in front of the jury *(group 1)*;
- what Rudy Baylor thinks and does not tell the jurors *(group 2)*;
pages 87-89
b. Share your findings.

4. Whole class.
a. Read the extract again and list:
- the points Rudy emphasises;
- the aspects he mentions but does not insist on.
pages 87-89
b. Share your findings with the class and explain his choices.

Recap → List the different devices Rudy uses to persuade the jurors.

LANGUAGE TOOLS

★ **WORDS** → p. 166

Introducing arguments
- to be**gin** with, to start with
- first/**first**ly ; **se**cond/**se**condly, last but not least...
- point out, stress, **em**phasise

Reparation
- fi**nan**cial compen**sa**tions, in**dem**nity, **da**mages, fine

★ **GRAMMAR** → p. 167

***Do* in affirmative sentences**
→ They did kill my son.

TRAINING TASK

Staging a speech

Act out Rudy's speech to the jury

1. In groups. Each group will focus on one of the points developed by Rudy Baylor (p. 162). Write the actual words Rudy may have used to address the jury.

2. On stage: deliver the speech with the help of the details given in the paragraph you have studied (tone of voice, gestures, etc.), emphasising the important points.

The jury

1 What is the jury's role?

- Listen to the interview and list the jury's different tasks.

track 56

The jury's role in American courtrooms.

2 Guilty or not guilty?

Here is a real case that took place in Woburn, Massachusetts: a lawsuit brought by a group of families who claimed that two companies,* WR Grace *and* Beatrice Foods*, polluted the wells that supplied their drinking water, ultimately causing their children to die of leukemia.

The day they began their formal deliberations, the clerk brought all the evidence up to the jury room – it took him several trips – and the list of questions that had been devised for them to answer. Jean Coulsey studied the questions in astonishment. And she wasn't the only one surprised by them. The others looked confused and perplexed, too. William Vogel remembered saying, "I thought we were just supposed to find them guilty or innocent." [...]

"Now what are we going to do?" asked Coulsey.

Vogel suggested they begin by taking a vote to see where everyone stood. [...]

As Vogel understood it, the first question asked whether the chemicals from Beatrice had gotten to the wells before May 22, 1979, the date the wells had closed. To him, that was essentially the "guilty" or "not guilty" question. He read that first question aloud to the other jurors and asked for a show of hands from those who believed Beatrice was liable. Jean Coulsey and Linda Kaplan promptly raised their hands. When no one else raised a hand, Vogel raised his. Finally Vincent O'Rourke, the postal employee, a very shy and retiring man, slowly raised his hand.

Then Vogel said: "Not guilty?"

Harriet Clarke held up her hand. Robert Fox, the only juror who had not yet voted, said he was undecided and would abstain for the moment.

Vogel posed the same question for Grace. The results were only slightly different. This time Robert Fox joined Harriet Clarke in finding Grace not liable. [...]

The jurors set to work that afternoon. [...] It quickly became apparent that although Robert Fox had abstained on the initial vote, he felt Beatrice should not be held liable. By the afternoon of the second day, the discussion between Fox and Coulsey began to grow heated. The judge had allowed the jurors to take notes during the trial, and Fox had filled the pages of four note-books. He would read to the other jurors items from his notes that supported his point of view.

Coulsey had taken almost no notes. She felt intuitively that the companies were responsible, but she had difficulty articulating her thoughts and could not readily summon* facts the way Fox could. [...]

For his part, Fox grew increasingly frustrated in his efforts to engage Coulsey in rational debate about the facts. He paced around the table, demanding that Coulsey explain, that she give her reasons, that she point to the evidence. "There simply isn't enough proof," Fox told her. "You need a preponderance of the evidence. Show me a preponderance of the evidence." [...]

They deliberated on Monday and Tuesday with little progress. [...] On Tuesday afternoon, Fox suggested they declare a deadlock and report to the judge that they could not arrive at a unanimous decision.

Jonathan Harr, *A Civil Action* (1996)

* evoke

1. **Read the introduction**. Explain what you have understood about this case.
2. **Read the text**, focusing on people's names. Discuss what you have understood.
3. Read the text again. Highlight and discuss:
   - the jurors' feelings;
   - details about the discussion between Fox and Coulsey.

   pages 90-91
4. **Explain** why Fox suggests they declare a deadlock (line 39).
5. If you want to know the verdict, turn to your Workbook.

   pages 91-92

Recap → Say what kind of power a jury has.

LANGUAGE TOOLS

★ WORDS → p. 166

Deliberating

- sum**mon** facts, sup**port** a **view**point, take a **vote**, ab**stain** on a vote
- find somebody **guil**ty/**in**nocent, be**lieve** somebody **li**able

Responsibility

- lia**bil**ity = accounta**bil**ity
- blame, debt, fi**nan**cial obli**ga**tion

TRAINING TASK

Reaching a verdict

In groups, choose one of two cases studied in the chapter.

1. *Woburn families against* WR Grace *and* Beatrice Foods

Act out the scene above. Follow your teacher's instructions.

2. *The Blacks against* Great Benefit Life Insurance

a. Imagine the jurors' deliberations at the end of the case. Make notes and decide on the verdict.

b. Act out the deliberation scene.

★ WORDS

❶ Courtroom vocabulary

Here are words and expressions you can hear in a courtroom. Match them with their definitions. Use a dictionary if needed.

Words/expressions
1. Objection!
2. (Objection) sustained
3. (Objection) overruled
4. "Do you swear to tell the truth, the whole truth and nothing but the truth?" "I do".
5. This testimony is irrelevant to the facts of the case.
6. Leading (question)
7. Sentence

Definitions
a. The oath taken/promise made by a witness before being questioned.
b. Used by the opposing side when they think the witness has not been questioned properly.
c. Rejected: the judge decides the questions may continue.
d. Accepted: the judge agrees that the questioning should not continue.
e. The punishment given.
f. Used to mean that what is being said has nothing to do with the case.
g. Used to show that the answer to the question is suggested.

❷ Adverbs

a. To emphasise your statements you can use adverbs such as:

- *very, extremely, quite, really, rather, so, fairly, too, utterly*

Use a dictionary to classify them in a grid like the one on the right, according to their degrees of intensity.

+	++	+++
...	very	...

b. Write four sentences expressing what you think of Great Benefit, Leo Drummond, or Rudy Baylor.

More exercises in your Workbook ▶ p. 92-93

★ PRONUNCIATION

❸ Intonation in dialogue

track 57

"What are you going to do with the money ↗ ?"

Dans un échange, l'intonation montante indique généralement que la personne qui parle demande l'avis de son interlocuteur (confirmation, réfutation ou explication). L'intonation descendante, par contre, accompagne un énoncé qui n'appelle pas directement de réplique ou de commentaire.

The following dialogue is taken from a trial:
"Would you mind telling the jury how many times you met the victim?"
"Please answer the question I have asked you."
"I suppose I met her about five or six times."
"Were these all pre-arranged appointments or just chance encounters? "
"They were all fixed appointments... except for the last time."
"And the last occasion was on the day the victim was found dead, wasn't it?"
"Are you asking me or telling me?"

a. Read these sentences and make sure you understand their meanings. Decide whether they have a rising (↗) or falling (↘) intonation.

b. Listen to the extract and check your answers.

c. With one of your classmates, act out the scene.

More exercises in your Workbook ▶ p.93

★ GRAMMAR

Not only... also, hardly... when, never...

Observe

A. They not only want the two hundred thousand dollars they are entitled to, they also want extra damages.
→ Not only do they want the two hundred thousand dollars they are entitled to, they also want extra damages.
B. A company has never been sentenced to pay such heavy damages.
→ Never has a company been sentenced to pay such heavy damages.
C. He had hardly purchased his insurance policy when he fell ill.
→ Hardly had he purchased his insurance policy when he fell ill.

Quel est le point commun aux mots soulignés ?
Comparez chaque paire de phrases.
Expliquez les changements opérés et l'effet produit.

Practise

4 **After attending a trial for the first time you write a letter to a friend about this unique experience.**

Dear XXX,

Never had I seen a trial before. It was a fabulous experience. Not only. . . .

Do in affirmative sentences

Observe

A. I do intend to sue Great Benefit, even if I may lose.
B. I disagree. Your company did kill my son.
C. "Are you telling me they did know the truth?"
D. "He isn't ready to help us."
"You're wrong: he does want to give us a hand".

Observez les éléments soulignés dans les phrases ci-dessus. Pourquoi sont-ils employés ?

g → Précis grammatical ⑮ p. 197

Practise

5 **Rephrase the following statements to be more assertive. Then practise saying them aloud.**

a. "The jurors think the company is guilty, you can be sure of it."
b. "Are you certain the boy was cured?"
"Yes. They discovered the vaccine in time."
c. "I'm telling you Mr and Mrs Black paid their premiums regularly."
d. "Listen to me! It happened because of your inhuman methods."

More exercises in your Workbook ▶ p.94

Stratégies

Argumenter pour convaincre

Convaincre signifie obtenir l'assentiment de quelqu'un, voire l'amener à changer d'avis, en utilisant certains procédés argumentatifs.

1 Rendez vos arguments irréfutables

a. Étayez les faits et justifiez les preuves.

b. Présentez-les logiquement et simplement pour qu'ils soient facilement compréhensibles.
→ *The medical procedure is far from experimental. There have been numerous transplants in the five past years.*

Utilisez des mots de liaison :

Paradoxe	Condition	Cause	Conséquence
(al)though, yet, still, however, despite, in spite of...	*if, unless, in case, provided, as long as...*	*because, as, since*	*so, therefore, consequently, that's why...*

→ À vous

The Rainmaker **: Leo Drummond prépare sa plaidoirie.**
Choisissez l'un des deux faits ci-dessous. Par écrit, expliquez-le et avancez des preuves (vous pouvez inventer des éléments).

1. *The policy specifically excludes transplants for every organ transplantable.*
2. *Bone marrow transplants are not an accepted and routine method of treating leukemia.*

2 Utilisez les procédés qui rendront ces arguments plus percutants

Procédés	Exemples
Utilisez des répétitions.	→ *"They call them punitive damages. I call them ridiculous. I call it greed."* → *"There's no tomorrow, no second chance in court, no other jury waiting to help them."*
Demandez aux témoins de répéter leurs affirmations.	→ *"I beg your pardon," I say loudly. "I didn't hear you."* → *"Would you mind repeating/speaking louder?"*
Ménagez des pauses : • pour laisser l'interlocuteur comprendre le message • pour maintenir l'attention par des changements de rythme.	

Procédés	Exemples
Remettez en cause les points de vue exprimés par d'autres personnes.	→ *"**You say** your company cannot be held responsible. However, the evidence shows...."*
Mettez en valeur les aspects que vous voulez privilégier.	→ *"Not only do... but..."* → *"It is the plaintiff who..."* g → Précis grammatical (18) p. 200
Impliquez l'auditoire : • demandez à ceux auxquels vous vous adressez de se mettre à la place des autres ; • personnalisez votre propos.	→ *"Imagine what it would be like to be slowly and painfully dying when you know you should be getting the treatment to which you're entitled."* → *"If you don't stop Great Benefit, you could be next."*

→ *À vous*

Reprenez le discours de Leo Drummond (p. 158) et introduisez certains de ces procédés.

3 Utilisez le langage corporel

a. Le regard

Regardez vos interlocuteurs pour maintenir leur attention et exercer une pression sur eux.

b. Les mouvements

Utilisez des éléments qui relèvent du théâtre : déplacez-vous, appuyez vos propos par un geste de la main, montrez des choses.

c. La voix

Soyez sûr de vous et calme, mais sachez aussi varier vos intonations, votre ton et votre débit.

→ *À vous*

Écoutez Rudy Baylor s'adressant au jury, puis entraînez-vous à dire ce même texte. track 59

"This is a very important day for my clients because it's their only chance to receive justice from Great Benefit. There's no tomorrow, no second chance in court, no other jury waiting to help them. Consider Dot and what she's been through. Think of Donny Ray. Imagine what it would be like to be slowly and painfully dying when you know you should be getting the treatment to which you're entitled. "

Auto-évaluation

Argumenter pour convaincre

↑ A drive-through restaurant

Lisez les éléments du cas ci-dessous :

Mrs Dodge poursuit en justice un grand nom de la restauration rapide. Vous avez suivi l'audience du tribunal dans le public et vous vous demandez ce que le jury va décider.

What you know about the case

- Mrs Stella Dodge, 79 years old.
- Bought a cup of coffee from the drive-through window of a fast food restaurant in California;
- was in the passenger's seat of her car, and her son Ray parked the car so that she could add cream and sugar to her coffee;
- placed the coffee cup between her knees and opened the lid of the plastic cup;
- spilled the entire cup of coffee on her lap;
- her cotton trousers absorbed the coffee and held it against her skin;
- suffered third-degree burns and remained in the hospital for eight days;
- two years of medical treatment followed.

a. Préparez un dialogue en binômes.
Vous n'avez pas le même point de vue sur l'éventuelle décision du jury.

- Décidez quel rôle vous allez jouer.
- Notez les arguments (bien sûr, vous pouvez en inventer) ; choisissez les procédés que vous allez privilégier pour convaincre votre interlocuteur que vous avez raison.

Vous pouvez organiser votre brouillon de cette façon :

Arguments	Procédés utilisés pour convaincre
...	...

b. Jouez le dialogue.

Deux autres élèves vont évaluer comment vous effectuez votre performance afin de vous aider à l'améliorer.

Faites le point

a. Vérifiez votre production.

Auto-corrigé ▶ www.didierpassword.fr

b. Situez votre niveau dans le tableau ci-dessous.

Niveaux	Mes compétences
B1-1	J'ai pu avancer des arguments simples et directs.
B1-2	J'ai pu avancer des arguments de manière claire et méthodique en soulignant les éléments pertinents grâce à des connecteurs logiques.
	J'ai pu contredire mon interlocuteur.
B1-3	J'ai pu avancer des arguments en utilisant des procédés variés.
	J'ai pu utiliser des questions rhétoriques.
B2	J'ai pu m'écarter des arguments préparés pour réagir aux points intéressants soulevés par mon interlocuteur.

FINAL TASKS

In court

task 1

Speaking

Stage a trial in class

Role Play: you are taking part in the National High School Mock Trial Championship.

The case:

Jimmy underwent an operation and came out of hospital suffering from an infection due to bacterial contamination.

His mother is suing the doctor.

- Your teacher will give you a card similar to the one above with the part you have to play.

1. Get ready

- **Whole class**: read the cards and make sure you understand them. Discuss the main ideas.
- **In groups**: imagine the framework of the trial.
- **On your own**: learn your part.

2. Action!

- **In groups**: act out the trial.

task 2

Reading

Find out who is speaking in court

Your teacher will give you extracts from different statements made in court. Read each of them, then find out who said what. The characters:

- A witness for the defense
- The defense attorney
- The judge
- etc.

Reading test

- Your teacher will give you a text: read it carefully, then answer the questions.

Einstein's Chauffeur

The podium hides half my body but it cannot hide my trembling hands. I take a deep breath, place his glasses on my nose, and look down at his notes. They are in German. I can't read German. Why? Because I'm from Pittsburgh. I shouldn't even be up here.

I look around the amphitheatre full of researchers: there are grey heads, white heads, bald heads and young heads with alert, enthusiastic expressions. A hall full of physicists who want to learn from me. I'm a chauffeur, and I'm here to teach Relativity.

I clear my throat and take a drink of water. At the back of the amphitheatre I see a familiar figure dressed in my dark chauffeur's uniform, sitting on a stool with my cap pulled down over his eyes. Even from here I can see his white hair. He sits up and I see the quick, childish smile come across his face. He sticks his tongue out at me.

Now the crowd is becoming agitated. There is a noise of chairs moving, and I'm thinking they can smell my fear, they've got to know what's up. But now my boss is smiling and I can feel his warmth right from the back of the hall.

I can't blame him. He didn't force me to do this. I gave him the idea and he just... persuaded me. I've been driving him for a couple of months now, and one thing I can tell you for certain, it's hard to say no to the professor.

Just last week, as I was driving Professor Einstein back from a lecture in Baltimore, I remember his calm Austrian accent coming from the back of the car.

"Harry, did you enjoy the speech I made this evening?"

"Oh, absolutely, sir."

"Yes... I saw that you were enjoying it. I had a very good view."

"Sir?"

"It appears to me that you were in a state of repose at the back of the auditorium. Is that correct?"

I slowed down a little, and glanced up at him in the mirror.

"Repose? What do you mean, sir?"

"You were asleep, yes. That is correct, is it not?"

I took a second to think about that. There wasn't any anger in his voice, just curiosity. I guess you'd call it a desire for knowledge. His dark eyes were watching me in the mirror.

"Well, I wouldn't say I was asleep—"

"Harry, we have, how do you put it... we have been on the road for some months now, yes? And although for many people across America my theory is new, you have heard me explain it at least twenty times, is that correct?"

"Twenty-three times, sir."

He chuckled and slapped his knees. "Exactly. I can see it clearly. Now, you cannot read a book twenty-three times and expect to stay interested, can you?"

"No sir, I imagine that would be difficult."

He sat back for a few minutes and I drove on through the rain. It was an easy drive back to the hotel, but I was going slowly as I thought he had something more to say.

"Harry," he said at last. "Am I boring?"

"Oh, no, sir."

"But my speech is boring you, yes?"

"Oh no, Mr. Einstein. I wouldn't say that at all. I guess I've just heard the old Theory of Relativity so many times, I could give your speech myself."

"Really?" For a moment I thought I'd gone too far. He sounded angry.

"Please, prove it," he said.

"Well, sir..." I began. And I gave him his introduction, word for word. He sat back in the seat, laughing softly.

"I don't mean to be disrespectful, sir, it's just that I have a good memory—"

"An excellent memory," he said. "And what about the central theme, hmm?"

I gave him the rest of the speech, without having any idea what it all meant. I even did it with an Austrian accent, as I'd spent a long time sitting at the back of lecture halls mouthing out the words as he said them.

"Fascinating," he said when I'd finished. "I couldn't have put it any better! I can't blame you for falling asleep. I've often felt a little drowsy myself, saying the same thing each time."

"But it's important, Mr. Einstein! I'm sure lots of people hang on to your every word!"

"Yes..."

"One day it could even make you famous."

He sat back in the seat so I couldn't see him, and we drove on for another few minutes. Then he bounced forward, wringing his hands in his lap, his eyes wide and childish.

"Stop the car."

I pulled over to the side of the road, and we sat for a few minutes. I remember the sound of the rain on the roof, like a hundred ticking clocks, and the shape of the physicist in the back of the cab, thinking.

"I think we can have a little fun, yes? Some refreshment. We go to Dartmouth next week... no one there knows me, not yet... no one knows what I look like. So, why not you go and give the speech, and I take a little repose at the back, yes?" He pulled at his bow tie and smiled in the dark.

I should have said no. Straight away I should have slammed the door on the idea, but Professor Einstein is one of those people it's very difficult to refuse. More than that, he's the kind of man who'll make you believe you can do anything. Anything I found difficult he'd just laugh away.

Over the next three days Professor Einstein spent a great deal of time explaining Relativity to me in simple terms a child might understand. He drew me pictures of a lift in a skyscraper, then one of trains pulling away from another, and while I was no closer to understanding what the theory meant, his drive and his confidence was enough to make me agree to exchange clothes before we left the Dartmouth hotel, and he even persuaded me to let him drive us through the grounds of the university to the Physics Department.

So here I am at the front of this great hall, staring at the sheet of paper. I'm trying to remember what he told me in the hotel, but all I can see are trains and skyscrapers spinning away into a black hole. The other thing I can see is me getting discovered and handing my uniform to my boss for the last time. Einstein's tweed jacket is tight around my shoulders, and only now am I aware of how much smaller he is than me.

The faces at the front are all enthusiastic and attentive; I see one young man, sharp-eyed like a fox, his pen poised over his paper. I take a final look at my chauffeur at the back of the hall. He's already slumped in repose, his white hair frothing out from under his cap.

I begin.

I move through the speech, speaking slowly and carefully, not understanding a word I'm saying, but pretty soon I'm delivering the whole kaboodle word for word, just as we'd rehearsed it in the hotel. Just as the professor had told me, over and over again, "Don't think, Harry, don't think about it all. Just let the words come out in the right order." At first I'm numb, beyond thinking, but pretty soon I'm forgetting myself and just giving a good performance. Before I know it I'm finishing and feeling very clever and flushed with success as I gather up Einstein's notes.

Before anyone can stick up a hand to ask a question I'm rushing down off the stage, the professor's papers clasped to my chest, the hall ringing with the sound of applause.

I could do this all week, I'm thinking. The hell with it. Let Einstein drive. I see him stand up at the back, clapping delightedly, smiling like the proudest uncle in the world. As if in a dream I go towards him—

—and the fox-faced student steps in front of me, speaking breathlessly.

"Excuse me, Professor. I very much enjoyed your talk."

"Why, thank you," I murmur, trying to push past.

"Perhaps if you could just elucidate on one point..."

The clapping is dying down and soon the other lecturers and researchers can hear what's being said. The Professor is now standing beside me but saying nothing. My knees are starting to tremble again, I feel the cold rise up in my guts once more.

"Elucidate," I mumble. What does that mean?

I look over at Albert Einstein for help, but he just carries on looking proudly at me and not saying a word.

"Yes, sir," the student goes on. "You see, you argued that the principle proposed by Newton..."

I lose him from there on in. I have no idea what to say, I can only let him finish and wait for him to find me out. I wish Professor Einstein would come out and rescue me, but he just takes out the car keys and says, in a terrible Pittsburgh accent, "Shall I wait outside, sir?"

The student is waiting, his pencil is poised on his pad. I notice four other students waiting in the same way, their pens quivering like stings. Over their shoulders I see Einstein stick out his tongue again, and suddenly it feels like his voice is speaking through me, his words slow and patient and logical.

I look straight at the student and put on my best Austrian accent.

"The answer to that is very simple," I say cheerfully. "Why, it's so simple, I'm going to let my chauffeur answer it!"

Peter Flynn, *Hemingways's chihuahua and other mysteries* (2011)

A Horse and Two Goats

Of the seven hundred thousand villages dotting the map of India, in which the majority of India's five hundred million live, flourish, and die, Kritam was probably the tiniest, indicated on the district survey map by a microscopic dot [...]. But its size did not prevent its giving itself the grandiose name Kritam, which meant in Tamil "coronet" or "crown" on the brow of this subcontinent. The village consisted of less than thirty houses, only one of them built with brick and cement. Painted a brilliant yellow and blue all over with gorgeous carvings of gods and gargoyles on its balustrade, it was known as the Big House. The other houses, distributed in four streets, were generally of bamboo thatch, straw, mud, and other unspecified material. Muni's was the last house in the fourth street, beyond which stretched the fields. In his prosperous days Muni had owned a flock of forty sheep and goats and sallied forth every morning driving the flock to the highway a couple of miles away. There he would sit on a pedestal of a clay statue of a horse while his cattle grazed around. [...]

His fortunes had declined gradually, unnoticed. From a flock of forty which he drove into a pen at night, his stock had now come down to two goats, which were not worth the rent of a half rupee a month the Big House charged for the use of the pen in their backyard. And so the two goats were tethered to the trunk of a drumstick tree which grew in front of his hut. [...] This morning, unleashing the goats from the drumstick tree, Muni started out, driving them ahead and uttering weird cries from time to time in order to urge them on. He passed through the village with his head bowed in thought. [...]

He avoided looking at anyone; they all professed to be so high up, and everyone else in the village had more money than he. "I am the poorest fellow in our caste and no wonder that they spurn me, but I won't look at them either," and so he passed on with his eyes downcast along the edge of the street [...]. Only on the outskirts did he lift his head and look up. He urged and bullied the goats until they meandered along to the foot of the horse statue on the edge of the village. He sat on its pedestal for the rest of the day. The advantage of this was that he could watch the highway and see the lorries and buses pass through to the hills, and it gave him a sense of belonging to a larger world. The pedestal of the statue was broad enough for him to move around as the sun traveled up and westward; or he could also crouch under the belly of the horse, for shade.

The horse was nearly life-size, moulded out of clay, baked, burnt, and brightly coloured, and reared its head proudly, prancing its forelegs in the air and flourishing its tail in a loop; beside the horse stood a warrior with scythe-like mustachios, bulging eyes, and aquiline nose. [...] The horse itself was said to have been as white as a dhobi-washed sheet, and had had on its back a cover of pure brocade of red and black lace, matching the multicolored sash around the waist of the warrior. But none in the village remembered the splendor as no one noticed its existence. Even Muni, who spent all his waking hours at its foot, never bothered to look up. It was untouched even by the young vandals of the village who gashed tree trunks with knives and tried to topple off milestones and inscribed lewd designs on all walls. [...]

Muni sat at the foot of the statue, watching his two goats graze in the arid soil among the cactus and lantana bushes. He looked at the sun; it was tilted westward no doubt, but it was not the time to go back home; if he went too early, his wife would have no food for him [...].

He noticed now a new sort of vehicle coming down at full-speed. It looked like both a motorcar and a bus. He used to be intrigued by the novelty of such spectacles, but of late work was going on at the source of the river on the mountain and an assortment of people and traffic went past him, and he took it all casually and described to his wife, later in the day, everything he say. Today, while he observed the yellow vehicle coming down, he was wondering how to describe it later to his wife when it sputtered and stopped in front of him. A red-faced foreigner, who had been driving it, got down and went around it, stooping, looking, and poking under the vehicle; then he straightened himself up, looked at the dashboard, stared in Muni's direction, and approached him. "Excuse me, is there a gas station nearby, or do I have to wait until another car comes —" He suddenly looked up at the clay horse and cried, "Marvelous," without completing his sentence. [...]

The red-faced man wore khaki clothes — evidently a policeman or a soldier. Muni said to himself, "He will chase or shoot if I start running. Some dogs chase only those who run — oh, Shiva protect me. I don't know why this man should be after me." Meanwhile the foreigner cried, "Marvelous!" again, nodding his head. He paced around the statue with his eyes fixed on it. Muni sat frozen for a while, and then fidgeted and tried to edge away. Now the other man suddenly pressed his palms together in a salute, smiled, and said, "Namaste! How do you do?"

At which Muni spoke the only English expressions he had learnt, "Yes, no." Having exhausted his English vocabulary, he started in Tamil: "My name is Muni. These two goats are mine [...]."

The foreigner faithfully looked in the direction indicated by Muni's fingers, gazed for a while at the two goats and the rocks, and with a puzzled expression took out his silver cigarette case and lit a cigarette. Suddenly remembering the courtesies of the season, he asked, "Do you smoke?" Muni answered "Yes, no." Whereupon the red-faced man took a cigarette and gave it to Muni, who received it with surprise, having had no offer of a smoke from anyone for years now. [...] Muni drew a deep puff and started coughing; it was racking, no doubt, but extremely pleasant. When his cough subsided he wiped his eyes and took stock of the situation, understating that the other man was not an Inquisitor of any kind. Yet, in order to make sure, he remained wary. No need to run away from a man who gave him such a potent smoke. His head was reeling from the effect of one of those strong American cigarettes made with roasted tobacco. The man said, "I come from New York," took out a wallet from his hip pocket, and presented his card.

Muni shrank away from the card. Perhaps he was trying to present a warrant and arrest him. Beware of khaki, one part of his mind warned. Take all the cigarettes or bhang or whatever is offered, but don't get caught. Beware of khaki. [...] The Tamil language gushed through Muni in an unimpeded flow. He said, "Before God, sir, Bhagwan, who sees everything, I tell you, sir, that we know nothing of the case. If the murder was committed, whoever did it will not escape. Bhagwan is all-seeing. Don't ask me about it. I know nothing." A body had been found mutilated and thrown under a tamarind tree at the border between Kritam and Kuppam a few weeks before, giving rise to much gossip and speculation. Muni added an explanation. "Anything is possible there. People over there will stop at nothing." The foreigner nodded his head and listened courteously though he understood nothing.

"I am sure you know when this horse was made," said the red man and smiled ingratiatingly.

Muni reacted to the relaxed atmosphere by smiling himself, and pleased, "Please go away, sir, I know nothing. I promise we will hold him for you if we see any bad character around, and we will bury him up to his neck in a coconut pit if he tries to escape; but our village has always had a clean record. Must definitely be the other village."

Now the red man implored, "Please, please, I will speak slowly, please try to understand me. Can't you understand even a simple word of English? Everyone

in this country seems to know English. I have gotten along with English everywhere in this country, but you don't speak it. Have you any religious or spiritual scruples against English speech?" [...]

Muni felt totally confused but decided the best thing would be to make an attempt to get away from this place. He tried to edge out, saying, "Must go home," and turned to go. The other seized his shoulder and said desperately, "Is there no one, absolutely no one here, to translate for me?" He looked up and down the road, which was deserted in this hot afternoon; a sudden gust of wind churned up the dust and dead leaves on the roadside into a ghostly column and propelled it towards the mountain road. The stranger almost pinioned Muni's back to the statue and asked, "Isn't this statue yours? Why don't you sell it to me?"

The old man now understood the reference to the horse, thought for a second, and said in his own language, "I was an urchin this high when I heard my grandfather explain this horse and warrior, and my grandfather himself was this high when he heard his grandfather, whose grandfather —"

The other man interrupted him. "I don't want to seem to have stopped here for nothing. I will offer you a good price for this," he said, indicating the horse. He had concluded without the least doubt that Muni owned this mud horse. Perhaps he guessed by the way he sat on his pedestal, like other souvenir sellers in this country presiding over their wares. [...]

Muni, now assured that the subject was the horse [...] said, "This is our guardian, it means death to our adversaries. At the end of Kali Yuga, this world and all other worlds will be destroyed, and the Redeemer will come in the shape of a horse called 'Kalki'; this horse will come to life and gallop and trample down all bad men. [...]

The visitor, feeling that he had spent too much time already, said, "Tell me, will you accept a hundred rupees or not for the horse? I'd love to take the whiskered soldier also but no space for him this year. I'll have to cancel my air ticket and take a boat home, I suppose. [...] I have a station wagon as you see. I can push the seat back and take the horse in if you will lend me a hand with it."

"Do you know Mahabharata? Krishna was the eight avatar of Vishnu, incarnated to help the Five Brothers regain their kingdom. When Krishna was a baby he danced on the thousand hooded giant serpent and trampled it to death; and then he suckled the breasts of the demoness and left them flat as a disc, though when she came to him her bosoms were large, like mounds of earth on the banks of a dug-up canal." He indicated two mounds with his hands. The stranger was completely mystified by the gesture. For the first time he said, "I really wonder what are you saying because your answer is crucial. We have come to the point when we should be ready to talk business."

"When the tenth avatar comes, do you know where you and I will be?" asked the old man.

"Lend me a hand and I can lift off the horse from its pedestal after picking out the cement at the joints. We can do anything if we have a basis of understanding."

At this stage the mutual mystification was complete, and there was no need even to carry on a guessing game at the meaning of words. The old man chattered away in a spirit of balancing off the credits and debits of conversational exchange, and said in order to be on the credit side, " O, honourable one, I hope God has blessed you with numerous progeny. I say this because you seem to be a good man, willing to stay beside an old man and talk to him, while all day I have none to talk to except when somebody stops to ask for a piece of tobacco. But I seldom have it, tobacco is not what it used to be at one time, and I have given up chewing. I cannot afford it nowadays." Noting the other's interest in his speech, Muni felt encouraged to ask, "How many children have you?" with appropriate gestures with his hands. Realizing that a question was being asked, the red man replied, "I said a hundred," which encouraged Muni to go into details. "How many of your children are boys and how many girls? Where are they? Is your daughter married? Is it difficult to find a son-in-law in your country also?"

In answer to these questions the red man dashed his hands into his pocket and brought forth his wallet in order to take immediate advantage of the bearish trend in the market. He flourished a hundred-rupee currency note and said, "Well, this is what I meant."

The old man now realized that some financial element was entering their talk. He peered closely at the currency note, the like of which he had never seen in his life; he knew the five and ten by their colours although always in other people's hands, while his own earning at that time was in coppers and nickels. What was this man flourishing the note for? Perhaps asking for change. He laughed to himself at the notion of anyone coming to him for changing a thousand- or ten-thousand-rupee note. He said with a grin, "Ask our village headman, who is also a moneylender; he can change even a lakh of rupees in gold sovereigns if you prefer it that way [...]." His eyes traveled to his goats nosing about, attempting to wrest nutrition from minute greenery peeping out of rock and dry earth.

The foreigner followed his look and decided that it would be a sound policy to show an interest in the old man's pets. He went up casually to them and stroked their backs with every show of courteous attention. Now the truth dawned on the old man. His dream of a lifetime was about to be realized. He understood that the red man was actually making an offer for the goats. He had reared them up in hope of selling them some day and, with the capital, opening a small shop on this very spot. Sitting here, watching towards the hills, he had often dreamed how he would put up a thatched roof here, spread a gunnysack out on the ground, and display on it fried nuts, colored sweets, and green coconut for the thirsty and famished wayfarers on the highway, which was sometimes very busy. The animals were not prize ones for a cattle show, but he had spent his occasional savings to provide them some fancy diet now and then, and they did not look too bad. While he was reflecting thus, the red man shook his hand and left on his palm one hundred rupees in tens now, suddenly realizing that this was what the old man was asking. "It is all for you or you may share it if you have a partner."

The old man pointed at the station wagon and asked, "Are you carrying them off in that?"

"Yes, of course," said the other, understanding the transportation part of it.

The old man said, "This will be their first ride in a motorcar. Carry them off after I get out of sight, otherwise they will never follow you, but only me even if I am travelling on the path to Yama Loka." He laughed at his own joke, brought his palms together in a salute, turned around and went off, and was soon out of sight beyond a clump of thicket.

The red man looked at the goats grazing peacefully. Perched on the pedestal of the horse, as the westerly sun touched off the ancient faded colours of the statue with a fresh splendor, he ruminated, "He must be gone to fetch some help, I suppose!" and settled down to wait. When a truck came downhill, he stopped it and got the help of a couple of men to detach the horse from its pedestal and place it in his station wagon. He gave them five rupees each, and for a further payment they siphoned off gas from the truck, and helped him to start his engine.

R. K. Narayan, *The Grandmother's Tale and Selected Stories* (1994)

SOMMAIRE

L'énoncé : quelques définitions préalables

I. LE GROUPE NOMINAL

II. LE GROUPE VERBAL

III. LA PHRASE

L'ÉNONCÉ : QUELQUES DÉFINITIONS PRÉALABLES

Parler une langue, c'est **exprimer des idées**, les partager, les confronter. Ces idées sont véhiculées à travers des énoncés, messages écrits ou oraux, simples (ex : *« Pardon » / « Laure parle anglais. »*) ou complexes (ex : *« Bien que Laure ne soit jamais allée en Angleterre, elle parle anglais couramment. »*), que l'on produit en contexte, dans **une situation donnée**. Cette situation s'appelle **la situation d'énonciation**. Elle met en scène un **énonciateur** (celui qui produit l'énoncé) et un **co-énonciateur** (le destinataire de l'énoncé).

Ce précis grammatical vous aidera :
– à repérer et analyser les formes que peuvent prendre les groupes nominaux, les groupes verbaux et les phrases en anglais.
– à mieux saisir leurs sens et ainsi à mieux les utiliser lors des différentes situations de communication dans lesquelles vous vous trouverez.

Quelques définitions utiles

Adjectif :	Mot qui détermine et qualifie un nom/groupe nominal.
Adverbe :	Mot qui modifie le sens d'un verbe, d'un adjectif, d'un autre adverbe ou d'une phrase.
Agent :	Celui qui fait l'action.
Auxiliaire :	mot qui permet de construire diverses formes verbales. On l'utilise notamment pour former des énoncés négatifs et interrogatifs. Trois auxiliaires en anglais : *DO, BE, HAVE,* auxquels s'ajoutent les auxiliaires modaux.
Base verbale :	→ Voir : *Infinitif*
Coordination :	Juxtaposition de deux noms/groupes nominaux/groupes adjectivaux/ propositions liés entre eux par une conjonction de coordination (ex : *and, but, so, consequently, however*).
Infinitif :	Forme nue du verbe, appelée aussi « base verbale » (ex : *walk, work, eat, sing*).
Préposition :	Mot qui permet d'introduire un complément (ex : *at, by, from, in, on*).
Proposition :	Ensemble de mots composé en général d'un sujet et d'un groupe verbal.
Subordination :	Lien entre une proposition subordonnée rattachée à une proposition principale par une conjonction de subordination (ex : *although, whereas, while*).
Verbe transitif :	Verbe suivi d'un complément direct ou indirect (par opposition à « verbe intransitif »).

I — Le groupe nominal

En anglais, le nom est **déterminé** par des éléments qui viennent se placer directement à sa gauche. Les compléments que l'on trouve à sa droite relèvent de l'**expansion** du groupe nominal.

Détermination du nom			Nom	Expansion du nom
• article • adjectif démonstratif • quantifieur • génitif /adjectif possessif	adjectif (s) qualificatif(s)	nom	nom	proposition(s) relative(s)

Their frightening video report, which was about environmental disasters, came out on TV yesterday.

1 Noms dénombrables et indénombrables

a. Noms dénombrables

Ces noms renvoient à des éléments distincts que l'on peut séparer, quantifier à l'aide d'adjectifs numéraux *(one, two, three)* ou de quantifieurs *(much, many, a lot of...)*.

pen → ten pens *flower → a bunch of flowers* *book → many books*

b. Noms indénombrables

Ces noms renvoient à quelque chose de global, envisagé comme un tout. Ils n'ont qu'une forme singulier et le verbe qui suit est lui aussi singulier. Parmi eux, on trouve des termes qui renvoient à des activités *(swimming, reading)*, des catégories *(wood, sand, tea)*, des notions abstraites *(knowledge, luck, peace, freedom, courage)*. Certains sont quantifiables :

money → a lot of money *coffee → a cup of coffee* *bread → a loaf of bread*

⚠ **Certains noms dénombrables en français sont indénombrables en anglais :**

Français	Anglais
bagage / bagages	*luggage*
meuble / meubles	*furniture*
information / informations	*information*
conseil / conseils	*advice*

Si l'on souhaite faire référence à un ou plusieurs de ces éléments, il faut utiliser *'a piece of' (a piece of luggage/furniture, two pieces of information/advice)*.

2 Dérivation et composition

a. Dérivation

Les noms, adjectifs et adverbes dérivés sont formés à partir d'un « mot racine » auquel on ajoute un ou plusieurs préfixes (avant la racine) et/ou suffixe(s) (après la racine). Ce principe est très actif en anglais et permet de transformer un nom en adjectif ou en adverbe, un verbe en nom, etc. :

happy → unhappy, happiness, happily
friend → friendly, friendship
play → player, playful

Préfixes		Exemples
sens privatif ou contraire	*a-, anti-, dis-, il-, im-, in-, ir-, mal-, mis-, non-, un-*	*amoral, dislike, illegal, impossible, irregular, misunderstand, unreasonable*
référence temporelle	*after-, neo-, post-, pre-*	*afterthought, postgraduate, premature*
Suffixes		**Exemples**
absence ou approximation	*-less, -ish*	*hopeless, greyish*
activité ou action	*-al, -ation, -ing, -ment*	*arrival, negociation, reading, development*
agent	*- ant, -er, -ess, -or*	*attendant, driver, actress, actor*
catégorie ou nationalité	*-ese, -ian, -ish, -ism, -ist*	*Chinese, Italian, Turkish, capitalism, extremist*
état	*-dom, -hood, -ness, -ship*	*freedom, brotherhood, hopelessness, friendship*
matière ou manière de faire	*-y, -ly*	*silky, softly*

b. Composition

• Les noms et adjectifs composés sont formés de deux éléments. Le deuxième élément est le mot principal ; le premier élément joue le rôle d'adjectif : il vient préciser le sens du deuxième élément et c'est souvent lui qui est accentué (→ *Précis de prononciation p. 212*).

a tea room   *a chat room*   *a living-room*   *a dining room*

• Lorsqu'ils sont formés de deux noms, les noms composés peuvent prendre les formes **NN** *(a raincoat)*, **NØN** *(a golden boy)* ou **N-N** *(a post-office)*.

• Ils peuvent aussi être formés d'un nom et d'une base verbale: **N + BV-er** *(a bus driver)*, **N + BV-ing** *(rock climbing)* ou **BV-ing + N** *(a cleaning woman)*.

LES DÉTERMINANTS DU NOM

3 Articles et adjectifs démonstratifs

Le système des articles en anglais diffère largement du français : comme on ne distingue pas le masculin et le féminin, il n'y a pas d'articles de sens masculin ou féminin. Le choix de l'article ou de l'adjectif démonstratif se fait en fonction :
- du sens que l'on souhaite véhiculer (général ou particulier) ;
- de la catégorie (dénombrable ou non) du nom.

a. Article indéfini *a/an*

Il permet de mentionner UN élément pour la première fois.

Give me a banana, please.   *There was a student in the library.*   *I will buy a bike.*

⚠ **Si le nom commence par une consonne ou par le son [j]** *(university/year)*, **on utilisera l'article** ***a***.
S'il commence par une voyelle ou un «h» non aspiré – qu'on ne prononce pas *(hour/honour/heir)*, **on utilisera l'article** ***an*** (→ *Précis de prononciation p. 214*).
I would like an orange first.   *We have been waiting for an hour.*

Emplois particuliers

- L'article *a* peut aussi faire référence à un élément représentatif d'une classe.

A dog can become dangerous if you don't feed him.
→ Un chien peut devenir dangereux si on ne le nourrit pas.
Everybody needs a computer today.
→ Tout le monde a besoin d'un ordinateur de nos jours.

Ici, on parle d'un chien ou d'un ordinateur en général.

- Contrairement au français, les **noms de métiers** sont toujours précédés de l'article *a*.

He is a baker. *She works as a secretary.*

b. Article défini *the*

Il permet de déterminer UN OU PLUSIEURS éléments particuliers dont on a déjà parlé ou qui sont connus du co-énonciateur. Cet élément peut être caractérisé par :

- Les compléments qui le précèdent ou le suivent :
  The girl I met yesterday *is their niece.* *At the end* of the film, *she started to cry.*
- La situation ou le contexte dans lesquels on se trouve :
  Will you buy me the book? (sous-entendu « le livre dont je t'ai parlé »)
  Give me the salt, please. (sous-entendu « le sel qui est sur la table »)
- Leur unicité, leur spécificité, leur renvoi à la connaissance générale du monde :
  the British anthem, the French government, the Atlantic ocean
  the earth, the sun, the sky, the moon, the internet...

c. Article zéro Ø

Il permet de faire référence à UN ENSEMBLE d'éléments (pluriel de *a/an*) ou à une classe/sous-classe, lorsqu'il est associé à des noms dénombrables pluriels.

Ø Whales are amazing animals. *Ø Babies often cry.* *I am afraid of Ø black cats.*

Lorsqu'il est associé à des noms indénombrables, il a une valeur généralisante.

Ø Money doesn't make happiness. *Ø Freedom is a basic human right.*

Lorsqu'un nom propre est précédé d'un titre ou d'une fonction, il n'y a jamais d'article. Il en va de même pour les noms de pays et les langues.

Ø Queen Elizabeth, *Ø President Obama.* *Ø France is north of Ø Spain.*
Ø Chinese is a lovely language. *I love speaking Ø English.*

d. Adjectifs démonstratifs

Les adjectifs démonstratifs ***this*** (pluriel ***these***) et ***that*** (pluriel ***those***) correspondent aux déterminants français « ce/cet(te)/ces » mais n'ont pas les mêmes caractéristiques.

This/ These	+ qque chose dont l'énonciateur n'a pas encore parlé, qui n'est connu que de lui.	• *This is my new boyfriend. His name is Patrick.* (personne nouvellement présentée) • *Can you lend me this book, please?* (*'this book'* : information nouvelle)
That/ Those	+ qque chose dont l'énonciateur a déjà parlé ou qui est déjà connu du co-énonciateur.	• *Have you heard what happened? Oh yes, I've heard about that story!* (histoire connue du co-énonciateur)

⚠ ***This* et *that* peuvent aussi être pronoms ou adverbes.**
Give me this!
(*'this'* remplace un nom → « Donne moi ceci immédiatement ! »)
He has just found 100 dollars but he does not look that happy.
(*'that'* restreint le sens de *'happy'* → Il vient de trouver 100 dollars mais il n'a pas l'air si heureux que ça)

4 Quantifieurs

Les quantifieurs permettent de spécifier la quantité donnée d'un nom ou d'un groupe nominal. Cette quantité peut être précise, chiffrée, ou plus indicative. Les quantifieurs varient selon la nature (dénombrable ou non) du nom qu'ils déterminent.

	Quantifieurs	Exemples : noms dénombrables	Exemples : noms indénombrables
Quantité nulle	*no* (négation absolue)	*There were no flowers in his garden.* (aucune)	*She has no money to buy a new car.* (pas du tout)
	not any	*There were not any flowers in his garden.*	*She hasn't got any money to buy a new car.*
	none *no one*	*None of them can help me.* (aucun d'eux)	*No one can help me.* (personne)
Petite quantité	*(a) little* (+ sing.)	/	*She has (a) little money on her account* (un peu/ peu de)
	(a) few (+ plur.)	*There were only (a) few flowers in his garden* (quelques/peu de)	/
Grande quantité	*(not) much* *(too) much* (+ sing.)	/	*She has (not) much/ too much money on her bank account* (peu de/ beaucoup de/trop de)
	(not) many *(too) many* (+ plur.)	*There are (not) many/too many flowers in his garden.* (pas de/ beaucoup de/trop de)	/
	a lot of / lots of / loads of / plenty of	*There are a lot of flowers in his garden* (beaucoup de)	*She has a lot of money on her bank account* (beaucoup de)
Quantité non précisée	*Some* - dans un énoncé affirmatif - dans un énoncé interrogatif (on s'attend à une réponse positive)	*Some books are very boring.* (certains) *Did you buy some books at the market?* (des/quelques)	*Give me some money, please.* (de/un peu de) *Would you have some money, please?* (de/un peu de)
	Any - dans un énoncé affirmatif - dans un énoncé interrogatif (on ne sait pas quelle sera la réponse, on demande « à tout hasard »)	*I can read any book, I don't mind.* (n'importe quel) *Did you buy any books at the market?* (des)	/ *Does she have any money?* (de)

	Quantifieurs	Exemples
De l'unité à la totalité	***One***	*Only one guest came to his party.* (un et un seul)
	Both	*Both families were proud of them.* (les deux)
	Each (+ sing.)	*Each child has a right to education.* (chaque)
	Every (+ sing.)	*Every child has a right to education.* (tous/chacun d'eux)
	Nombres précis	*Only three thousand children go to school in his country.* *Hundreds/thousands of children ...*
	Most (+ plur.)	*Most children like sweets.* (la plupart)
	The whole (+sing.)	*The whole village was flooded.* (tout entier)
	All	*All the village(s) was(were) flooded.* (tout, tous)
	Either ... or ***Neither ... nor***	*Either you or your sister can stay*.(soit... soit...) *Neither you nor your sister can stay.* (ni... ni...)

5 Génitif *(...'s)* et adjectifs possessifs

a. Utilisations du génitif

Le génitif indique un lien entre deux personnes, deux objets ou une personne et un objet. Ce lien est marqué par la présence de *« 's »*. Le premier élément détermine le second. Le lien qui unit les deux éléments peut être :

- un lien de propriété : *Mike's bike is broken.* → Le vélo de Mike est cassé.
- un lien de parenté : *I have met Mike's sister.* → J'ai rencontré la sœur de Mike.
- un lien relationnel : *Mike's friends are great!* → Les amis de Mike sont formidables !

NB : On remarquera qu'en français cette relation est souvent marquée par la préposition « de ».

On peut également trouver *« 's »* pour indiquer :

- un repère dans l'espace : *London's musicals are exceptional.* *America's buildings are huge.*
- un lieu : *I went to the baker's.* *I went to my uncle's.*
- un repère temporel : *Today's cars are very expensive.* *Last year's protests were violent.*
- une durée : *After a day's work, I'm always exhausted.* *I have a two-month holiday.*

Lorsque le mot qui précède « *'s* » est au pluriel, on indique uniquement le lien par l'apostrophe *(my cousins' house)*. Par contre, lorsque son pluriel est irrégulier, on maintient « *'s* » *(the children's games)*. Si ce mot est un nom singulier qui se termine par un « *-s* », on pourra ou non maintenir le « *'s* » *(James' book ou James's book)*.

b. Adjectifs possessifs

Les adjectifs possessifs marquent un lien (de possession, mais pas toujours) entre deux éléments.

I	*you*	*he*	*she*	*it*	*we*	*you*	*they*
my	*your*	*his*	*her*	*its*	*our*	*your*	*their*

Ils s'accordent en genre et en nombre avec l'élément auquel ils se rapportent, et non pas avec le nom qui suit comme en français.

Mike likes his aunt very much. *Carla often plays with her brother.*

6 Adjectifs qualificatifs et comparaison

a. Règles fondamentales

• En anglais, les adjectifs qualificatifs sont toujours invariables (ne s'accordent ni en genre, ni en nombre) et sont toujours placés devant le nom, en position épithète, quel que soit leur nombre.

Mary is an intelligent pretty young girl.

• Lorsque plusieurs adjectifs qualifient un même nom, on les place selon un ordre allant du + subjectif au + objectif :

adj. + subjectif ----------- adj. + objectif – nom
opinion / taille / âge / couleur / origine / matière – nom

A nice tall young Asian girl *A beautiful comfortable new silky jersey*

b. Comparatifs et superlatifs réguliers

Comparatif	Superlatif
Il permet de comparer **2 éléments entre eux**. Il existe **3 types** de comparatifs : • le comparatif de supériorité (plus... que) • le comparatif d'(in)égalité [(pas) aussi ... que] • le comparatif d'infériorité (moins... que)	Il permet de comparer **1 élément à tous les autres**. Il existe **2 types** de superlatifs : • le superlatif d'infériorité (le moins...) • le superlatif de supériorité (le plus...).

	Comparatif	Superlatif
infériorité	***less*** + adj. + ***than*** (moins + adj. + que...) *Mary is less selfish than her brother*	***the least*** + adj. (le/la/les moins + adj. ...) *Mary is the least selfish girl I've ever met.*
égalité inégalité	***(not) as*** + adj. + ***as*** [(pas) aussi + adj. + que] *Clara is (not) as tall as her twin sister*	
supériorité	• **Adjectifs longs*** ***more*** + adj. + ***than*** (plus + adj. + que) *The blue car is more expensive than the yellow one.*	• **Adjectifs longs*** ***the most*** + adj. (le/la/les plus + adj. ...) *This blue car is the most beautiful car ever made.*
supériorité	• **Adjectifs courts**** adj. + ***-er*** + ***than*** *The blue car is cheaper than the red one.*	• **Adjectifs courts**** adj. + ***-est*** *This is the cheapest car I've ever bought.*

***Adjectifs longs** (2 syllabes – sauf ceux terminés en *-er*, *-y*, *-ow*, et *-le* ou plus) :
stupid, interesting, wonderful, extraordinary

****Adjectifs courts** (1 syllabe ou de 2 syllabes terminés par *-er*, *-y*, *-ow*, et *-le*) :
big, fat, young, short *clever, pretty, narrow, subtle*

c. Comparatifs et superlatifs irréguliers

	Comparatif	Superlatif
Good	*better*	*the best*
Bad	*worse*	*the worst*
Far	*farther/further*	*the farthest/furthest*

d. Expression de l'accroissement

	Adjectifs courts	Adjectifs longs
De plus en plus...	*Sweets are cheaper and cheaper.*	*Vegetables are more and more expensive.*
De moins en moins...	*Computers are less and less expensive.*	

LES COMPLÉMENTS DU NOM

7 Noms et propositions relatives

• Deux types de propositions relatives permettent de compléter le sens d'un nom :

- les **propositions relatives déterminatives** (ou restrictives)

  The students who had finished left quickly. (a)

- les **propositions relatives non déterminatives**

  The students, who had finished, left quickly.. (b)

La nature de la proposition relative change le sens de l'énoncé. En (a), seuls les étudiants qui avaient terminé sont partis. En (b), il s'agit de tous les étudiants : la relative placée entre virgules n'est qu'un simple ajout d'information.

• On utilise le pronom relatif ***who*** (ou ***that***) si le mot qui précède est sujet de la phrase et renvoie à une personne ; on utilise ***which*** (ou ***that***) si le mot qui précède est sujet ou objet de la phrase et renvoie à de l'inanimé, et ***where*** si le mot qui précède renvoie à un lieu.

⚠ **Parfois (en position objet) le pronom relatif n'apparaît pas et peut être sous-entendu.**
The museum (which/that) I visited was quite old.
The girl (that) I met last week is fantastic!

• Il existe deux autres pronoms relatifs : ***whose*** (qui exprime l'appartenance) et ***whom*** qui est l'équivalent de ***who*** et s'emploie lorsque le mot qui précède est en position objet.

My uncle, whose car broke down yesterday, did not go on holidays.
→ Mon oncle, dont la voiture est tombée en panne hier, n'est pas parti en vacances.

My aunt, whom you met yesterday, lives in London.
→ Ma tante, que tu as rencontrée hier, habite à Londres.

They consulted the lawyer (whom) they had met in London.
→ Ils consultèrent l'avocat qu'ils avaient rencontré à Londres.

⚠ **Attention à la traduction de** « dont » **: en français, il ne renvoie pas systématiquement à l'appartenance.**
L'homme dont je t'ai parlé est ingénieur.
The man (whom) I told you about is an engineer.

⚠ ***Who's*** (= *who is* : « qui est » **ou** *who has* : « qui a ») ≠ ***whose*** (« dont »).

LES SUBSTITUTS DU NOM

8 Pronoms *(personnels, réfléchis, possessifs, réciproques)*

Par définition, les pronoms remplacent les noms auxquels ils font référence (« pro-nom » : « pour le nom »). Il existe 5 catégories de pronoms qui peuvent occuper différentes fonctions dans la phrase :

1. pronoms personnels (sujets)	2. pronoms personnels (compléments)	3. pronoms possessifs	4. pronoms réfléchis	5. pronoms réciproques
I	*me*	*mine*	*myself*	
you	*you*	*yours*	*yourself*	
he	*him*	*his*	*himself*	
she	*her*	*hers*	*herself*	*each other*
it	*it*	*its*	*itself*	*one another*
we	*us*	*ours*	*ourselves*	
you	*you*	*yours*	*yourselves*	
they	*them*	*theirs*	*themselves*	

1 et 2 : Les pronoms personnels sujets et compléments remplacent des noms en position sujet ou complément.

*Mary loves Peter → She loves him (**She** = sujet, **him** = complément)*
Georges broke a vase → He broke it.

En anglais, on n'emploie pas deux fois le pronom sujet. On marque simplement l'insistance à l'oral.
Moi, j'aime vraiment la course à pied → *I really like running.*

Attention à la traduction d'un groupe nominal composé d'un double sujet car le français et l'anglais n'ont pas recours aux mêmes pronoms.
Mon cousin et moi habitons Montpellier → *My cousin and I live in Montpellier.*

3 : Les pronoms possessifs permettent de renvoyer à l'objet possédé en évitant les répétitions.
Don't touch this dress, it's my dress. → Don't touch this dress, it's mine.

4 : Les pronoms réfléchis s'emploient lorsque le sujet et l'objet renvoient à la même personne.
He looked at himself in the mirror (***himself*** = lui-même)
≠ He looked at him in the mirror (***him*** = une autre personne)

- On peut également les utiliser pour insister sur une personne/un objet.
  Pourquoi ne le fais-tu pas toi-même ? → *Why don't you do it yourself?*
- Ils permettent parfois de traduire certains verbes pronominaux.
  Elle s'est blessée → *She hurt herself.*

5 : Les pronoms réciproques expriment l'idée d'un échange, d'une relation entre deux ***(each other)*** ou plusieurs personnes ***(one another)***. Ils indiquent que les sujets concernés agissent l'un envers l'autre. On les emploie souvent dans le cas de verbes pronominaux français.

His uncle and aunt respect each other.
→ Son oncle et sa tante ont du respect l'un pour l'autre.
They all know one another.
→ Ils se connaissent tous.

II — Le groupe verbal

Contrairement au français, l'anglais ne compte que **2 temps** : le passé et le présent.
À ces deux temps s'ajoutent **2 aspects** : *have -en* (auxiliaire *Have* + participe passé) et *be -ing* (auxiliaire *Be* + base verbale *-ing*) qui permettent d'apporter de nombreuses nuances de sens.
Le système verbal anglais n'est donc pas du tout comparable au système français : à un temps grammatical français peuvent correspondre plusieurs formes verbales anglaises et inversement.

Informer	Présent simple/Prétérit
Effectuer un bilan	*have -en:* Present perfect/Past perfect
Justifier Réagir	*be -ing:* Présent *be -ing*/Passé *be -ing* Modalité : auxiliaires modaux
Repérer des faits	Marqueurs temporels : *ago, for, since*

INFORMER

Lorsque l'énonciateur présente des faits à simple titre d'information (pour annoncer ou informer), il utilise le présent simple ou le prétérit.

9 Présent simple et préterit

a. Présent simple

• **Formation** : Base verbale (BV) à toutes les personnes ; *-s* final à la 3e personne du singulier.

• **À la forme négative**, on utilise l'auxiliaire *Do* au présent auquel on ajoute *not* (forme contractée : *n't*). À la forme interrogative, on place l'auxiliaire *Do* devant le sujet. (voir 15)

I/you/we/they work. *He/she/it works.*
I don't work. *Do you work?* *He doesn't work.* *Does he work?*

• **On utilise le présent simple pour** :
1. énoncer des faits
Water boils at 100°C. *The sun rises on the east.* *She likes strawberries.*
2. raconter une histoire (présent de narration)
So he goes to work, and when he comes back, he discovers the truth.
3. renvoyer à un événement à venir
His family arrives at 10 a.m. tomorrow.
Who speaks after Mark? Peter does but then Mary enters the stage.

b. Le prétérit

• **Formation** : BV + *-d* ou *-ed* pour les verbes réguliers.
⚠ Verbes irréguliers *(voir liste p. 204-205)*.

• **On utilise l'auxiliaire** *Do* (*Did* au passé) pour former des énoncés négatifs ou interrogatifs.
I/you/he/she/it/we/you/they worked. *I didn't work.* *Did she work?*

• **On utilise le prétérit**, temps du récit, pour faire référence à une action passée, souvent datée, et révolue. Le prétérit exprime une coupure avec le présent, et dans certains cas avec la réalité (voir 19 prétérit modal). On peut le traduire en français par un passé composé, un passé simple ou un imparfait.
The wolf asked the little girl where she was going to.
→ Le loup demanda à la fillette où elle allait.
When I was younger, I played the violin. → Quand j'étais plus jeune, je jouais du violon.

⚠ ***Used to*** **est uniquement employé pour marquer une rupture totale avec le présent.**
I used to go swimming when I was young → (sous-entendu : « Je ne nage plus »).

EFFECTUER UN BILAN

Lorsque l'énonciateur porte un certain regard sur un événement, notamment lorsqu'il souhaite indiquer les conséquences d'un événement passé sur la situation d'énonciation, il utilise le *present perfect* ou le *past perfect*.

⑩ *Present perfect* et *past perfect*: *have* + participe passé

a. *Present perfect*

• **Formation** : auxiliaire ***have*** **au présent + participe passé** (BV + *-d* ou *-ed*, ou 3e colonne des verbes irréguliers *(voir liste p. 204-205)*.

• Comme ***have*** est auxiliaire, c'est lui qui est conjugué, qui s'accorde avec le sujet auquel il se rapporte, qui porte la marque de la négation ***(not/n't)*** dans les énoncés négatifs et qui est placé devant le sujet dans les énoncés interrogatifs.

I/you/we/they have worked *He/she/it has worked* *I haven't worked* *Has he worked?*

• **On utilise le *present perfect*** pour : présenter le(s) résultat(s) présent(s) d'une action passée, pour faire le bilan d'une situation passée, ou parler d'une action qui a démarré dans le passé et se poursuit au moment où l'on parle. On peut le traduire en français par du passé composé ou du présent.

He has lost his keys. → Il a perdu ses clés. (résultat : il ne peut plus rentrer chez lui)
I have worked here for 3 years. → Je travaille ici depuis 3 ans. (fait toujours d'actualité)

b. *Past perfect*

• **Formation** : auxiliaire ***have*** **au passé + participe passé.**

I/you/he/she/it/we/you/they had worked *We hadn't worked* *Had they worked?*

• Le *past perfect* correspond en général au *present perfect* dans un contexte passé. On l'utilise dans des discours rapportés ou pour effectuer des retours en arrière explicatifs. Il équivaut au plus-que-parfait français.

He told me that they had not come because they were sick.
→ Il m'a dit qu'ils n'étaient pas venus car ils étaient malades.

EXPLIQUER, RÉAGIR

Lorsque l'énonciateur souhaite expliquer, justifier, réagir à une situation il utilise l'aspect ***be -ing***, ou bien les auxiliaires de modalité.

⑪ L'aspect *be -ing*

a. Au présent

• Formation : auxiliaire ***be*** au présent + BV ***-ing***

• Comme ***be*** est auxiliaire, c'est lui qui est conjugué, qui s'accorde avec le sujet auquel il se rapporte, qui porte la marque de la négation ***(not/n't)*** dans les énoncés négatifs et qui est placé devant le sujet dans les énoncés interrogatifs.

I am working. *you/we/they are working.* *he/she/it is working.*
We are not/aren't working. *Are they working?*

• On utilise le présent ***be -ing*** pour:
1. justifier des propos ou une situation
I'm doing my homework, don't disturb me, please!
→ j'explique pourquoi je ne veux pas être dérangé.
I'm going to London next weekend. → j'explique pourquoi je ne serai pas là.
2. réagir à des propos ou à une situation
I'm sorry but I'm not cooking again. → J'en ai assez, j'ai déjà cuisiné hier et avant-hier.
He is always complaining about something. → C'est lassant, il se plaint toujours.

b. Au passé

• Formation : Auxiliaire ***be*** **au passé + BV *-ing*.**
I/he/she/it was working. *you/we/they were working.* *Were they working?*

• On utilise le passé ***be -ing*** lorsqu'on veut expliquer/commenter des faits qui se sont déroulés dans le passé. On peut le traduire en français par un imparfait.
I was reading a novel when my friends called to invite me out.
→ Je lisais un roman lorsque mes amis m'ont appelée pour m'inviter à sortir.
Le passé ***be -ing*** permet de dire ce que je faisais à l'arrivée de mes amis (pour expliquer/justifier ma présence chez moi, ou pour expliquer pourquoi j'étais libre et ai pu accepter l'invitation...).

c. Au *present perfect* et *past perfect*

• L'énonciateur peut choisir de combiner l'aspect ***have -en*** à l'aspect ***be -ing*** au présent ou au passé. Dans ce cas, c'est ***have*** qui est conjugué, qui porte la marque de la négation et qui est inversé dans les énoncés interrogatifs.
They have been working *I haven't been working* *Has she been working?*
We had been working *They hadn't been working* *Had he been working?*

• Le *present perfect* + ***be -ing***, combine la valeur du *present perfect* simple (l'énonciateur fait le constat d'un fait passé) et celle de ***be-ing*** (il explique / justifie / réagit à ce fait passé).
You cough a lot; that's because you've been smoking too much!
→ Tu tousses beaucoup, c'est parce que tu as trop fumé !

• Le *past perfect* + ***be -ing*** correspond à du *present perfect* + ***be -ing*** dans un contexte passé.
I realised you had been smoking too much when I heard you cough.
→ Je me suis rendu compte que tu avais trop fumé quand je t'ai entendu tousser.

12 Auxiliaires modaux

a. Définition et caractéristiques des auxiliaires modaux

• Ils permettent de donner son point de vue sur le lien qui existe entre le sujet et le verbe auquel il est associé, ou sur les chances de réalisation d'un événement.

• Comme les auxiliaires ***do***, ***be*** et ***have***, ils sont suivis de ***not*** dans les énoncés négatifs et sont placés devant le sujet dans les énoncés interrogatifs.
• Toutefois, contrairement à eux, ils n'ont pas de formes conjuguées, ils ont simplement une forme présent et une forme passé (sauf l'auxiliaire ***must***), et ils sont toujours suivis d'une base verbale (jamais suivis de ***to***, de V-***ing*** ou d'un autre modal).

b. Les deux sens des auxiliaires modaux

Auxiliaire modal	Sens 1 Lien sujet - verbe	Sens 2 Chances de réalisation d'un événement
may ***might***	**Permission** *May I open the window?* **Interdiction** *You may not talk to me like that!*	***May:*** **Hypothèse** *She may come or not, I don't know.* ***Might:*** **Hypothèse plus faible** *She might come but only if you invite her.*

Auxiliaire modal	Sens 1 Lien sujet - verbe	Sens 2 Chances de réalisation d'un événement
must *(+ needn't)*	**Obligation/nécessité** *You must work hard or you will fail your exam.* **Interdiction** *You mustn't shout in a church.* ⚠ **Absence d'obligation/nécessité** *You needn't wait so long.*	**Quasi certitude** *She has just got married: she must be so happy!*
can *could*	**Capacité** • au présent : *He can sing, dance and play the guitar at the same time: he is a great artist!* • au passé : *When he was young, he could sing, dance and play the guitar at the same time: he was a great artist!* • au conditionnel : *She could work more, don't you think?* **Incapacité** • au présent : *He cannot run long distances because his knees hurt.* • au passé : *When he was young, he could not run long distances.* **Permission** *You can go out with your friends but only if you come back before 5 p.m.* **Interdiction** *You cannot go out, that's all!*	**Probabilité** • au présent : *We can meet wild animals here, so get prepared!* **Probabilité plus incertaine** • au passé : *We could meet wild animals here but I doubt it.* **Impossibilité certaine** *There cannot be any wild animals here, trust me. There's too much noise.*
will *would*	**Volonté** *Listen to us, will you?* **Refus** *I won't listen to you; your opinion is unacceptable.* **Volonté atténuée** *I would listen to you, but honestly, I have to go.* Je t'écouterais bien mais... **Caractéristique/habitude du sujet (actuelle ou passée)** *He will watch TV endlessly if I don't tell him to stop.* *He would watch TV endlessly when he was a kid.*	**Sens futur** *One day I will go to America!* **Conditionnel (fait irréel)** • présent : *I would travel with him if he wanted to.* Je voyagerais avec lui si... • passé : *I would have travelled with him if he had wanted to.* J'aurais voyagé avec lui si...
shall *should*	**Suggestion (forme interrogative)** *Shall we go to a restaurant tonight?* Et si nous allions au restaurant ? **Conseil** *You should listen to him more.* Tu devrais l'écouter davantage. **Reproche/regret** *You should have listened to him more.* Tu aurais dû l'écouter davantage.	**Probabilité forte** *He should win a lot of money at the lottery.* Il devrait gagner beaucoup d'argent à la loterie.

c. Sens 1 des auxiliaires modaux et équivalents

Il existe des verbes/tournures verbales qui expriment des idées équivalentes à celles véhiculées par les auxiliaires modaux lorsqu'ils sont employés avec le sens 1. Lorsque l'énonciateur utilise ces verbes, il n'exprime alors plus son point de vue, mais énonce un état de fait.

Sens 1	Formes modales	équivalents	Exemples
Capacité/ Incapacité	*can*	*be able to*	• au présent : *He is able to sing, dance and play an instrument at the same time: he is a great artist!* • au passé : *When he was young, he was able to sing, dance and play an instrument at the same time: he was a great artist!*
	cannot	*not be able to* *be unable to*	• au présent : *He is not able to/is unable to run long distances because his knees hurt.* • au passé : *When he was young, he was not able to/he was unable to run long distances.*
Permission/ Interdiction	*can* *may*	*be allowed to*	• *You are allowed to go out with your friends but only if you come back before 5 p.m.* • *Am I allowed to open the window?*
	cannot *may not* *must not* *shall not*	*not be allowed to* *be forbidden to*	• *You are not allowed to go out, that's all!* • *You are not allowed to talk to me like that!* • *It is forbidden to shout in a church.*
Obligation/ Absence d'obligation	*must*	*have to*	• *You have to work hard or you will fail your exam.*
	(+ need'nt)	*don't have to*	• *You don't have to wait so long.*
Volonté/ Refus	*will*	*want to*	
	will not	*don't want to/ not be willing to*	*I am not willing to/don't want to listen to you, your opinion is unacceptable.*

REPÉRER DES FAITS

13 *Ago, for, since*

a. *Ago*

Ago est un adverbe de temps qui renvoie au **passé**.
Il est donc associé à du prétérit + complément de temps.

I left Moscow three years ago → J'ai quitté Moscou il y a trois ans.

b. *For*

For est une préposition qui indique une **durée**.
Elle est souvent (mais pas toujours) associée à du *present perfect*.

We have walked for three hours. It's time to have a rest.
→ Cela fait trois heures que nous marchons, il est temps de faire une pause.
I have walked for three hours before getting to the train station.
→ J'ai marché pendant trois heures avant d'arriver à la gare.

c. *Since*

Since est une préposition qui indique le **début**, le point de départ d'un événement. Elle est souvent associée à du *present perfect* et correspond à la préposition française « depuis ».

I have met him only twice since last March.
→ Je ne l'ai vu que deux fois depuis mars dernier.

PARLER DE L'AVENIR

14 *Will*, présent simple, présent *be -ing*, *be going to* + V

Comme il n'y a pas véritablement de temps « futur » en anglais, l'énonciateur a différents moyens de renvoyer à l'avenir.

Expressions	Valeurs	Exemples
Will	Prédit, prévoit ce qui va se passer indépendamment de la situation présente.	*It will rain tomorrow.*
Présent simple	Informe quelqu'un d'un événement prévu, prédéterminé.	*His train arrives at 3 p.m. tomorrow, so be on time!*
Présent ***be -ing***	Présente l'événement futur comme une explication de la situation présente.	*I'm seeing Mike at 2 p.m. so I can't come with you.*
Be going to + V	Présente l'événement futur comme certain, lié de près à la situation présente.	*It's going to rain, look at those clouds!*

III — La phrase

DE L'ÉNONCÉ SIMPLE…

15 Déclarer, interroger, demander confirmation, répondre

a. Déclarer (affirmations et négations)

Parmi les énoncés déclaratifs, on trouve:

- les **affirmations** qui suivent l'ordre **S (+ Aux.) + V + Complément(s)**.
  Tom has bought a new car. *Mary studied in Los Angeles last year.*
- les **négations** qui suivent l'ordre **S + Aux. + Not + V + Complément(s)**.

Lorsque le verbe est au présent ou au prétérit (sans auxiliaire), on utilise l'auxiliaire ***do*** (***did*** au passé) suivi de la négation ***not***. Si le verbe est déjà accompagné d'un auxiliaire (***have***, ***be*** ou auxiliaire modal), la négation porte directement sur l'auxiliaire.

Tom has not bought a new car. *Mary will not study in Los Angeles next year.*

> ⚠ **Auxiliaire *do* de reprise**
> Parfois, on utilise l'auxiliaire *do* pour reprendre des propos antérieurs en évitant de répéter le verbe, pour marquer l'insistance, ou pour corriger et réaffirmer un fait qui aurait été nié ou mis en doute.
> *He said he would come and he did.* (sous-entendu : *and he did come*)
> *Are you sure you like me? Of course, I do like you!* (valeur d'insistance)
> *Why didn't you go to London? I did go to London!* (correction + réaffirmation)

b. Interroger (*yes/no questions, Wh- questions*, questions brèves)

• Parmi les énoncés interrogatifs, on trouve :

1. **les questions fermées** (ou *yes-no questions*) qui attendent une réponse de type *'yes', 'no', 'maybe'*.

2. **les questions ouvertes** (ou *Wh- questions*) qui attendent une réponse développée avec des informations précises. Toutes deux suivent l'ordre:

(pronom interrogatif) + Aux. + S + V + Complément(s)?

(1) *Did Paul visit the cathedral yesterday?* *Has Tom bought a new car?*
(2) *When did Paul visit the cathedral?* *What has Tom bought?*

Les pronoms interrogatifs commencent tous par *'wh-'* : ***who, what, which, when, where, why, whose, how*** (qui commençait également autrefois par «wh-») et ses composés, ***how much/how many/ how old/how tall/ long/how far/how big/ how often***.

> ⚠ **Lorsque le pronom interrogatif porte sur l'identité du sujet *(who)* OU sur le sujet d'action *(what)*, l'ordre sera :** *Who* + Aux. + V.
>
> *Who is coming?* *Who will work with us?* *What happened?*

• **Les questions brèves** permettent de rebondir sur les propos de quelqu'un en évitant de répéter ce qui vient d'être dit. Pour cela, on reprend simplement l'auxiliaire.

I have never met him. Have you? (sous-entendu : *Have you met him?*)

Elles permettent aussi de marquer la surprise face aux propos qui viennent d'être exprimés.

- *I have worked in a factory for 10 years.*
- *Have you?* (En français, on pourra traduire par « Ah bon ? »)

c. Demander confirmation (*Tag questions*)

Les *Tags*, spécificité anglaise que l'on traduit souvent en français par «n'est-ce pas ?» permettent de demander confirmation de ce qui a été déclaré. Ils transforment une affirmation ou une négation en question.

She is a great actress, isn't she? *She isn't a great actress, is she?*
He can't be his father, can he? *He will sing at the show, won't he?*

(intonation : → voir précis de prononciation p. 213)

d. Répondre

Les réponses brèves permettent de répondre à une question en évitant les répétitions.

- *Have you finished your homework?*
- *Yes, I have. / No, I haven't.*

« moi aussi »	*So* + Aux. + S	• *'I love chocolate.' 'So do I.'* (moi aussi) • *'They went to New York.' 'So did we.'* (nous aussi)
« moi non plus »	***Neither*** + Aux. + S	• *'We haven't gone to Paris.' 'Neither have they.'* (eux non plus) • *'He cannot come.' 'Neither can she.'* (elle non plus)
« moi si » « moi non »	Reprise auxiliaire, forme opposée	• *'I love chocolate.' 'I don't.'* (moi non) • *'We haven't gone to the concert.' 'They have.'* (eux si)

16 S'exclamer, donner des ordres

a. S'exclamer (*What (a)/such (a)* + (Adj.) N, *How/so* + Adj.)

Si l'exclamation porte sur un groupe nominal, on utilise ***What/such (a)*** + Groupe Nominal ; si elle porte sur un groupe adjectival, on utilise ***How/so*** + Groupe Adjectival.

	Groupe nominal		Groupe adjectival
what (a) + adj. + nom (+ S + V)!	*What a pretty girl (she is)!* Quelle jolie fille! *What strong men (they are)!* *What an actress!* *What actors!*	***how*** + adj. (+ S + V)!	*How pretty (she is)!* Comme elle est jolie! Qu'est-ce qu'elle est jolie! *How strong (they are)!*
S + V + ***such (a)*** (+ adj.) + nom	*She is such a pretty girl!* C'est une si jolie fille! *They are such strong men!* *She is such an actress!* *They are such actors!*	S + V + ***so*** (+ adj.)	*She is so pretty!* Elle est si jolie! *They are so strong!*

b. Donner des ordres (impératif)

Formation de l'**impératif** : base verbale ou **impératif négatif** : ***Don't*** + base verbale.

Pars maintenant ! *Leave now!* Ne pars pas maintenant ! *Don't leave now!*

NB : Si l'on souhaite faire une **suggestion**, on utilise l'expression ***Let's*** + base verbale.

Allons au cinéma ! *Let's go to cinema!* Ne les oublions pas ! *Let's not forget them!*

...VERS L'ÉNONCÉ COMPLEXE

17 Rapporter des propos : du discours direct au discours indirect

Comme en français, on utilise le discours indirect pour rapporter les propos de quelqu'un.
Le passage du discours direct au discours indirect implique des changements au niveau de la ponctuation (disparition des guillemets), des pronoms (sujet → complément, ***this*** → ***that***), des adjectifs et pronoms possessifs, des temps (présent → passé) et des adverbes de lieu et de temps (***here*** → ***there*** ; ***yesterday*** → ***the day before*** ; ***tomorrow*** → ***the day after***).
Les propos rapportés sont souvent introduits par la conjonction de subordination *that* et par des verbes tels que ***say, tell, answer, reply, retort, explain...***

Paul: 'I found it here yesterday'
→ Paul said that he had found it there the day before.

Tina: 'I will come with you tomorrow'
→ Tina said that she would come with us the day after.

⚠ **D'autres changements peuvent apparaître selon le type de phrases.**

- **Interrogatives indirectes**

Suppression du point d'interrogation et de l'inversion Aux. + S

Paul: 'Are you eating with us?' → Paul asked me if I was eating with them.

'How many books has she read?' → Paul wondered how many books she had read.

- **Impératifs indirects**

Ajout de *'to'* ou *'not to'* devant le verbe.

Tina: 'Stay here!' → Tina told me to stay there.
'Don't stay here!' → Tina told me not to stay there.

18 Mettre en relief des éléments d'un énoncé

a. Tournures emphatiques *(what ... is // It is... that...)*

• Lorsqu'on présente des faits de manière neutre, sans mise en relief, l'ordre des mots suit le schéma traditionnel S + V + Complément(s) propre aux énoncés déclaratifs.

Prince William studied biology at Eton.

• Si on souhaite mettre en avant une information particulière, on peut réorganiser l'énoncé.

1. *It is/was at Eton that Prince William studied.*
2. *It is/was biology that Prince William studied.*
3. *It is/was Prince William who studied biology at Eton.*

Dans l'exemple 1, l'information *'at Eton'* est mise en relief, dans l'exemple 2, c'est *'biology'* qui est mise en avant et dans l'exemple 3, *'Prince William'*.
Ce type d'énoncés s'appelle une « **clivée** » et suit toujours le même schéma :
It + be **+ information mise en relief +** ***who/that*** **+ proposition**.

• On peut aussi présenter l'information de cette manière :

What Prince William studied is/was biology.

Dans ce cas, l'information mise en avant est celle placée en bout de phrase, ici *'biology'* et le schéma sera : ***What*** **+ proposition +** ***be*** **+ information mise en relief**.

b. Formes passives

An army of 500 troops saved the civilians. (forme active)
1. *The civilians were saved by an army of 500 troops.* (forme passive)
2. *This library has been built recently.*
3. *Girls are said to learn faster than boys.*

Lorsqu'on emploie une forme passive, l'objet de l'action est mis en relief et devient en conséquence sujet de la phrase. On y a recours :

• soit pour mettre l'accent sur la victime ou le bénéficiaire de l'action (1),
• soit parce que la personne à l'origine de l'action (l'agent) est inconnue, évidente, sans importance ou parce qu'on ne souhaite pas la mentionner (2),
• soit pour présenter une généralité, une rumeur, une croyance (3).

Comme on l'observe dans les exemples ci-dessus, l'énoncé prend la forme :

Sujet + ***be*** **+ participe passé du verbe (+ préposition** ***'by'*** **+ agent).**

Be porte la marque du temps et/ou de l'aspect et peut être accompagné d'un modal.

NB : La forme passive est beaucoup plus fréquente en anglais qu'en français. Très souvent, lorsqu'une phrase commence par « on » en français, on la traduira par une forme passive en anglais.

On a cloné de nombreux animaux l'an dernier → *Many animals were cloned last year.*
On m'a dit que tu ne viendrais pas → *I was told that you would not come.*

c. Inversion du sujet

La mise en relief de termes négatifs tels que ***not only, never, hardly*** placés en début de phrase transforme la structure de celle-ci.

Not only did I have to wake up early, but I also had to work hard.

19 Imaginer des faits, exprimer un souhait ou un regret

a. Pour renvoyer à des faits non réels (hypothétiques, imaginés ou souhaités)

On peut avoir recours à des propositions subordonnées en *if*. La condition exprimée par la proposition hypothétique introduite par *if* a pour conséquence le résultat exprimé dans la proposition principale: *'If* X, *then* Y'. La réalisation de Y dépend donc de la réalisation de X.

- **Hypothèse réalisable : *'If* + présent *... will'***

  If he learns the rules (X), *he will play well* (Y).
  If he doesn't learn the rules, he will not play well.

- **Hypothèse plus incertaine : *'If* + prétérit modal *... would'***

  If he learnt the rules, he would play well.

On parle dans ce cas « d'irréel » du présent. La forme prétérit *'learnt'* ne renvoie pas à une action passée mais à une situation souhaitée ou imaginée. Cette coupure avec la réalité est exprimée par le prétérit modal.

- **Hypothèse non réalisée : *'If* + past perfect modal *... would have -en'***

  If he had learnt the rules, he would have played well.

On parle dans ce cas « d'irréel du passé » car les actions ***learn*** et ***play well*** n'ont jamais eu lieu. Comme dans la tournure précédente, la forme *past perfect* ***had learned*** ne renvoie pas ici à une action antérieure au moment passé, mais à une action qui n'a jamais eu lieu.

NB : On remarquera que ces tournures sont comparables au français.
1. S'il apprend les règles, il jouera bien.
2. S'il apprenait les règles (ce qu'il ne fait pas), il jouerait bien.
3. S'il avait appris les règles (ce qu'il n'a pas fait), il aurait bien joué.

b. Pour exprimer un souhait

On peut utiliser le verbe ***wish*** + prétérit modal.

I wish I had more money. *I wish I could win at the lottery next weekend.*

Là encore, *had* ou *could* ne renvoient pas à des situations passées mais à des situations souhaitées, irréelles, en décalage avec la réalité.

c. Pour exprimer un regret

On peut utiliser le verbe ***wish*** + *past perfect modal*.

I wish I had not written that letter.

Ici, ***wish*** renvoie à une action passée que l'on aurait souhaitée autre.

20 Étoffer des énoncés : propositions coordonnées et subordonnées

Lorsqu'on souhaite exprimer une pensée de façon plus riche et plus précise, on peut étoffer les énoncés grâce à des propositions coordonnées ou subordonnées.

a. Propositions coordonnées

Propositions indépendantes, liées entre elles par une conjonction de coordination.

Conjonctions de coordination	Exemples de propositions coordonnées
Cause : ***because, since, for, as***	*He came with us because/since he felt lonely*
Conséquence : ***so, therefore, consequently, as a consequence, thus, that's why***	• *I'm feeling sick, so/thus/therefore I'm going to stay home.* • *He won the lottery, that's why he has bought a new car!*
Choix/alternative : ***or, otherwise, or else***	*You should listen to him, otherwise you will regret it.*
Opposition : ***but, yet, however, nevertheless***	*He's quite rich. Yet, he doesn't spend much money.*
Concession : ***despite, in spite of*** (malgré)	*Despite/in spite of his strength, he can't make it.*

b. Propositions subordonnées:

Propositions liées entre elles par une conjonction de subordination. Leur syntaxe est liée: la proposition subordonnée dépend de la proposition principale. On trouve les propositions subordonnées circonstancielles et les propositions subordonnées complétives.

Propositions subordonnées circonstancielles	Exemples
Temps : ***when*** (lorsque), ***before*** (avant que), ***after*** (après que), ***until*** (jusqu'à ce que), ***as soon as*** (dès que)	• *When he was a child, he used to play badminton.* • *He played tennis until he was 12.* • *As soon as she realised her mistake, she started to cry.*
Simultanéité : ***while*** (pendant que)	• *He cooked the meal while they were washing the dishes.*
Concession/paradoxe : ***(Al)though, even though*** (alors/bien que), ***even if*** (même si)	• *Although/even though she loves him, she doesn't want to marry him.* • *I won't go, even if he asks me to.*
Condition : ***if, provided*** (à condition que), ***unless*** (à moins que)	• *If you work better, you will be rewarded.* • *Unless you work better, you will not be rewarded.*
Opposition : ***whereas/while*** (tandis que)	• *She wanted to go to Nepal whereas/while he wanted to go to Kenya.*
But : ***so that, in order to, so as to***	• *She studied biology in order to/so as to become a doctor.* • *She studied biology so that she could become a doctor.*

⚠ **Contrairement au français, lorsqu'une proposition subordonnée est introduite par *when* et renvoie à une prédiction future, le verbe est conjugué au présent.**

Lorsque je trouverai la réponse, je te le dirai.
When I find the answer, I will tell you.

Lorsque j'aurai trouvé la réponse, je te le dirai.
When I have found the answer, I will tell you.

Les propositions subordonnées complétives sont généralement introduites par la conjonction ***that*** mais cette conjonction est souvent sous-entendue. Elles permettent de compléter le sens d'un verbe (1) ou d'un adjectif (2).

1. *He told me (that) he wanted to go to Barcelona for the summer holidays.*
2. *I was afraid (that) he might refuse to help me.*

21 Exprimer l'action qu'exerce qqu'un sur qqu'un d'autre

Lorsqu'on souhaite exprimer l'action ou l'influence qu'exerce quelqu'un sur quelqu'un d'autre, on peut utiliser les propositions infinitives ou les structures causatives.

a. Propositions infinitives

S + V1 + Complément + *to* + V2

V1: ***allow, advise, ask, expect, force, get, order, prefer, tell, want.***

She wanted her parents to help her. *They asked their neighbour to stop being noisy.*
I will get her to go and see a doctor. *What do you prefer me to do for you?*

b. Structures causatives

S + V1 + Complément + V2

V1: ***make, have***

She made them clean their rooms. → Elle les a obligés à nettoyer leur chambre.
She had the gardener cut off the trees. → Elle a fait couper les arbres par le jardinier.

VERBES À PARTICULES

Rappel

- **Préposition** : mot qui permet d'introduire un complément (de lieu, de temps, de manière).
  He went to Dublin. *The train left at 7 a.m.* *They come from Italy.*
- **Verbe prépositionnel** : verbe qui fonctionne avec certaines prépositions uniquement.
  He is listening to music. *She waited for him.* *We will have to deal with this issue.*
- **Particule** : adverbe de forme identique aux prépositions mais contrairement à elles, il fait partie intégrante du verbe et en modifie le sens. Il peut se placer avant ou après le complément (si c'est un pronom, il se place après).
  Get out now! *He took off his coat./He took his coat off.* *Come in!*

PRINCIPALES PREPOSITIONS ET PARTICULES

about	à propos de, au sujet de, environ	*from*	de (provenance)
after	après	*in*	dans
against	contre	*of*	de (lien)
above	au dessus de	*off*	(arrêt)
across	à travers	*on*	sur (+ marche)
along	le long de	*out*	à l'extérieur de (+ épuisement)
at	à (lieu précis)	*over*	par-dessus
away	loin de	*through*	à travers (+ réussite)
back	derrière (retour)	*to*	à, vers, en direction de
by	par (moyen), près de	*under*	sous
down	en bas	*up*	en haut (+ apparition)
for	pour (destinataire)	*with*	avec

PRINCIPAUX VERBES A PARTICULES

break	*break down:* tomber en panne, rompre *break in(to):* entrer par effraction *break up:* rompre	keep	*keep out:* rester en dehors *keep up:* se maintenir
bring	*bring about:* provoquer *bring over:* amener, apporter *bring up:* élever (des enfants)	look	*look after:* prendre soin de *look back:* regarder derrière soi *look down (on):* regarder en bas, mépriser *look for:* chercher
come	*come in:* entrer *come along:* venir *come out:* sortir	put	*put aside:* mettre de côté *put off:* retarder *put on:* enfiler (un vêtement) *put up (with):* supporter
get	*get along (with):* s'entendre *get away:* partir, s'éloigner *get back:* revenir *get in:* arriver *get off:* sortir (d'un véhicule) *get out:* sortir *get up:* se lever	take	*take after:* ressembler à *take along:* emmener *take away:* emporter *take off:* enlever, ôter
give	*give away:* révéler, distribuer *give back:* rendre *give in:* se résoudre à, céder *give up:* abandonner, renoncer à	turn	*turn down:* refuser, baisser (le son) *turn into:* transformer *turn out:* s'avérer *turn up:* se présenter

base verbale	prétérit	participe passé	Traduction
awake	awoke	awoken	*se réveiller*
be	was / were	been	*être*
beat	beat	beaten	*battre*
become	became	become	*devenir*
awake begin	began	begun	*commencer*
bet	bet	bet	*parier*
blow	blew	blown	*souffler*
break	broke	broken	*casser, briser, rompre*
bring	brought /brɔːt/	brought /brɔːt/	*apporter*
broadcast	broadcast	broadcast	*diffuser (radio, etc.)*
build	built	built	*construire, bâtir*
burn	burnt	burnt	*brûler*
buy	bought /bɔːt/	bought /bɔːt/	*acheter*
catch	caught /kɔːt/	caught /kɔːt/	*attraper, saisir*
choose	chose	chosen	*choisir*
come	came	come	*venir*
cost	cost	cost	*coûter, valoir*
cut	cut	cut	*couper*
deal	dealt	dealt	*distribuer, donner*
do	did /dɪd/	done /dʌn/	*faire*
draw	drew /druː/	drawn /drɔːn/	*1. dessiner ; 2. tirer*
dream	dreamt	dreamt	*rêver*
drink	drank	drunk	*boire*
drive /draɪv/	drove	driven /drɪvən/	*conduire*
eat	ate	eaten	*manger*
fall	fell	fallen	*tomber*
feed	fed	fed	*nourrir*
feel	felt	felt	*1. (res)sentir, se sentir ; 2. toucher*
fight	fought /fɔːt/	fought /fɔːt/	*se battre, combattre*
find	found	found	*trouver*
fly	flew	flown	*voler*
forbid	forbade	forbidden	*interdire*
forecast	forecast	forecast	*prévoir, prédire*
foresee	foresaw	foreseen	*prévoir*
forget	forgot	forgotten	*oublier*
forgive	forgave	forgiven	*pardonner*
freeze	froze	frozen	*geler*
get	got	got	*1. obtenir ; 2. devenir*
give	gave	given	*donner*
go	went /went/	gone /gɒn/	*aller*
grow	grew	grown	*grandir, croître, faire pousser*
have	had	had	*avoir, posséder*
hear	heard	heard	*entendre*
hide /haɪd/	hid /hɪd/	hidden /hɪdən/	*(se) cacher*
hit	hit	hit	*frapper*
hold	held	held	*tenir*
hurt	hurt	hurt	*blesser, vexer, faire mal*
keep	kept	kept	*garder*
know	knew	known	*savoir, connaître*
lead	led	led	*mener, diriger*
learn	learnt	learnt	*étudier, apprendre*
leave	left	left	*1. partir ; 2. quitter*
lend	lent	lent	*prêter*
let	let	let	*1. laisser, permettre ; 2. louer*
lie	lay	lain	*être allongé, être couché*
light /laɪt/	lit /lɪt/	lit /lɪt/	*éclairer, allumer*
lose	lost	lost	*perdre*
make	made	made	*fabriquer, faire*

base verbale	prétérit	participe passé	Traduction
mean	meant	meant	*signifier*
meet	met	met	*rencontrer*
mistake	mistook	mistaken	*se tromper sur*
misunderstand	misunderstood	misunderstood	*mal comprendre*
overcome	overcame	overcome	*surmonter, vaincre*
pay	paid	paid	*payer*
put	put	put	*poser, mettre*
quit	quit	quit	*abandonner, quitter*
read /ri:d/	read /red/	read /red/	*lire*
ride	rode	ridden	*monter cheval, moto, vélo*
ring	rang	rung	*sonner*
rise	rose	risen	*s'élever, se lever*
run	ran	run	*courir*
say	said /sed/	said /sed/	*dire*
see	saw /sɔ:/	seen /si:n/	*voir*
sell	sold	sold	*vendre*
send	sent	sent	*envoyer*
set	set	set	*1. poser ; 2. (se) situer ; 3. fixer (date) ; 4. se coucher (soleil)*
shake	shook	shaken	*1. secouer ; 2. trembler*
shine	shone	shone	*briller*
shoot	shot	shot	*tirer (fusil, arc, etc.)*
show	showed	shown	*montrer*
shut	shut	shut	*fermer*
sing	sang	sung	*chanter*
sink	sank	sunk	*couler, s'enfoncer, sombrer*
sit	sat	sat	*être assis*
sleep	slept	slept	*dormir*
smell	smelt	smelt	*sentir (odeur)*
speak	spoke	spoken	*parler*
speed	sped	sped	*aller vite*
spell	spelt	spelt	*épeler*
spend	spent	spent	*dépenser*
spill	spilt	spilt	*renverser (liquide)*
split	split	split	*(se) séparer*
spoil	spoilt	spoilt	*1. gâcher ; 2. gâter (enfant)*
spread	spread	spread	*1. étaler, étendre ; 2. se répandre*
stand	stood	stood	*se tenir debout*
steal	stole	stolen	*dérober, voler*
stick	stuck	stuck	*coller*
strike	struck	struck	*frapper*
swear	swore	sworn	*jurer*
sweep	swept	swept	*balayer*
swim	swam	swum	*nager*
take	took	taken	*prendre*
teach	taught /tɔ:t/	taught /tɔ:t/	*enseigner*
tell	told	told	*1. dire ; 2. raconter*
think	thought /θɔ:t/	thought /θɔ:t/	*penser*
throw	threw	thrown	*lancer, jeter*
understand	understood	understood	*comprendre*
undertake	undertook	undertaken	*entreprendre*
undo	undid	undone	*défaire*
upset	upset	upset	*1. bouleverser ; 2. renverser*
wake	woke	woken	*réveiller*
wear	wore	worn	*porter (vêtements)*
weep	wept	wept	*pleurer*
win	won /wʌn/	won /wʌn/	*gagner*
withdraw	withdrew /wɪðˌdru:/	withdrawn /wɪðˌdrɔ:n/	*(se) retirer*
write /raɪt/	wrote /rəʊt/	written /ˌrɪtən/	*écrire*

SOMMAIRE

LE RYTHME

L'INTONATION

L'ACCENTUATION

LES PHONÈMES

LE RYTHME

"English is a time-stressed language"

À la différence du français, où toutes les syllabes ont la même importance, l'anglais est une langue accentuée : certaines syllabes sont prononcées plus fortement que d'autres.

❶ Le rythme à l'intérieur du mot

track 60

Prenons le même métier en français et en anglais :

- **photographe** /ˈfɔˈtɒˈgraf/
  en français 3 syllabes qui sont toutes accentuées.
- ***photographer*** /fəˈtɒgrəfə/
  en anglais 4 syllabes dont une seule est accentuée et trois réduites.

❷ Le rythme à l'intérieur de l'énoncé

track 61

Prenons le début classique d'un conte en français et en anglais :

	mots	syllabes	syllabes accentuées	syllabes réduites
Il était une fois sur une île magique...	8	10	10	0
Once upon a time on a magical island...	8	12	5	7

La **réduction** (dans notre exemple 7 syllabes réduites sur 12) est un phénomène **très important** : c'est l'une des **clés** de l'anglais oral. C'est cette réduction qui diminue l'importance des mots non accentués (appelés **formes faibles**) et met en valeur ceux qui sont accentués (**formes fortes**).

Dans une chaîne parlée, les mots réduits ou **formes faibles**, sont parfois difficiles à entendre, car ce sont les mots prononcés plus clairement, les **formes fortes**, qui transmettent les informations principales. Ainsi, si l'on connaît le contexte et que l'on saisit les formes fortes, on peut comprendre un message sans difficulté.

Observons ces deux énoncés en anglais :

track 62

1. *There was a man standing at the corner of the street.*
2. *Large cars waste petrol*

Dans une langue où les **formes fortes** reviennent à **intervalles réguliers**, il y a plusieurs constats importants à faire :

- dans le premier énoncé, il y a des moments d'**accélération** *(there was a / at the / of the)* et des moments de **ralentissement** *(man standing)*. C'est de là que vient l'impression que l'anglais est une « langue rapide » ;
- dans le deuxième énoncé, où on ne trouve que des formes fortes car tous les mots portent le sens, tout est **ralenti** ;
- il faut, en anglais, **autant de temps** pour dire le premier énoncé que le deuxième.

Le rythme de l'anglais provient de cette alternance entre formes fortes et formes faibles.

L'INTONATION

L'intonation est un moyen, propre à la langue orale, de transmettre des informations au-delà des mots. Ces informations sont toujours subjectives et sont le résultat d'un choix opéré par l'énonciateur. Le repérage de l'intonation peut aider à comprendre le sentiment et l'avis de l'énonciateur.

Chaque forme intonative a une fonction différente.

❸ Intonation descendante (↘)

L'énonciateur transmet des informations, souvent factuelles, sans attendre une réponse, une validation ou une confirmation.
Les francophones doivent s'entraîner à faire descendre l'intonation dans ces types d'énoncés pour éviter d'envoyer un message implicite « dites-moi si c'est correct » ou « est-ce la bonne réponse ? ».
On trouve généralement une intonation descendante dans les situations d'énonciation suivantes pour exprimer :

track 63

Situation d'énoncé	Intonation
une affirmation	*'I had an awful day at school.'* (↘) *'I hate Mondays.'* (↘)
une certitude, une vérité, un constat, une déclaration	*'We only have 30 minutes for lunch.'* (↘) *'There's always so much homework'* (↘)
une question ouverte commençant par *'WH'* (l'énonciateur attend une réponse assez prévisible)*	*'What class is your sister in?'* (↘) *'What's your best subject?'* (↘) *'How was your day?'* (↘)

* mais si l'énonciateur n'a aucune idée de la réponse, on pourra aussi imaginer des situations où une question commençant par un mot interrogatif entraîne une intonation finale montante. Par exemple, en parlant d'un problème « insoluble » :

'How did you find the answer ?' (↗)

❹ Intonation montante (↗)

L'énonciateur demande une confirmation, une suite ou un avis. On trouve généralement une intonation montante dans les situations d'énonciation suivantes :

track 63

Situation d'énoncé	Intonation
une incertitude, un doute	*'I think there's a Maths test next week.'* (↗)
des propos inachevés	*'I can't remember what our teacher said, but...'* (↗)
une énumération	*'I've got so much to do - History, French, English...'* (↗)
une question fermée (réponse par *'Yes/No'*)	*'Have you started your revision yet?'* (↗)
une demande de confirmation ou d'information supplémentaire*	*'He said something about our next test, didn't he?'* (↗)

* mais un *tag question* s'utilise parfois pour faire admettre des évidences et des vérités avérées. Dans ce cas, l'intonation finale sera descendante :

'A teacher's life is easier than ours, isn't it?' (↘)

❺ Intonation emphatique et contrastive

■ Emphatique

L'énonciateur peut choisir d'accentuer plus fortement un mot pour transmettre un sentiment, une appréciation ou un point de vue et charger ainsi son énoncé d'implicite :

track 64

'You should see your doctor.' (tu as mauvaise mine)
*'You **should** see your doctor.'* (c'est plus que conseillé)
*'You should **see** your doctor.'* (inutile de lui téléphoner)
*'You should see **your** doctor.'* (pas un docteur qui ne te connaît pas)
*'You should see your **doctor**.'* (pas ton dentiste)

■ Contrastive

L'énonciateur utilise l'intonation pour faire une comparaison entre deux personnes ou choses en insistant plus fortement sur l'un et/ou l'autre de ces deux éléments :

track 65

*'**Your** time-table is much easier than **mine**.'*
*'My **dad** agrees but my **mum** thinks it's an awful idea.'*

❻ Les groupes intonatifs (ou « groupes de souffle »)

Si à l'écrit on trouve des virgules, des points et d'autres signes de ponctuation, la langue orale divise les informations en blocs que l'on appelle en français des **groupes intonatifs** (ou groupes de souffle) et en anglais ***tone units***.

Ces blocs d'informations sont entrecoupés de pauses plus ou moins longues. Dans chaque bloc, un mot (le plus important pour le sens) est accentué plus fortement que les autres.

track 66

A : |*'We went camping again'*|
B : |*'Did you enjoy it ?'*|
A : |*'Yeah!↗ It was great↘* | *As soon as we arrived* | *it started raining.*|
B : |*'It didn't rain* | *all the time ?'*|
A : |*'No,*| *only for a week.*| *But we only stayed*| *for two weeks'.*|

L'ACCENTUATION

❼ Accentuation à l'intérieur du mot

a. La réduction vocalique

track 67

Comparons la prononciation de *Canada* en anglais et en français :

- en anglais, la première syllabe ressort très nettement : *Canada* ;
- en français, les trois syllabes ont une importance égale : Canada.

Dans les transcriptions phonétiques, la syllabe accentuée est précédée par le signe ˈ :
Canada s'écrirait donc /ˈkænədə/.

L'une des caractéristiques essentielles de l'anglais oral concerne la façon de faire ressortir la syllabe accentuée : **c'est en réduisant l'importance des syllabes non accentuées que la syllabe accentuée ressort tout naturellement** ; ce phénomène s'appelle la **réduction vocalique**.

La première syllabe de ***Ca**nada* ressort parce que l'on réduit les deux autres : /ˈkænədə/.

track 68

⟶ À vous

Entraînez-vous à prononcer les noms des pays suivants en respectant la syllabe accentuée (ici soulignée) et la réduction des syllabes non accentuées.

Algeria, America, Brazil, Bulgaria, China, Germany, Holland, Hungary, India, Italy, Jamaica, Japan, Kenya, Morocco, Poland, Portugal, Sri Lanka, Sweden, Switzerland, Tunisia, etc.

On peut dresser une liste de terminaisons neutres (qui se trouvent à la fin de beaucoup de mots de plusieurs syllabes en position non accentuée) avec leur prononciation :

track 69

Terminaisons neutres	Prononciation	Exemples
-er / -or	[ə]	*sister, brother, later, author, better daughter, etc.*
-age	[ɪdʒ]	*cottage, village, manage, damage, cabbage, etc*
-et	[ɪt]	*carpet, ticket, basket, pocket, bracket, cricket, etc.*
-est	[ɪst]	*biggest, smallest, harvest, forest, interest, etc*
-ness	[nəs]	*darkness, madness, loneliness, dirtiness, etc.*
-less	[ləs]	*hopeless, useless, heartless, luckless, etc.*
-able/ -ible	[əbəl]	*capable, readable, avoidable, feasible, etc.*
-ful	[fəl]	*useful, handful, hopeful, successful, thoughtful, etc.*

8 Accentuation et nature du mot

La majorité des mots en anglais sont accentués sur la première syllabe : *kitchen, cupboard, garden, vehicle*, etc. Les exceptions sont de deux ordres.

a. Les préfixés

Les mots commençant par un préfixe *(a-, be-, com-, de-, mis-, re-, sur-, in-, im-, ex-, etc.)* ont une très grande tendance à ne pas accentuer le préfixe et à retenir la deuxième syllabe pour l'accentuation : *propose, expose, impose, suppose, etc.*

Beaucoup de **préfixés** en anglais comportent seulement **deux syllabes** et sont à la fois **nom** et **verbe**. On peut les diviser en **trois** catégories :

track 70

- la très grande majorité est accentuée sur la deuxième syllabe (o ˈO) :
  address, attack, control, debate, defeat, divide, regret, repeat, report, respect, result, reply, return, support, surprise...

track 71

- un nombre limité d'exceptions est accentué sur la première syllabe (ˈO o) :
  combat, comfort, comment, distance, envy, exit, offer, outline, pardon, profit, promise, rescue
- les « **paires alternantes** » : certains mots de deux syllabes sont à la fois noms et verbes.

- en tant que **nom**, ces mots s'accentuent ˈO o,
- et en tant que **verbe** o ˈO :

track 72

→ À vous

Entraînez-vous à prononcer chacun des mots ci-dessous, une première fois en tant que nom, une deuxième fois en tant que verbe, en respectant la bonne accentuation dans les deux cas :

addict, conflict, contract, contrast, convict, escort, exploit, export, extract, increase insult, object, present, progress, project, protest, rebel, record, subject, suspect

Vérifiez en écoutant l'enregistrement.

b. Les mots à « terminaison contraignante »

Certaines terminaisons orthographiques déterminent la place de l'accentuation, par exemple, les mots se terminant par *-ion, -ic, -ity*.

Les noms

terminaisons	place de l'accentuation	exceptions
-ade	*lemonade*	*marmelade, decade*
-ese	*Chinese, Japanese*	–
-ee, -oo	*refugee, tattoo*	*coffee, toffee*
-esse, -ette	*finesse, cassette*	*cigarette, clarinette*
-ion, ian	*education, librarian*	*television*
-ity, -ety	*electricity, society*	–
-ogy, -ophy, -omy	*biology, philosophy, economy*	–
-osis, -itis	*diagnosis, appendicitis*	–

Les adjectifs

- La terminaison *-ic (ironic, symbolic)* : elle place l'accentuation sur la syllabe qui la précède.
- Autres terminaisons courantes pour les adjectifs : *-al, -ent, -ant, -ar, -ous*.

À part quelques exceptions, quand la terminaison est précédée d'une seule consonne, on trouve l'accentuation à **deux** syllabes avant la fin de l'adjectif (exemples : *tolerant, original, generous*).

- Quand la terminaison est précédée de deux consonnes ou d'une consonne + une voyelle, l'accentuation se place sur l'avant-dernière syllabe (exemples : *reluctant, delicious, peculiar*)

track 73

→ À vous

Entraînez-vous à prononcer les adjectifs suivants en respectant la syllabe accentuée et la réduction des syllabes non accentuées :

competent, criminal, dangerous, enormous, ignorant, important, intelligent, militant, parental, popular, principal, religious, ridiculous, sentimental, suspicious, universal, etc.

Vérifiez en écoutant l'enregistrement.

Les adverbes

Le suffixe adverbial *-ly* ajoute une syllabe à un adjectif :

(final → finally, happy → happily...) mais **ne modifie pas le schéma accentuel.**

Sauf pour les adjectifs se terminant en *-ary* :

('necessary → ˌneces'sarily, 'primary → ˌpri'marily...)

■ Les verbes

Les verbes ont souvent une terminaison forte, c'est-à-dire un son voyelle assez fort tel que *-ate, -fy, -ize, -ute*.

Dans les verbes de trois syllabes ou plus, ces terminaisons fortes repoussent l'accentuation à deux syllabes avant la terminaison :

track 74

*com**mu**nicate, an**ti**cipate, **re**cognize, **sa**tisfy, **ex**ecute...*

Dans les verbes de deux syllabes par contre, ces terminaisons fortes retiennent généralement l'accentuation :

*cre**ate**, frus**trate**, re**ply**, sur**prise**, sa**lute**...*

9 Accentuation secondaire

Nous avons déjà vu (« Le rythme » page 207) que l'anglais oral se caractérise par une alternance entre forme pleine (O) et forme réduite (o).

Aucun mot, et ceci sans exception, ne peut commencer par deux syllabes réduites.

Le schéma accentuel o o **O** en début d'un mot **est donc impossible**.

Pour éviter de commencer par deux syllabes réduites, la première reçoit une accentuation secondaire (accentuation un peu moins forte que l'accentuation principale) qui est signalée dans les transcriptions phonétiques par un tiret vertical qui se place en bas (ˌ) avant la syllabe recevant l'accentuation secondaire.

track 75

kangaroo /ˌkæŋgəˈruː/ [O o **O**]

refugee /ˌrefjuˈdʒiː/ [O o **O**]

afternoon /ˌæftəˈnuːn/ [O o **O**]

La terminaison ***-tion*** se trouve souvent aussi sur la troisième et parfois sur la quatrième syllabe d'un mot. On trouve dans ce cas une accentuation secondaire sur la première ou deuxième syllabe :

education /ˌedjuˈkeɪʃən/ [ˌO o ˈ**O** o]

communication /kəˌmjuːnɪˈkeɪʃən/ [o ˌO o ˈ **O** o]
(ici l'accentuation secondaire se place sur la syllabe accentuée dans le dérivant *com**mu**nicate*).

10 Accentuation à l'intérieur de l'énoncé

a. Formes fortes et formes faibles

À l'intérieur de l'énoncé, l'anglais oral privilégie toujours les mots qui véhiculent le sens. Ces mots que l'on appelle souvent les « **formes fortes** » doivent ressortir clairement et distinctement.

Pour cela :

- on retient la forme pleine du mot, c'est-à-dire de sa syllabe accentuée ;
- on « réduit » les mots, souvent grammaticaux, qui ne véhiculent pas le sens, appelés les « formes faibles ». En voici un exemple qui vient de Unit 7 *Utopia* :

- en **gras** les syllabes à faire ressortir (les formes fortes),
- en rouge les mots à réduire (les formes faibles).

track 76

"I **think** I **know** what you **mean**. You **think** that **I** have **done** you a **service**; so you **feel** yourself **bound** to **give** me **something** which I am **not** to **give** to a **neighbour**, **unless he** has **done something special** for **me**. I have **heard** of this **kind** of **thing**; **but pardon** me for **saying**, that it **seems** to **us** a **troublesome** and **roundabout custom**; and we **don't know** **how** to **manage it**."

Il existe quelques situations où les formes faibles (souvent des mots grammaticaux) doivent être accentuées.

b. L'emphase

track 77

La forme pleine permet d'insister :

'Maybe you didn't see me, but I ***was*** *there.'*

c. La négation

Une forme négative apporte une information importante dans un énoncé, elle est donc accentuée :

track 78

1. *'His sister can swim very well'*
2. *'His sister* ***can't*** *swim very well'*

d. Les « mots isolés » ou *stranding*

Beaucoup de mots, de par leur fonction grammaticale, sont destinés à être suivis d'un complément d'information (modal + base verbale, préposition + nom, etc.). Dans ce cas, ils sont réduits :

track 79

'He was waiting for the bus'

- ***was*** est normalement suivi d'une forme verbale. Il est donc réduit en /wəz/
- ***for*** est normalement suivi d'un nom. Il est aussi réduit, ici en /fə/

track 80

'I don't know what he was waiting ***for*** *but he was later than I* ***was****'*

Ici, on retrouve ***for*** et ***was*** (à la fin) dans une position « d'isolement » (en anglais ***stranding***) où ils ne sont plus suivis de leur complément logique. C'est dans ce cas qu'ils sont réalisés avec une forme forte : ***was*** /wɒz/ et ***for*** /fɔː/.

LES PHONÈMES

Le phonème est à l'oral ce qu'est la lettre orthographique à l'écrit. Il est important de faire une distinction claire entre les lettres orthographiques (ce qu'on lit et écrit) et les phonèmes (ce qu'on entend et prononce). On va donc respecter le code <lettre> et /son/ et on pourra dire, par exemple, que <ch> se prononce /ʃ/ en français (cher) mais /tʃ/ en anglais *(cheese)*.

Tout comme à l'écrit, il y a des consonnes et des voyelles.

On trouve en anglais :
- 24 phonèmes consonnes (20 en français)
- 20 phonèmes voyelles (16 en français)

11 Les consonnes : voisées et non voisées

Il suffit de se couvrir les oreilles et de prononcer /s/ suivi de /z/ ou /f/ suivi de /v/ pour entendre un bourdonnement. On remarque aussi ce phénomène de vibration en mettant les doigts sur les cordes vocales. On constate donc que les cordes vocales vibrent avec certaines consonnes (**voisées**) alors que d'autres se prononcent sans les cordes vocales (**non voisées**).

track 81

NON VOISÉES		VOISÉES	
p	*pin, apple, cheap*	**b**	*bin, able, club*
t	*time, fifteen, eat*	**d**	*dream, garden, bed*
f	*free, physics, laugh*	**v**	*very, evening, dive*
k	*kit, quit, back*	**g**	*green, English, bag*
s	*swim, centre, bus*	**z**	*zero, buzz, dogs*
ʃ	*fashion, nation*	**ʒ**	*measure, vision*
θ	*three, author, bath*	**ð**	*this, mother, bathe*
tʃ	*China, match, nature*	**dʒ**	*John, age, soldier*
		l	*live, hello, feel*
		m	*many, summer, dumb*
		n	*no, know, any, alone*
		ŋ	*sing, young, thanks*
		r	*ring, sorry, marriage*
		w	*window, when*
		j	*you, young, uniform*
h	*here, hard, who*		

Quelques consonnes posent problème aux francophones :

- **La lettre <h>** existe bien sûr en français. On ne l'entend pas mais elle manifeste néanmoins sa présence, par exemple : le haricot, le héros, le hibou mais l'habitude, l'héroïne, l'hippopotame...

En anglais, la lettre orthographique <h> est toujours prononcée /h/ au début d'un mot sauf dans *hour, honour, honest* et *heir*. Comme en français, c'est la raison pour laquelle on a :

> *a hero, a house, a happy hitch-hiker* mais *an hour, an heir,*
> *an honourable person, an honest offer, etc.*

- **<th>** : en anglais pour bien prononcer /θ/ *(three, thin, think...)* et /ð/ *(the, this, there...)*, il faut que le bout de la langue empêche les dents de se fermer.

Une consonne « voisée » a tendance à entraîner naturellement une autre consonne « voisée » :

> *exact* : le < x > se prononce **/gz/** (deux consonnes « voisées »)
> *taxi* : < x > se prononce **/ks/** (« non voisées »)

C'est ce phénomène qui explique la prononciation des :

- pluriels : *cats* /ts/, *dogs* /gz/...
- génitifs : *Eric's* /ks/, *Dave's* /vz/...
- formes verbales se terminant en <ed> : *worked* /kt/, *lived* /vd/...

12 Prononciation du <ed>

Les verbes en anglais **ne se conjuguent pas** mais se signalent à l'oral de différentes façons :

- la terminaison verbale <ed> se prononce /t/, /d/ ou /ɪd/ ;
- lorsqu'il ne s'agit plus de suffixe verbal, le <ed> revient à une prononciation syllabique /ɪd/.

Dans ce cas, il s'agit d'un adjectif que l'on trouve dans : *wicked, wretched, naked, sacred, crooked...*

13 Les voyelles

a. Les mots repères

Il y a 20 sons voyelles en anglais. Leur prononciation peut varier d'un pays à l'autre (États-Unis, Australie, Canada, etc.) ou d'une région à l'autre (nord et sud du Royaume Uni, etc.).

Malgré les différents accents, ces sons voyelles présentent certaines caractéristiques invariables. Il est donc très utile de s'entraîner à associer le son voyelle des mots au mot repère du tableau situé sur le rabat II de la couverture de votre manuel. C'est ainsi que l'on peut associer :

track 82

love		*cup*
want		*clock*
law	***is the same sound as***	*door*
parent		*chair*
most		*snow*
danger		*day*

→ *À vous*

Entraînez-vous à trouver le mot repère qui correspond au son voyelle accentué de ces mots :

dive, hope, some, race, blue, great, come, wood, meat, catch, tent, with, where, teacher, money, person, people, country, daughter...

b. Voyelles longues, voyelles courtes

Lopposition entre les voyelles dites **« longues »** et **« courtes »** est une caractéristique de l'anglais oral. Il est important de bien marquer la distinction entre ces « paires » car une confusion peut être l'origine d'un changement de sens et donc d'une incompréhension.

track 83

'Don't hit it, heat it!'
'Look at the heel, not the hill!'
'What a cheek ! What a chick!'

'Look at the heel, not the hill!'

c. Les diphtongues

Les diphtongues constituent une autre particularité de l'anglais oral. Il y en a 8 mais les plus fréquentes sont celles que l'on trouve dans *day, eye, snow* et *cow*.

Références iconographiques

Couverture : Philippe Brault / Agence VU - **6, 12 :** The Right Image / Wildlight - **14, hg :** Gardel Bertrand / hemis.fr - **15, b** : Catalin Petolea / Fotolia.com ; **bd :** Eli Jamei / Corbis ; **bg :** Image Source / Getty Images ; **bm :** Joson / Corbis ; **h :** Biosphoto / Mike Leonard / Auscape - **16, b :** Mitch Reardon / Getty Images ; **hg :** Biosphoto / Jean-Paul Ferrero / Auscape ; **hm :** Catherine Karnow / Corbis - **17, b :** "Honey Ant Hunt" by Tim Leura Tjapaltjarri © Estate of the artist 2011 licensed by Aboriginal Artists Agency / National Museum of Australia, Camberra ; **h :** Nick Haslam / Alamy - **18, b :** ZSSD / Getty Images - **19, hd, bm :** "Working Together" by Jennifer Taylor ; **hg, bd :** "Mulga Tree Seed Dreaming" by Lyndsay Bird Mpetyane, Central Art - Aboriginal Art Store - **20 :** Paul Almasy / Corbis - **21 :** Lonely Planet Images / Alamy - **24 :** Liba Taylor / Corbis - **25, bd :** Maria Taglienti-Molinari / Getty Images ; **bg :** AnnCuttingSelect / Alamy ; **hd :** Australian Government, Aboriginal Tourism Australia ; **md :** Derek Latta / Getty Images - **6, 26 :** plainpicture / Folio Images - **28, bg :** Jose Luis Pelaez, Inc. / Corbis ; **hd :** Facebook.com ; **hg :** Cortesia / AFP - **29, 1 :** Bebo.com ; **2 :** Librarything.com ; **3 :** Linkedin.com ; **4 :** Twitter.com ; **5 :** Reproduced with permission of Yahoo! Inc. © 2011 Yahoo! Inc. FLICKR and the FLICKR logo are registered trademarks of Yahoo! Inc. ; **h :** The Nielsen Company - **30, b :** Joshua Grigby (oil on canvas) by Thomas Gainsborough (1727-88)Private Collection/Photo © Agnew's, London, UK/ The Bridgeman Art LibraryNationality - **h :** Lana Sundman / Alamy - **31, bd :** www.CartoonStock.com ; **bg :** www.joyoftech.com - **32 :** Raul Arboleda / AFP - **33, bd :** © Greenpeace ; **bg :** With permission of Vision Forum Ministries ; **bm :** WireImage / Getty Images - **35 :** www.CartoonStock.com - **38 :** David Horsey, Hearst Newspapers - **6, 40 :** Ladd Co / Warner Brothers / The Kobal Collection - **42 :** www.zazzle.com - **43, bd :** Bettman / Corbis ; **bg :** Reuters / Corbis ; **hg :** Getty Images ; **mg :** NY Daily News via Getty Images - **44 :** Collection ChristopheL - **47, bd :** DC Comics ; **hg :** Paramount / The Kobal Collection - **48 :** Collection ChristopheL - **52, h :** Photodisc / Getty ; **m :** Gio Barto / Getty Images - **53, bd :** Universal / The Kobal Collection ; **bg :** 20TH Century Fox / Dreamworks / The Kobal Collection ; **hd :** Sunrgia - **8, 54 :** Heeb Christian / hemis.fr - **54, hd :** Damon Miller / Fotolia.com - **56, 1 :** VisionsofAmerica / Joe Sohm / Getty Images ; **2 :** Du Boisberranger Jean / hemis.fr ; **3 :** François Le Diascorn / Rapho ; **4 :** Aurélia Galicher ; **hg :** f 1.2 / Alamy - **57, bd :** Weijmans Media Group – Helmond, the Netherlands / Sunshine Photo ; **hg :** *Route 66* by Luning, Jim. Copyright 2011 in the format Textbook via Copyright Clearance Center. - **58, bd :** Raymond Forbes / Age Fotostock ; **hd :** David Robert Eastley / Alamy ; **hg :** Holger Leue / AGE ; **md :** Car Culture / Getty Images ; **mg :** Aurélia Galicher - **59, b :** Sashkin - Fotolia.com ; **h :** Peter Turnley / Corbis - **60, 61, bg :** Paul Edmondson / Getty Images ; **hd :** Richard Lee / http://westernswingsummer2010.blogspot.com - **60, mm :** Stuckey's Corporation - **61, bg, bd :** John Elk III / AGE ; **hg, bd :** Yasushi Akimoto amanaimages RF / Getty Images - **63 :** Bettmann / Corbis - **64 :** Heritage Images / Leemage - **65, d :** Caro / Alamy ; **g :** John Elk III / Alamy ; **m :** Jack Sullivan / Alamy - **68 :** Front cover of ON THE ROAD by Jack Kerouac (Penguin Books, 1972, 2000). Copyright © Jack Kerouac, 1955, 1957. - **69, 1 :** François Le Diascorn / Rapho ; **2 :** Bagdad Café ; **3 :** Jean-Marc GIBAOUX / GAMMA ; **4 :** Heeb Christian / hemis.fr ; **5 :** Richard Cummins / Alamy - **71, b :** Bettmann / Corbis ; **h :** Theo Allofs / Corbis - **8, 72 :** Sunrgia - **74 :** Getty Images / AFP - **75 :** From the "How to Be Bristish Collection" © LGP, Brighton, UK, www.lgpcards.com - **77 :** Jupiterimages - **79, b :** Foodfolio / AGE ; **h :** John Lund / Matt Holmes / Blend Images / Corbis - **81, b :** Stewart Ferguson / Camerapress / Gamma ; **h :** Chad Ehlers / Getty Images - **8, 88 :** AP / Sipa - **90 :** Popperfoto / Getty Images - **91, b** : Rue des Archives / BCA ; **h :** www.illdigital.com - **92, 93 :** Bettman / Corbis - **93, b :** Photo by Mike Keckhaver / Courtesy of Encyclopedia of Arkansas History and Culture - **94 :** Sean Qualls - **96 :** Rebecca Feind - **97, b :** Jess Hurd / Report Digital - Rea ; **h :** Thomas MacMillan/New Haven Independent - **99, b :** Bettman / Corbis ; **h :** The Granger Collection NYC/Rue des Archives - **103 :** Bettman / Corbis - **104, b :** Getty Images ; **h :** Wilfredo Lee / AP / Sipa - **105, bd** : Bettmann / Corbis ; **bg :** *Tuscaloosa News*, 05/11/2008 - **8, 106 :** Luc Schuiten, Archiborescence - **108 :** OutreachMedia, Auroville. Photographe : Dominique Darr - **109, b :** OutreachMedia, Auroville. Photographe : John Mandeen ; **h :** www.auroville.org - **110 :** Chris Maluszynski / Moment / Agence VU - **111 :** Doyle Yoder - **113, b :** David Muir / Masterfile - **114 :** *The Giver* by Loïs Lowry, HarperCollins 2008 - **115 :** Lucy Lou - **116 :** africanpictures / akg-images - **118 :** Jack Sullivan / Alamy - **120 :** www.CartoonStock.com - **121 :** Wouter van den Bos / Danube Foundation - **10, 122 :** www.angelacatlin.com - **124, h :** Paul McErlane / Alamy - **125, b :** Stephen Saks Photography / Alamy ; **h :** NBC Universal - **127, b :** James Nachtwey ; **h :** REUTERS / Paul McErlane - **128, b :** The Wave, 1917 (oil on canvas) by Christopher Richard Wynne Nevinson (1889-1946) © Yale Center for British Art, Paul Mellon Fund, USA // The Bridgeman Art Library ; **m :** Geray Sweeney / Corbis - **129 :** IIC / Axiom / Getty Images - **130 :** Belfast Telegraph - **132 :** Abaca / PA - **133 :** AntipasM / Alamy - **134 :** Stephen Saks Photography / Alamy - **135 :** H. & D. Zielske/Look/Photononstop - **10, 136 :** "From Time Magazine, 3/10/1997 © 1997 Time Inc. Used under license" - **138, bd :** Luis Domingo / AGE ; **hd :** BBC Motion Gallery ; Science Photo Library RF / AGE ; **139, h :** Jim Incledon / Newsteam / Sipa - **140, bg :** Getty Images ; **hd :** Kevin Wheal / Alamy ; **hg :** Evening News / Associated Newspapers Ltd - **141, b :** flashpics - Fotolia.com ; **h :** ABCNews.com - **142 :** "Vintage Book Jacket" copyright © 2006 by Vintage Book, a division of Random House, Inc., from NEVER LET ME GO by Kazuo Ishiguro. Used by permission of Alfred A. Knopf, a division of Random House, Inc. - **143, bd :** www.CartoonStock.com ; **bg :** www.CartoonStock.com - **145, bd :** "From Newsweek, March 1997 © 1997 The Newsweek / Daily Beast Company LLC. All rights reserved. Used by permission and protected by the Copyright Laws of the United States. The printing, copying, redistribution, or restransmission of the Material without express written permission is prohibited." - **151, h :** Fuse / Getty Images - **152, b :** MAD architects, Beijing ; **h :** Xinhua / Zuma / Réa - **153, b :** Yousuf Karsh / Camerapress / Gamma ; **h :** Collection ChristopheL - **10, 156 :** Collection ChristopheL - **158 :** andibyte - Fotolia.com - **159, h :** Collection ChristopheL - **160 :** Collection ChristopheL - **163, b :** Ocean / Corbis ; **h :** Collection ChristopheL - **164 :** Creative Studio Heineman / Getty Images - **170 :** Owaki / Kulla / Corbis - **171 :** Maukun - Fotolia.com ; **154 :** Philippe HUPP / GAMMA ; **155 :** DC Comics, Promethea Book 4, Chapter 5, 2002

Références des textes

14 : Jewel Topsfield / Courtesy of *The Age* - **18 :** *The Songlines* © Bruce Chatwin 1987 published by Random House UK - **30 :** Christine Rosen, « Virtual Friendship and the New Narcissism », *The New Atlantis* (2007) - **32 :** *The Facebook Effect* Copyright © 2010 by David Kirkpatrick first published by Simon and Schuster - **44 :** *The Last Don* Copyright © Mario Puzo, 1996, reissued by Arrow Books 2009 - **46 :** *My Only Son*, Christopher Gambino, Nicole Productions 2004 - **60 :** Written by Felicia Fairchild, Executive Director, Saugatuck-Douglas Convention & Visitors Bureau, Saugatuck, Michigan - **62 :** "Chapter 12", from THE GRAPES OF WRATH by John Steinbeck, copyright 1939, renewed © 1967 by John Steinbeck. Used by permission of Viking Penguin, a division of Penguin Group (USA) Inc. - **70 :** "The Road Not Taken" from the book THE POETRY OF ROBERT FROST edited by Edward Connery Lathem. Copyright © 1969 by Henry Holt and Company. Reprinted by permission of Henry Holt and Company, LLC. - **71 :** Reprinted by permission of SLL/Sterling Lord Literistic, Inc. Copyright 1955, by Jack Kerouac. Copyright renewed by Stella Kerouac, 1983. Copyright renewed by Stella Kerouac and Jan Kerouac, 1985. - **74, 75 :** http://www.cultureshocksblog.us/; http://nclrc.org/cultureclub/ - **76 :** "Knopf Book Cover" copyright © 2004 by Alfred A. Knopf, a division of Random House, Inc., from THE LOVE WIFE by Gish Jen. Used by permission of Alfred A. Knopf, a division of Random House, Inc. - **78 :** Excerpt from INTERPRETER OF MALADIES by Jhumpa Lahiri. Copyright © 1999 by Jhumpa Lahiri. Reprinted by permission of Houghton Mifflin Harcourt Publishing Company. All rights reserved. - **80 :** "Letter of Mother" by Chenjerai Hove, excerpt from "Stavanger City of Culture", Stavanger, Norway - **90 :** From The New York Times, 19th October © 1968 The New York Times. All rights reserved. Used by permission and protected by the Copyright Laws of The United States. The printing, copying, redistribution, or retransmission of this Content without express written permission is prohibited. - **92 :** *A Mighty Long Way* © 2009 by Carlotta Walls LaNier published by One World Book - **93 :** From The New York Times, 24th September © 1957 The New York Times. All rights reserved. Used by permission and protected by the Copyright Laws of The United States. The printing, copying, redistribution, or retransmission of this Content without express written permission is prohibited. - **94 :** *Warriors don't cry*, Orginal edition copyright © 1994 by Melba Beals, Simon and Schuster - **95 :** From *Sula by* Toni Morrison, published by Chattao and Windus. Reprinted by permis-sion of The Random House Group Ltd. - **96 :** Excerpted material from *Silent Gesture* by Tommie Smith. Used by permission of Temple University Press. © 2007 by Temple University. All Rights Reserved. - **100 :** Copyright Guardian News & Media Ltd 2008 - **102 :** From The New York Times, 17th October © 2005, The New York Times. All right reserved. Used by permission and protected by the Copyright Law of the United States. The printing, copying, redistribution, or retransmission of this Content without permission is prohibited. - **107 :** From ROSA PARK: MY STORY by Rosa Parks with Jim Haskins, copyright © 1992 by Rosa Parks. Used by Permission of Dial Books for Young Readers, A Division of Penguin Young Readers Group, A Member of Penguin Books (USA) Inc., 345 Hudson Street New York, NY 10014. All rights reserved. - **109 :** www.auroville.org - **110, 111 :** Mission to Amish People - **114 :** Excerpt from THE GIVER by Loïs Lowry. Copyright © 1993 by Loïs Lowry. Reprinted by permission of Houghton Mifflin Harcourt Publishing Company. All rights reserved. - **126 :** Extract from "The Wall Reader" by Fiona Barr, Daniel J. Casey, Stories by Contemporary Irish Women (Syracuse: Syracuse University Press, 1990.) - **128:** Excerpt from THE CURE AT TROY: A VERSION OF SOPHOCLES' PHILOCTETES by Seamus Heaney. Copyright © 1990 by Seamus Heaney. Reprinted by permission of Farrar, Straus and Giroux, LLC. - **138 :** Telegraph Media Group Limited 2008 - **139 :** Content by Hugh Collins © 2010 AOL Inc. Used with permession. - **141 :** ABCNews.com - **142 :** *Never Let me Go*, Kuzuo Ishiguro, Faber and Faber Ltd - **144 :** BRAVE NEW WORLD by Aldous Huxley. © 1932, 1946 by Aldous Huxley. Reprinted with the permission of Georges Borchardt, Inc., on behalf of the Aldous and Laura Huxley Trust. All rights reserved. - **153 :** Fom I, ROBOT by Isaac Asimov, copyright 1950 by Isaac Asimov. Used by permission of Bantam Books, a division of Random House, Inc. **155:** 2002, The Estate of Philip K. Dick - **164 :** *A Civil Action* © 1995, 1996 by Jonathan Harr published by Vintage Books - **158, 161, 162, 164-165 :** *The Rainmaker* © John Grisham 1995 published by Arrow Books - **174-177 :** *Hemingways's chihuahua and other mysteries de* Peter Flynn, Editions Didier 2011 - **178-183 :** Excerpt from "A Horse and Two Goats" by R. K. NarayanCopyright © 1970 by R. K. Narayan Used by permission of the Wallace Literary Agency, Inc.

Références sonores

Piste 4 : Australian Government Indigenous Newslines www.indigenous.gov.au
Piste 6 : Extrait de l'émission « Behind The News », ABC
Piste 11 : Extrait de l'émission « Online Social Networks No Longer Just for Teens », NPR
Piste 18 : Extrait du documentaire « Al Capone: The Untouchable Legend »
Piste 21 : Extrait de l'émission « The 100 most important American musical works of the 20th century » : "Route 66", NPR
Piste 25 : Extrait du documentaire « Route 66 », Journeyman Picture
Piste 27 : Chanson « Route 66 » par The Replacements, Warner Music
Piste 33 : Chanson « Me and Bobby McGee » par Kris Kristofferson, Sony Music
Piste 37 : Extrait de l'émission « The Legacy of the "Little Rock Nine" »
Piste 38 : Extrait du documentaire « Claudette Colvin: Twice Toward Justice by Author Phillip Hoose »
Piste 41: Discours de Martin Luther King, Martin Luther King Estate.
Piste 42 : Chanson « We Shall Overcome » par Joan Baez, Vanguard Records
Piste 45 : Excerpt from THE CURE AT TROY: A VERSION OF SOPHOCLES' PHILOCTETES by Seamus Heaney. Copyright © 1990 by Seamus Heaney. Reprinted by permission of Farrar, Straus and Giroux, LLC.